Preventing Deadly Conflict

War and Conflict in the Modern World

Preventing Deadly Conflict

I. William Zartman

polity

First published in 2015 by Polity Press

Polity Press
65 Bridge Street
Cambridge CB2 1UR, UK

Polity Press
350 Main Street
Malden, MA 02148, USA

ISBN-13: 978-0-7456-8691-2
ISBN-13: 978-0-7456-8692-9(pb)

A catalogue record for this book is available from the British Library.

Library of Congress Cataloging-in-Publication Data

Zartman, I. William.
  Preventing deadly conflict / I. William Zartman.
    pages cm
  Includes bibliographical references.
  ISBN 978-0-7456-8691-2 (hardback) -- ISBN 978-0-7456-8692-9 (pbk.) 1. Conflict management. 2. Crisis management. 3. War--Prevention. 4. Violence--Prevention. 5. Responsibility to protect (International law) I. Title.
  JZ5538.Z37 2015
  303.6--dc23

Typeset in 10.25 on 13 pt Scala by
Servis Filmsetting Ltd, Stockport, Cheshire
Printed and bound in the UK by Clays Ltd, St. Ives PLC

For further information on Polity, visit our website: politybooks.com

To my dedicated friends in the ultimate phases of the prevention business, Martti Ahtisaari, Alvaro de Soto and Lakhdar Brahimi

Contents

Acknowledgments

I am deeply grateful to Prof. James Piscatori, director of the Global Security Institute of Durham University for arranging my monastic stay in Durham to write this book, and to Prof. David Held, Master of University College, for having taken me under the College roof. St Cuthbert's spirit hath wrought much inspiration.

Introduction: The Fatal Attraction of Prevention

Prevention of deadly conflict is a life-long challenge. It is a challenge of preparedness for the whole course of a conflict, from its early potential for escalation to a final paroxysm of violence. It demands pro-active attention to keep conflicts – differences of opinion and position – at the level where they can be managed and resolved through normal politics and normal diplomacy. This is the essence of World Order, as it is the pillar of the institutionalized life of domestic order. Yet it must be recognized that there is nothing natural about prevention. Conflict begins and escalates for a reason, and to arrest its course demands a deliberate effort. It requires promoting, practicing, and perfecting, and that is the message of this book, a concept-based analysis for action.

To provide appropriate guidelines for analysis and policy, the matter of conflict and prevention must be differentiated in terms of both immediacy and issues. The choice of mechanisms, methods, and measures of prevention depends on the point in the evolution of the conflict, from gestation to pre-crisis, at which they are applied. A right response at the wrong time is a wrong response. Similarly, conflict and prevention are not the same across all issue areas; a toolbox with only hammers is not good for all jobs. Distinctions are needed between the dynamics of escalation in different issues and appropriate ways of arresting them. These distinctions are what is distinctive about this work.

The understanding and practice of prevention begins with

its nature as a paradox. On one hand, conflict is a natural, important, and useful element inherent in human behavior. As such, it involves strongly held, committed, even existential motives from which individuals and states are not likely to be dissuaded. On the other hand, literally innumerable conflicts have been prevented from escalating to serious political contention and to violence; the existing World Order rests on pervasive prevention of deadly conflict. Statesmen and doctors, weathermen and firemen, among others, continually talk of prevention, but live on the insufficiency of their efforts. Beginning in January 1992, the first-ever meeting of heads of state and government of the Security Council concluded with a call for "analysis and recommendations on ways of strengthening ... the capacity of the United Nations for preventive diplomacy" (pp. 117–18) that produced Secretary-General Boutros Boutros Ghali's (1992a) pioneering *Agenda for Peace*, welcomed by the Security Council and the General Assembly at the end of the year (Boutros Ghali, 1992a, 1992b, 1995). No one has yet been decorated for preventing World War III, which has not yet happened. But most countries do have a national hero who refused to be prevented from leading a bloody, patriotic campaign for independence. National security through national defense requires (and is accorded) about 200 times more in most countries' budgets for military security than for diplomacy, the preventive and preferable alternative to war. The list of contradictions about prevention could continue. This study of prevention offers itself as an analytical guidebook through this maze, in order to facilitate the understanding of practice and prevention for both the analysis and practice.

This book aims at presenting a comprehensive view of prevention of deadly conflict. It will bring together earlier treatments of the broad subject and draw in the many case studies and more narrowly focused treatments of parts of the subject. In doing so, it pays particular attention to the important but still inconclusive debate on the Responsibility to Protect (R2P); it situates prevention within the larger context of World Order, which exists despite its imperfections; it regards prevention as necessary and valuable but running against the current of difficulties inherent in an anarchic sovereign state system (and therefore requiring specific, creative attention); and it sees prevention, not as an imposition of big established states (Westphalian, Weberian, Western, nuclear, status quo), but as the first step to evolutionary change and the peaceful settlement of disputes among universally motivated peoples and states, at a much lower cost in population and productivity. The ethics of prevention will be discussed in the next section, but would-be preventers should remember that violent escalating conflict is a symptom of a causal problem of some sort, and de-escalating the conflict disarms the forces who demand attention to their problem; disarmament (conflict management) carries with it the promise of settlement (conflict resolution). Efforts at prevention must be complemented by efforts at solution, or the prevention will not hold.

The book begins with an examination of the fatal attraction of prevention and the associated concept of conflict, and brings the two together in an analysis of the challenges involved in conflict prevention, laying out the reasons why the goal persists and how to make a contribution to its final realization. The argument will then turn from a broad consideration to a "vertical" division into specific issue areas that have their own prevention practices, and a "horizontal" division of the topic by levels of immediacy into early, mid-term, pre-crisis, and post-crisis prevention. The treatment will close with an evaluation of the challenges to be overcome for better conflict prevention in the future. It will emphasize what can be learned from the structures and strategies of prevention that have often been successful in overcoming the attitudes

toward conflict and how they can be improved with constructive use and development. We can learn from what we have
done and left undone, and do more, better.

For the visually minded, figure I encapsulates the idea.[1]
Conflict ratchets its way from a passive state of incompat-
ibilities to active confrontation, escalating toward and into
violence. That process is not a smooth progression but a
bumpy path of intensification with its ups and down that provide opportunities for would-be preventers to seize and exploit,
to counter and inhibit that escalation. Long-term norms provide standards for handling conflict from its beginnings to the
end, wherever in the conflict cycle that end may occur. Mid-
term mechanisms for conflict management and resolution
work to reverse the course of the cycle before it reaches the
threshold of violence. If those efforts fail, last-minute methods are indicated to prevent a crisis and then to wind down
the conflict so that the mechanisms and norms can redirect its
course through management toward resolution. Even as the
conflict moves away from the threshold of violence toward the
threshold of (de)activation, post-crisis measures are needed
to prevent recidivism and re-emergence of the conflict even
when ostensibly managed but not fully resolved. Each of these
efforts acts within the context provided by the others, homing
in on particular phases of the conflict cycle as it spins through
escalation and de-escalation. The norms, mechanism, methods, and measures of prevention act as brakes on that spin
and help the conflict fall back into the hands of normal politics
and diplomacy.

Given the omnipresence of conflict inherent in human and
interstate relations, prevention of its escalation into violence
through its management and resolution is a fundamental
component of the post-World War II and post-Cold War systems of World Order. The functioning and yet-to-be-perfected
prevention of violent conflict is not just a set of techniques

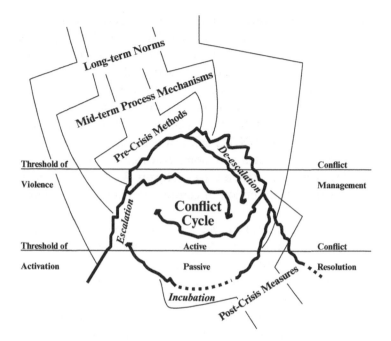

Figure 1 Conflict prevention.

for dampening inter- and intrastate behavior. It is a set of norms and practices that hold World Order together and keep relations functioning normally and effectively, allowing them to move on to other, more creative and positive matters (Zartman 2009; Jones et al. 2014). The norms and practices of prevention are not perfect but the instances that escape their effects are all the more striking for their exceptional character. The system operates through the individual and uncoordinated activities of members of the international community and through their coordinated actions in international institutions – norms and organizations. For those who would question the existence of a World Order and mistake exceptions and imperfections for normalcy, the widespread practice of prevention should be recognized as pervasive patterns consensually followed to maintain basic, regular responses to deviant challenges. Were it not so, international politics would indeed be total anarchy, wasting all time and energy in unregulated conflict and unprevented violence. With no authority or even coordinator to organize those activities and actions, the United Nations Security Council (UNSC) and General Assembly (UNGA) being only the tool and toy of their member states, states and non-governmental organizations (NGOs) have to do it themselves. Thus is World Order constituted, with the prevention of conflict escalation and violence as its key function.

Rather than introduce yet another definition of "Deadly Conflict Prevention," this discussion begins with the definition of Boutros Ghali (1992b, ¶20): *"action to prevent disputes from arising between parties, prevent existing disputes from escalating into [violent] conflicts, and to limit the spread of the latter when they occur"* (cf. Lund 1996; Holl 1997; Wallensteen 1998; Miall et al. 1999; Zartman 2001; Carment & Schnabel 2003). This identification, however (like most of the others), is circular: It tells what to prevent but it defines prevention as preventing. To avoid that problem, prevention can be further defined as *"measures to inhibit actions that can lead to deadly violence."* In these characterizations, prevention, in relation with peace-making, peace-keeping and peace-building, is recognized as a fundament of the World Order system. "This wider mission for the world Organization . . . [is] to seek to identify at the earliest possible stage situations that could produce conflict, and to try through diplomacy to remove the sources of danger before violence" (Boutros Ghali 1995, ¶¶16, 15). Prevention has to include all possible "actions," not just diplomacy, and has to consider the aftermath of violence into the "peace-building" efforts to bring the conflict fully to an end and prevent new conflict from arising, a circular and continuing effort, as the rest of Boutros Ghali's (1995, ¶21) definitions emphasize. An examination of violent conflict cannot begin with the violence, any more than one can study a person's development starting at age 21. One has to understand the pre-violent stage to understand where the violence comes from and therefore focus prevention on the conflict before it reaches violence.

A number of further facets of the prism of prevention are introduced within this definition. To prevent means, first of all, to warn (French *prévenir*). One has to know what is coming, either generally or specifically, in order to prevent it from arriving. The object is conflict or disputes susceptible of escalating to violence, to be discussed further below. The second notion is to avoid, inhibit, or stop something from happening, or at least reduce or limit its effects, all suggested in the UN definition. The action involves both managing and resolving the conflict; the term "handling" can be used here as a looser characterization that covers both management and resolution, also as discussed below. The conflict is not just to be left hanging when it is stopped; its re-escalation potential has to be reduced. To pursue the notion a bit further, conflict is turned aside in two ways: it is made either impossible or unthinkable. The first refers to structural efforts to prevent, the second to attitudinal changes. These two broad distinctions will also be developed more fully below. In either case, it is preferable to complement the prohibition with enablement, to add to the injunction "You can't do this" (or "Don't even think of it") an answer to the retort, "Well, what *can* I do?"

CHAPTER ONE

The Inevitability and Value of Conflict

As long as people hold different views of the same subject, there is conflict, classically defined as an incompatibility of positions (e.g. Hobbes 1964 [1651]: 83; Raven & Kuglanski 1970: 70). As such, conflict is inherent in the existence of separate units, whether they be individuals, parties, societies, or states; humans predate the conflicts they bear but without conflicting views individual socio-political units would have no reason for separate existence. At this stage, conflict is merely passive or potential, and generally unpreventable. But when parties escalate their positions to an intersocial relationship, such as an attempt to assert their position over others, they have raised their conflict to an active stage, the threshold indicated in figure 1 (Coser 1956: 8). Two parties that value the same thing passively and then make efforts to get it, two parties who have their own beliefs and then make efforts to convert or deny the other, two parties which hold different strategies for reaching a goal and then make efforts to make their approach prevail, are all cases of moving from passive to active conflict.

These efforts are usually normal and to be expected, and we engage in competition, persuasion, and bargaining all the time. When we run into resistance, we increase our efforts, but usually within bounds established by social norms and the value of the object to us. The value of the object is a personal matter, but social or interpersonal norms have several effects. Like personal values, they impose limits on conflict behavior, but they also provide established or acceptable ways of conducting the conflict. We can bid or bargain for the coveted object, we can debate or separately schedule the different beliefs, we can vote or adjudicate over the rival strategies. Many of our differences and even active conflicts are governed by established norms, and the conflict, though active and escalated to a certain point, is managed and resolved appropriately and acceptably.

A witness called to the stand on the subject is Robin Hood, who stood at the opposite end from Little John at the one-log bridge. Their passive conflict soon escalated as they reached the middle of the bridge and they came to blows, until Little John flicked Robin Hood into the drink with his deft staff. (They then made up and went off together to join the Merry Men in Sherwood Forest.) This kind of action is not common practice anymore: one-lane bridges have priority signs and red lights, or if not we have more informal procedural norms such as "age before beauty," "first come first served," "ladies first," alphabetical listings, or even rolling dice. These are termed conflict management devices; they replace violence as an arbiter and they demote the pursuit of the conflict to a social or political level. In this case, of course, they do more, they resolve the conflict, which no longer exists once the two parties have crossed the bridge safely (and joined the Merry Men). A second witness on the subject is the Chinese premier, who proclaimed his country's claim against neighboring countries over most of the South China Sea and the reefs and rocks (and oil and fish) in it. Hoping to avoid the Robin-and-John means of conflict resolution, interested third parties, including the United States, urge resort to other modern procedural norms of World Order such as the International Court of Justice or negotiation. A third witness is Vladimir Putin, who trashed World Order norms and the tenth of the Ten Commandments and escalated conflicts over neighbors' internal governance and territory into aggression, showing that Robin and John are not just historical or mythical characters.

But conflict has a deeper meaning in our society: It is the essence of our political and economic system (Matthews 1995; Zartman 1995). Democracy is based on conflict and its management by accepted norms that prevent the conflict from rising to the level of violence. Democrats believe that debate, application, and accountability are the test of truth and effectiveness. Democracy is the right to choose and the right to repent. Voting for candidates and for legislation is an exercise in conflict management in active conflict. Rarely is it conflict resolution, as the parties tend to hold their incompatible views even if they lose the vote. But they have resorted to a procedural norm for handling conflict, which replaces older methods such as killing the rival or imposing an ideology. Thus conflict management and prevention are the bundle of procedures on which democracy rests.

The same holds for the economic system of free enterprise, based on competition (conflict) to establish the best product and the best price. The market manages conflict and preventive measures of regulation manage the market; conflict escalation often rises high, although it usually stops before violence. More broadly, conflict is the basis of scientific inquiry. Theories are advanced, contested, and tested, with research and evidence managing the conflict until temporary truces are established, awaiting the next paradigm shift and challenge (Kuhn 1962). Scientific truth is established by conflict.

The Historic Attraction and Failure of Prevention

Because active conflict is normal and inherent in all these areas of activity, for that very reason prevention is desirable to keep it from escalating out of hand, beyond its useful benefits. Prevention is locked into domestic governance systems as an important value that makes the system work, linking the management mechanism with the conflict situation. Prevention here is a neutral effect; it does not purposely favor any candidate, product, theory, or argument, but provides an accepted means for handling the conflict among them. We know what would happen if it did not work, because conquest, killings, coups, and concentration camps have a historical record and are the methods of handling levels of conflict that current societies seek to prevent.

Prevention is the basis of a stable political system like a stable World Order, operating so that citizens can live and function in security with a firm sense of expectations. Law is the regulation of expectations, and prevention serves to inhibit actions that fall outside the normal range of expectations, specifically those on the path to violence. It is not enough to stop violence; violence comes from somewhere for some reason, and prevention needs to deal with situations that can lead to violence, as well as those that have already become violent. It is inefficient to have to resort to the Robin-and-John means of conflict resolution when stop signs and stop lights (and behind them the law enforcement officer) will suffice, establishing reliable expectations and generally preventing violence. Thus prevention is a political expectation and has a historical attraction. We work to establish ways of handling conflicts to keep them short of violence, as part of the general political system but also with regard to specific areas such as domestic security, civil litigation, education standards, sports rankings, and other areas of conflict. Domestically, the record is rather solid, even though there are always traffic infractions, crimes of passion, cheating scandals, and rioting sports team supporters that get through the net of norms and mechanisms to contain violence.

The same type of expectation of prevention extends to attitudes toward conflicts with nature, although the record is less solid. People look for prevention of hurricane damage, earthquake destruction, climate change effects, unwanted births, or disease epidemics (or even just the flu). Where such conflicts cannot be prevented directly, the demand shifts to protection against their effects. The politics of conflict prevention with nature in turn become the subject of conflict among parties, as politicians are held accountable for the failure to prevent hurricane damage, scientists are fined for supposedly inadequate seismic warnings, tempers fray as temperatures and ocean levels rise without adequate state action, marches clash (and sometimes feed violence) over abortion issues, and HIV/AIDS prevention becomes a major political topic. Again norms for managing the ensuing interpersonal conflicts are generally solid, but the means for handling the conflicts with nature that underlie them still elude us.

Similar expectation of prevention is transferred to the international arena, where it becomes the ingredient of normal state relations. Prevention has been a constant theme of UN Secretaries-General, from the early times of Dag Hammarskjöld to Boutros Boutros Ghali, Kofi Annan, and Ban Ki-moon. Secretaries-General establish records and reputations based on their abilities for bringing peace and preventing war. As noted, the world organization was established as the institution of World Order with the purpose of proving a means for peaceful resolution of disputes and a prevention of violence as a means of pursuing conflicts. While the UN is no world government, its members aspire to the reduction of violence, the prevention of wars among states and even within them when such conflicts are seen as a threat to international peace and security and World Order. To do so, they pursue the development and reinforcement of accepted norms, mechanisms, and practices for managing and even resolving conflicts. They have established a series of such mechanisms that provide a network of norms for behavior and for handling such conflicts similar to those that govern the management of domestic conflicts. The UN Charter (chap. VII, art. 33.1) lists such measures, including "negotiation, enquiry, mediation, conciliation, arbitration, judicial settlement, resort to regional agencies or arrangements, or other peaceful means of their own choice." As for domestic conflicts, the international system contains courts, tribunals, dispute settlement bodies, and others. International organizations and institutions have set standards for behavior in regard to issues that feed international conflict. However, whereas domestic conflicts fall rather firmly within the network of norms because they are predictable by standard categories, international conflicts are much more *sui generis* than terms such as "war" or "rebellion" might suggest. People know what will happen if they break the law; states play on the margins.

Yet such marginal plays are rare, compared with the literally innumerable cases of conflict where normal relations have prevailed and where World Order has been maintained. In these rare cases, prevention faces formidable obstacles and challenges. Preventers, after all, are whistleblowers, trying to change the course of events as they see them gain momentum toward disaster. While the larger community of onlookers may benefit from prevention efforts on their behalf, the parties to the conflict regard the preventer as a meddler in their dedicated business. The preventer's challenge, like the whistleblower's, is to make the conflicting parties aware of the pitfalls on the path they have chosen and to offer detours from the road to violence. Significant obstacles, some structural but above all attitudinal, both within their own organizations and with the conflicting parties, make this pursuit more difficult.

These challenges can be enumerated as sovereignty, the barrier to interference; knowledge, the uncertainty of the causal chain into escalation and violence; prediction, the fallibility of foresight; early warning, the distractions of inertia and inattention; action, the problem of knowing how to break the causal chain; effectiveness, the encroachment of externalities and other distractions; protection, the mitigation of effects as an alternative to an aversion to events; and nonprevention, the attraction of the natural course of events and the hubris of the preventer. Each deserves a fuller treatment, not as absolute impediments but as challenges to be overcome if prevention is to work.

Sovereignty
The first challenge is of course the barrier that sovereignty erects against interference with its actions (Ban 2010, ¶10). States may well act capriciously, but they usually act on the basis of firm convictions, popularly supported, that their action is in the national interest, which carries a higher justification than mere and only loosely enforceable international norms. Indeed, a major norm of the UN and of international interaction is the sanctity of sovereignty, higher than the sanctity of human life, and it wreaks havoc, for example, with such prevention efforts as the Responsibility to Protect (R2P). In regard to rebellion, sovereignty impedes efforts to mediate or otherwise prevent domestic conflict, and the rebels are often motivated by their version of sovereign devotion to the cause, which provides a coat of justifying armor against efforts to manage the conflict. When a state is set on a course of action and its leaders – elected or self-chosen – are committed to it, it is difficult to turn them from the course of violence. Sovereignty allows a Putin to invade a Georgia or a Ukraine, a Chavez to imprison opponents and inflate the national currency, or a Museveni to sentence homosexual citizens to imprisonment, despite preventive efforts of the world community. Similarly, when a rebellion is committed

to achieve independence or to bring the Way of God or the self-determination of a nation to the people it purports to represent, arguments, sanctions, and inducements to turn to the peaceful path ring hollow.

Knowledge

Scientists and other knowledge specialists are professionally wary, and the greater the knowledge and specialization, the greater their reluctance to make causal statements with assurance. Policymakers and other knowledge consumers often mistake such scientific skepticism for evidential weakness, and so find support for inaction. Conflict is always overdetermined. Finding the "real reason" for a conflict is like looking for the source of an underground river; its courses are multiple and hidden. Conflict also feeds itself, so that the original causes and grievances are often overtaken by wrongs committed in its course, just as they are by scars from before this round began. Conflicts do not hold still; they snowball into greater complexity, and pulling off the outer layers for treatment only reveals a compound core. Especially, conflict management tries to separate the underlying grievances of the conflict from the means of pursuing them; it carries with it promise for conflict resolution that leaves the parties doubly frustrated and angry if not pursued. The causal landscape for serious conflict involves a wide field of many antecedents; in most cases they peter out before reaching hurricane force, although often re-emerging later in new dimensions, but in a few cases the multiple antecedents will converge to produce a crisis.

Given the multicausality of the conflict, where it may be multicausality itself that contributes to its obduracy, it is difficult to establish a causal chain that would enable preventers to break the links effectively. The causes of the Bosnian war (1992–8) began in 1537, Serbia's national day commemorating its defeat (sic) in Kosovo Polje (Field), and run through World War II with the Croat Ustashi, the collapse of Tito's Yugoslavia, the economic downturn, the enclaved territories, and simply the animal macho of the Yugoslav/ Serbian fighters. Some of these links in the chain are harder to sever than others. We do not know what it is that keeps half a millennium of memory alive, demanding revenge for its bearers (Ricoeur 2000; Rosoux 2001). We do not know the effect of economic change and of economic pressures on the conflicting parties, although much work (and as much controversy) is being devoted to the topic. We do not know how absolute sacred territories and how divisible indivisibles are (Albin 1991; Toft 2003; Norlén 2015). Work has gone into the social psychology and the power of emotional leadership, including its psycho-sexual impact, but we have little second-step knowledge on how to make such macho rabble-rousers climb down from the entrapment of their own popularity (Ury 1991). And, at the end, we have no knowledge about the way in which these variables interact to cause conflict and then to support prevention efforts.

Prediction

Prevention depends on prediction, a notoriously difficult action that also bedevils dealings with conflicts with nature (Lorenz 1972, 1993; Silver 2012). It is surprising how little attention is given to prediction in the prevention literature. Prediction errors are grouped by operations specialists and church liturgists as Type I error (unpredicted events, or sins of omission) and Type II error (unfulfilled predictions, or sins of commission) (Avenhaus & Krieger 2014). Each relates to the misinterpretation of evidence, but the two actually work together to weaken each other: Errors of commission make predictors wary and susceptible to errors of omission (the *Cry Wolf Problem*), and errors of omission press predictors not to make the same mistake again and so to make errors of commission. The problem in regard to nature conflicts is illustrated by the dilemma of a North Carolina governor in 2000. After ordering coastal evacuation because of an impending hurricane that then never made it to shore, arousing instead a storm of protests for the unnecessary disruption (Type II error), he decided to ignore warnings about the subsequent hurricane, causing an even bigger storm of protests when the hurricane actually landed (Type I error). The challenge is not merely to be able to identify tropical storms but to be able to identify those cases where the tropical storm actually turns into a hurricane. An analyst once exclaimed: "We're great at prediction; we've identified 100 of the last ten hurricanes."

Prediction becomes surer, the closer the event. This explains why distant predictions are hard to sell and why prediction is often too late and too difficult. Distant prediction deals with categories of events, where probability of a specific occurrence is variable. Academic articles and government files are filled with indications of coming wars and rumors of wars, even if the exact dates of the crash are not predictable, even up close. The US Agency for International Development (USAID) has its conflict assessment, the UN Development Program (UNDP) its early warning assessment, the International Monetary Fund (IMF) its Early Warning System which it coordinates with private sector systems, the US Central Intelligence Agency (CIA) its State Failure Task Force, the African Union (AU) its early warning project, SwissPeace's Early Tension and Data Analysis (FAST), Francophonie's early warning and rapid reaction system, the Fund for Peace its Failed States index, and the UN Charter its art. 99, stipulating that the Secretary-General may serve as an agent of early warning (which he has almost never done before the outbreak of hostilities). Playing backward to crisis antecedents is not the same thing as playing forward to determine which and how antecedents actually produce the crisis. It is in this area that more work needs to be done to produce reliable predictions, but until it is done, practitioners will feel justified in not taking predictions seriously or in substituting their feelings for more scientific – even if still imperfect – analyses.

Early Warning

It cannot be stated too often that early warnings abound, although they are not unambiguous. The real challenge is early awareness and early action, the ability to listen, hear, and act on early warnings (van Walraven 1998).[1] Surprises in this business are rare but deafness is widespread (Adelman 1998). Foreign affairs bureaucracies and political advisors are the screen between analysis and action, each operating for their own reasons to avoid action that can be seen as either operationally or politically risky (the *Bureaucratic Inertia Problem*). Inactivity is usually safer than engagement, and non-decisions in favor of inaction are often rational given the uncertainties involved in action: the present devil we know is seen as a safer bet than the future devil we don't know. Such an attitude may be regretted in hindsight in specific cases, but it is generally preferable and rational compared to overly eager or uninformed involvement in uncertain futures. But as so often occurs, the rational routine stands as a barrier to appropriate awareness for the unusual signs and events that, as noted, are characteristic of violent conflicts.

Even when early warnings are available, the road to effective action is mined with typical problems beyond scenario unreliability, the North Carolina governor's problem (the *Tropical Storm Problem*). There is the *Busy Fireman Problem*:[2] The normal bureaucratic organization is not set up to look for uncertain problems in the future, and so the common response is, "Don't bother me with smoke; can't you see I'm busy putting out fires?" The US and the European Community ignored the risk of Yugoslav disintegration because they were fixating on the Soviet-Russian and German problems at the time (Woodward 1995).[3] Another is the *Sleeping Dogs Problem*: Best not stir up things that show no signs of stirring on their own for the moment. The argument against declaring a Year of African Boundary Demarcation by the Organization of African Unity (OAU)/African Union (AU) to deal with the risk of boundary wars was that most undemarcated boundaries are untroubled at the moment and so the best preventive measure might be not to trouble untroubled trouble (Nordquist 2001). A fifth problem is the *Free Viewer Problem*, where the viewer claims that the danger is someone else's problem and will pass him by. This is the opposite of the *Free Rider Problem*, where the rider claims that the danger calls for someone else's solution from which he will benefit; free riders enjoy a collective good, whereas free viewers feel untouched by a collective bad (Olson 1968). While some developing countries have acted as free riders toward the risk of global warming as seen in the protocols of the Climate Change Convention, the US is currently adopting a position of free viewer toward the "alleged problem." Studies have shown that it takes personalized, imminent or rapidly increasing threats and warnings to capture attention, quite the contrary of warnings that are, by definition, early (Gilbert 2006).

The *Three Monkeys Problem* is simply the event the predictor missed (Type I error). People tend not to want to hear – or see or speak of – bad news; it is not only disquieting but if taken seriously would require some costly measures of prevention or preparation. In the years – and especially the year – preceding the first Gulf War, the US refused to believe that its friend Iraq would do such a thing (Jentleson 1994). The reverse is the *Cry Wolf Problem*, or warning fatigue (Type II error). The most important problem in early warnings is the uncertainty of their predictions – uncertain warnings of uncertain events. Even the most sophisticated attempts at solid predictors of future disasters have come up with antecedents but not predictors, leading to repeated Type II errors that set up the Type I error. Actually more frequent is the *Deny Wolf Problem*, which illustrates the difficulty of prediction. A situation becomes so standard that no effort is put into identifying when exceptions can/will occur, because they "can't happen." Analysts of Arab authoritarianism, Soviet totalitarianism, and terrorist fundamentalism all focused on unshakable explanations of the situation, leaving only incredulity before the rise of the Arab Spring, the fall of the Berlin Wall, and the negotiations with terrorists.

Other blinders to awareness include the *Sunk Cost Problem*. Parties put further denial efforts into covering up earlier denials, which will demand further denials and cover-ups in the subsequent round (Meerts 2005). EU officials, faced with the exposure of corruption in the late 1990s, denied the problem rather than fixing it, insuring that the problem would be larger when the next round of revelations came around, as it did. A related reaction is reinforcement, in which not denial but persistence in an inappropriate direction is the response, another version of entrapment. Here the warning is heard but it provokes a continued or exaggerated wrong action. Warned by George Washington and others of the Indian forest tactics in the French and Indian War, General Braddock reinforced his red-coated phalanx, making them even better targets for the ambush. Finally, there is the *Certainty Problem* (or *Effect*) whereby, as prospect theory indicates, things unlikely to occur are fully discounted and things likely are counted as certain, so that risk is perceptionally reduced (also referred to as the hyperbolic discount function in intertemporal choice) (Loewenstein 1989, 1992; Laibson 1997; McDermott 2009).

Examples, as a result, are too numerous (Zartman 2005). The US government declined to act in 1991–6 when told of the presence of Osama bin Laden in Sudan. The UN Secretariat turned a deaf ear to clear signals of impending genocide in Rwanda in 1993, viewing them as "routine announcements" (Salton 2014). The UN Security Council declined to send a peacekeeping force to Congo-Brazzaville in 1997 because the ceasefire was merely *de facto*, not *de jure*, but instead ordered a study of the causes of African conflicts, while the ensuing massacre was going on (Zartman 1998). The 1994 Rwanda genocide, the 2001 foot-and-mouth epidemic and unrelated anthrax mailings, the 2011 Fukushima tsunami disaster, the 2012 Assam violence, and the 2012 murder of the US Ambassador in Benghazi could have been averted by awareness of the warning evidence available at the time (Prunier, 1994; Enserink 2001; Bhattacharjee 2011; Normile 2011; Harris 2012).

Action

As important as the prediction problem is the "postdiction problem" of the same type. The causal road from policy to prevention of violent conflict is as obscure as the causal road to the conflict. Effective antidotes and countermeasures are not always strongly indicated. "What to prevent when and how" is a major operative as well as conceptual question. A pertinent categorization of action choices is set out in the R2P triptych, where the first "pillar" is that a sovereign state is to be responsible for the welfare of its citizens, the second is that other states are responsible for assisting it in its own responsibility, and the third is that other states are responsible for assuming the first state's responsibility if it fails to do so. Thus early prevention is the preferred course, first by the conflicted party itself and then by outsiders to assist others in preventing impending conflicts within their own borders. But early prevention is the most difficult to justify, for the chances of the foreseen event taking place are highly uncertain and, if prevented, can never be proven. The earlier the preventive intervention in the course of a conflict, the more difficult it is to make a telling claim, and yet it is early prevention that is preferable to crisis intervention in terms of human and economic losses (Cortright 1997).

The gap between the first and second pillars is the most significant; the first indicates action by the sovereign, conflicted state, whereas the second and the third indicate some interference in the state's sovereign affairs. The third pillar has received the most critical attention from commentators and policymakers, especially because its limits and guidelines still need to be worked out, but it is the second pillar that is arguably more important but more difficult for outside states. Finding the correct and effective way to head off an otherwise certain catastrophe or even lesser trouble is not evident. Warnings of governing errors from repression to simply ignoring the public were on the mark in Egypt after 2000; its rulers, from Hosni Mubarek through Mohammed Morsi to Abdul-Fattah al-Sisi, were told by outside powers that their policies would bring rebellion, but they paid no heed, with the predicted but not prevented result.

Preventing conflicts not yet violent from becoming so amounts to telling sovereign states not to pursue their conflict with external enemies. It means interference in policies a state believes are required for its security (Zartman et al. 2012). Governments carrying out a policy of violent conflict against an identified – and, almost necessarily, demonized – external enemy are not likely to take kindly to external attempts to interfere with their efforts for the defense of the country or regime. Warnings and intervention to prevent Israel from carrying out expansionist policies that arguably will take it to Masada, or Egypt from carrying out repressive policies that predictably were going to introduce a Muslim Brotherhood takeover, or Iran from carrying out nuclear policies that would assuredly feed its own persecution complex, inevitably complicate attempts to cultivate better relations with respective countries. On the other hand, "early late" prevention efforts, just before the conflict has reached the crisis or "too late" stage, run into the problem of overcoming the conflicting parties' overcommitment, which earlier action would have avoided.

Invocation of the third pillar – in Iraq, in Libya, in Ukraine and elsewhere in the Near Abroad, and finally in Syria – has caused as many second thoughts on the part of the users as it has on the part of potential targets. In addition to weapons of mass destruction, repressive government and an egregious ruler were justifying ills that would be removed by intervention in Iraq in 2003; only in regard to the third goal can success be claimed. In Libya in 2011, the egregious ruler was also removed, leaving a vacuum that replaced repressive order with repressive disorder. In Ukraine, Russia justified its interventions as the protection of Russians, Russophones, and Russophiles, indistinguishably, although the goal seemed to be the acquisition of neighboring territorial protectorates rather than the protection of neighboring populations. The debate continues on the appropriateness as well as the legitimacy of direct preventive interventions, delaying rapid response for action.

Effectiveness
It is difficult to document prevention. The fact that something didn't happen is prima facie evidence that it wasn't going to happen anyhow. Claims of successful prevention are apparent counterfactuals and make poor campaign material for the claimant. Neville Chamberlain was unable to make good on his claim that he kept war from happening. At best, claims that "he kept us out of war" were successful for Woodrow Wilson's and Franklin D. Roosevelt's election campaigns but

were soon belied by subsequent events and the presidents' own later decisions. Claims of effective last-minute interventions (if they succeed) are easier to document; no one would contest the success of the diplomatic interventions of Secretary Henry Kissinger and President Carter in preventing war between Israel and Egypt for more than three decades and counting, or of Finnish former President Martti Ahtisaari in preventing the continuation of war in Aceh and Kosovo.

Even when effective, however, prevention has its costs, counted as externalities or unintended side effects and opportunity costs, that need to be taken into account, but that are also hard to foresee and to document. Intervention from the outside is always a risky business in face of the oft-repeated maxim that "they should be left to work it out themselves." The intervention to prevent the worst in Libya and Yemen in 2011 by removing the Hydra head left lesser Hydra heads all over the land, an unforeseen consequence; the absence of intervention to prevent further waves of deadly killing in Syria in 2012, because "intervention carries risks," left a situation with all the risks realized in the form of competing Islamist ethnocide and the egregious ruler still in power. Yet the two lessons contradict each other. Such errors of commission and omission illustrate the need to evaluate the second-level consequences in calculating the effectiveness of a preventive policy.

Relatedly, there is the aftermath of the successful prevention that needs to be considered. A conflict managed will always leave some parties or parts of them feeling frustrated, certain that they could have won if they had not been prevented. The question of effectiveness concerns the degree of management or resolution (or management without resolution) achieved by the prevention initiative. A measure of total resolution is humanly and conceptually unlikely; prevention measures are more likely to address issues or steps on the way to resolution.

Late in the development of the conflict, they are even more likely to introduce conflict management, only suspending the danger of violence and preparing for resolution later on. As noted, management carries with it the promise of resolution, but it also lifts the pressure for resolution: why resolve when the conflict is no longer violent and the danger of an unfavorable resolution is always present? Cyrus Vance intervened for the US to remove the danger of violence in the Cyprus dispute in 1964, but he left it unresolved, as the world saw a decade and then four decades later. The same year, Somalia and Ethiopia signed a conflict management agreement, preventing the danger of continued war over the non-existent border. Somalia thought there was an inherent promise of a border settlement, Ethiopia thought the matter *was* settled, and so 15 years later when Somalia realized there was no border settlement, it launched into a war that was disastrous for the regime, and settled no border (Zartman 2005). Morocco and Algeria agreed to a border conflict management agreement brokered by the OAU that did not effectively ease tensions and prevent later border conflicts between the "enemy brothers" (Zartman 1989). The 1993 Oslo agreements, a remarkable exercise in Track 2 and then Track 1 diplomacy between Israelis and Palestinians, left so many questions unresolved when the negotiators returned home that neither party was willing to move into wholehearted implementation, and a daring measure of prevention fell victim to its own source of success – secret negotiation (Zartman 1996; Ross 2004).

Even when full resolution is the purported purpose of the measure to prevent continued conflict, the agents of prevention may find the conflict still alive. Frequently, it is simply the nature of a deep-seated conflict that prevents even comprehensive agreements from resolving all the old scores and sores. The independence agreements to prevent further war in Eritrea (1993), Timor Leste (2002), Kosovo (2008), and South Sudan (2011) were followed by renewed conflict, extremely violent in the first and fourth cases. The point is that risky and vulnerable efforts at prevention may have such uncertain chances of effectiveness that they discourage parties and, more importantly, peace-makers from pursuing them.

Protection
Consideration of prevention must also include efforts to deal with its failure. When it is not possible to stop conflict, it is better to turn attention to mitigating its effects. This is a common policy in confrontation with natural disasters, from US Interior Secretary Donald Hodel's 1987 comment on the ozone hole ("Buy a hat"), to flood and hurricane evacuation, and much can be learned from such efforts to protect against such conflicts with nature that one cannot prevent. Protection is often a more defensible, more successful, and less intrusive policy for preventing damage than trying to stop nature. River dwellers have learned to rely more on levees and elevations than on dams and diversions, and ultimately, simply on insurance, the most frequent form of protection against the effect of unpredictable disasters. Protection policies are often easier to sell than prevention efforts; they are immediate and sure, risk-reducing by definition, and generic in coverage (depending on the policy).

But not all risks are insurable, and not all insurance covers the lasting effects of conflict. Protection can be a cop-out, an alternative to serious attempts at prevention. Again, in conflicts with nature, some discussion has given up on efforts to prevent global warming, immediately costly with effects only in the distant future, and turns to measures to protect from the effects of inevitable conflict with nature when the conflict is lost. Businesses are especially sensitive to the risk of conflict; they benefit from stability and run from instability. The Arab Spring cost the affected countries much in foreign direct investment (FDI), just as business fled from Ivory Coast during its decade and a half of internal conflict. Yet protective flight is costly, and protective preparations for flight hamper business enterprise; it is in the interest of business to support prevention efforts. But the same reasoning can be applied to citizenry, rulers, and external friends.

Unable to prevent the 200,000 casualties of the Syrian civil war, the UNSC and the international community turned to the protection of the millions of refugees and internally displaced persons (IDPs) in neighboring countries and in Syria. Unable to prevent violence in eastern Congo, the UNSC sent Blue Helmets (with inadequate rules of engagement) to protect the populations. Unable to prevent the spread of HIV/AIDS, countries have turned their efforts to protection from its worst effects. Protection is an admission of preventive failure, but it is often useful as the second line of prevention against the event's effects.

Non-Prevention
Given these challenges, it is always tempting not to get involved in prevention, especially of other people's conflicts. Conflicting parties do not focus on prevention until they have to; their aim is to win the conflict and to mobilize the resources necessary to do so. Parties directly involved in a conflict examine the cost of prevention, by settlement for example, against the cost of staying in the conflict and seeking to prevail. Parties do not seek a settlement unless they find themselves stuck in an impasse that is costly to them, and this subjective perception must be reciprocal for both parties to turn from unilateral methods of pursuing the conflict to multilateral methods of seeking a solution (Zartman 2000). This condition, known as a mutually hurting stalemate, must also be accompanied by the mutual perception that both sides see a joint solution as possible. If conflict is to be prevented from escalating, it is

important to face the facts of costs and consequences. Such perceptions are relevant to conflict management and resolution in the upper levels of escalation, as costs of conflict rise while costs of settlement tend to remain constant. But they are also applicable to the early stages of conflict, when parties ready to engage would do well to count the cost of contending against the value of the prize, and consider prevention instead. Calculations of this type are too often avoided, making third-party efforts necessary.

Third parties are frequently necessary as the agents of prevention, since conflicting parties usually need help not only in finding solutions but, before that, in perceiving their costly stalemate and the need to prevent its aggravation. Although there is room for consideration of prevention in the abstract, without regard to the agent, or of prevention as an altruistic gesture often related to a party's self-image, like Norway in regard to Guatemala, Colombia, Palestine, and Sri Lanka, in real life preventers generally take on the challenge because the conflict hurts them, whether as an involved party or as a bystander. The motivating harm from the conflict can be specific, if the parties stand in the path of the conflict, like the US in the Middle East, or it can be more generalized, like Malta's efforts to promote a new Law of the Sea. So preventive interveners must always calculate the cost of intervention against the cost of staying out. Against such specifics stand the more numerous instances of third parties that want to "sit this one out" and not become involved. The costs of prevention, in efforts expended, in opportunity costs, and in relations with the conflicting parties, for them outweigh the calculated gains.

Compounding the element of pain as a cause for non-engagement is the element of risk, calculated as danger times certainty (Avenhaus & Sjöstedt 2009). Risk is frequently simply waved as a reason for inaction, as if certainty needs to be absolute for action to be taken. Risk has to be calculated against alternatives, including staying the course; "better the devil we know than the devil we don't know" is sound only depending how devilish each devil is and is likely to be. Risk calculations are often made on the basis of the last, most recent experience; "we are always fighting the last war" (Mnookin 2010; Kahneman 2011). The US policy of inaction on the Syrian crisis in 2013 combined these problems; the course was decided on the basis of experience in Iraq and then in Libya, without considering whether the situation and the proposed policy were the same, and the element of risk was cited as an absolute without taking into account the risk inherent in alternatives to the measures to reduce the risk.

A broader consideration, related to "let them work it out among themselves," is the "Let war have its chance" approach (Luttwak 1999). US policy in regard to Syria in 2013 and Bosnia in 1995 found its justification in this approach, if it finds any justification at all. Statistics tend to show that won wars have a better chance of creating durable outcomes than negotiated settlements. A general judgment on the world's great wars – World Wars I and II, the US Civil War, the Napoleonic Wars – approves the historical outcomes rather than some compromise during the conflict, even though prevention *before the wars* would doubtless achieve greater appreciation. Perhaps the judgment would be different on internal events, such as the French or Russian Revolution. Again, the result seems to favor prevention before the final clash but hands off in the ultimate stage of the conflict: "If you can't stop it, let someone win it."

Nonetheless, advocates of prevention need to face a final consideration: the ethics of imposing external efforts on parties who are deeply convinced of the rightness – and indeed the righteousness – of their cause. Citizens of most countries of the world enthusiastically celebrate the conflict that brought them independence and enshrine the national hero that led the conflict. It is a matter of some hubris to say such efforts were wrong and should have been prevented. Of course, one could turn the argument around and say that the cost should have been prevented, but in major conflicts where the stakes are high, it would be difficult to assure the outcome without the cost expended. Would-be preventers need first address their calling with a good deal of humility. There are indeed conflicts that could not and should not be prevented (although there is doubtless no unanimity on which ones they were). Arguably, the only way to have prevented World War II would have been to prevent the election of Adolf Hitler, which would have required earlier prevention of the vindictive Versailles Peace Treaty (or indeed of World War I) (Tuchman 1994). This is not a final injunction against prevention, but a statement that the ethical question needs to be examined in each case (but also that it should not stand as a *prima facie* barrier against action). The path between these considerations is indeed narrow, unclearly lit, and convoluted.

These issues have been raised, not to defeat the notion of prevention, but to consider objectively and evaluate the challenges that prevention must face. The prevention of conflict escalation and violence is a major undertaking, involving both courage and calculations. It is not a superficial effort or one to be advocated reflexively, but one that takes deep commitment and analysis

As a result, the history of prevention in international affairs is a very wavy matter. Hammarskjöld raised the approach, and died of it, in Congo in 1961. His immediate successors were less daring. Later, Xavier Perez de Cuellar revived the notion in practice, followed by Boutros Boutros Ghali, who raised it to a high intellectual level and was fired for it. Kofi Annan was more subtle, and effective; Ban Ki-moon has focused more on the development of R2P. In the US, prevention has scarcely been an appealing campaign theme. President Jimmy Carter took it as a mission to prevent another Arab–Israeli war, a shut-down of the Panama Canal, and a war in Southern Africa over Namibia, with varying degrees of success. George W. Bush used preemption instead. In Sweden, however, it has been a major thrust of Foreign Minister (and then UN General Assembly President and UN Deputy Secretary-General) Jan Eliasson during the Swedish presidency of the European Union (EU) in the first half of 2001. His interest provided the basis for a 1999 report, *Preventing Violent Conflict* (Sweden 1999). The focus was on developing a culture of prevention, for which the rationale and justification appeared to be almost self-evident. Although diplomatic measures were emphasized, military measures were also included, and there was little concern about the dangers of intervention or sovereign interference. The point is that although prevention of conflict escalation has been a constant expectation of foreign affairs practitioners and observers, it has proven difficult for them to live up to expectations and after a while it has been submerged by conflicts that were not prevented and needed priority attention.

The Reasons for Persistence and Optimism

These obstacles and challenges are real and debilitating. Yet the fact is that in the existing system of World Order, literally innumerable conflicts have been prevented. Only a few have made their way through the net of normalcy to grab the headlines. Both facts are striking. Most neighboring states can find something to fight about; any African state can have a border war if it wants (Zartman 1965); ethnic groups and Islamic rebels can destroy security in any Muslim or ethnically fractured country; the conflict between traditional and modern land ownership systems is the largest source of instability in the developing world; legal and illegal arms sales provide the means for any state or group to threaten its neighbor, internal or external; dwindling natural resources, and above all water, make national security and personal health a matter of international concern and conflict. Many other known sources of conflict abound in and between the countries of the world. Yet most of these conflicts never reach the stage of violence or even of active political contest. Most remain passive, potential, and those that are activated tend to be handled somewhere along the way before they reach violence. Somehow, those obstacles and challenges have been overcome. That is a comforting, reassuring fact, and one that should lead the inquiry into how this has been done.

For all their seeming frequency and their inhumane practices, the conflicts that still have to be prevented are unusual events. That is what makes them such newsworthy (or at least sensationalist) happenings and draws attention to their excesses. There has been only one genocide, at least of the magnitude of Rwanda, since World War II. Most African and Mideast states achieved their independence without violence, putting the few cases, from Algeria to Zimbabwe, in relief. The international community's involvement in Afghanistan and Iraq has drawn attention because of the huge losses and because the two cases stand alone, and public opinion will not take much more of it. The carnage of the rare events that stand out pushes the public to demand more and better prevention.

But the uncountable frequency of prevented conflict, compared with the rare but shocking events that have avoided the preventive net, offers an encouraging record and a rich field for investigation and learning. How were so many prevented, compared to the few that were not? How did the few get through the net? How does the system of World Order work? How was ever-present conflict dampened when its sources were universal and its motivations supported? What is the effect of stifling the natural tendency to pursue national security and aspirations to the end of available means? These are questions that this study examines, with the aim of improving and expanding the practice, and overcoming its challenges.

CHAPTER TWO

The Ubiquity of Prevention

In this chapter, the tone changes. Despite all the challenges, so much conflict has been prevented that something must be different in the many situations of potential or passive conflict that have not turned active and violent. It is important to learn the lessons and mechanisms of the successes of prevention in order to apply them to the instances of conflict that continue to appear. Most discussions of prevention have been generalized, as if there is one approach and one type of conflict to be prevented. Yet prevention of climate disasters can scarcely be studied in the same way as prevention of boundary disputes, and prevention of ethnic conflicts is different from prevention of global arms races. To become applicable, investigation of prevention must cut up the subject substantively and address different issue areas where prevention has been achieved. The issue areas considered in the present chapter are security, territorial, and ethnic conflicts; analysis of levels of immediacy will be considered in later chapters.

Conflict is an attitudinal problem; prevention is more readily a structural challenge. Converting attitudes of conflict requires a long and deep effort; the operative aim of conflict prevention is to create and maintain structures that inhibit the activation of conflict and channel activity into paths of management and resolution, whereby attitude change is then made easier. These structures constitute the framework of a World Order system, shaping the attitudes of the parties living in the structure. Overly escalated conflict becomes unthinkable because the inhabitants of the system collectively declare it undoable and make it so. Obviously this approach is not absolute: for structures to work on their own, attitudes need to change to fit, so there is a relation between the two, and there may even be some occasions where preventers can work on attitudes directly. For this, external efforts are best positioned, although not alone. It is easier for agencies not involved in a conflict to change the structures in which the participants operate, and changing structures is the best way to change attitudes. But for external preventers to intervene effectively, the goals and behaviors they pursue must be condoned by the international community, including the parties to the conflict and the bystanders. Therefore, this chapter will begin with the question of agency. Whether the prevention acts as a self-inhibition on the conflicting parties or as a legitimizer of third-party efforts, the impact derives from a shared notion of acceptable behavior that holds the World Order together.

Who Done It?

The ultimate actor in escalation prevention is the state or other body involved in the conflict, but parties to a conflict need help. So the actors necessarily follow the R2P gradation: the state first but third parties as necessary. There is much literature on the special needs and talents of various agents for handling various conflicts (de Callières 2002 [1716]; Bartoli 2009; Peck 2009; Zartman 2010). This book will not enter the depth of that debate, but a few words are necessary to place it within the framework used here.

Established conventions and practices are best buttressed by collective consensus, even if the actual actor is an individual state or person. World Order institutions, such as the UN, regional organizations, multilateral fora and protocols, NGOs

and intergovernmental organizations (IGOs) all help formal-
ize and authorize standard ways of handling conflicts, as will
be discussed in the specifics in the following chapters (Cohen
1999; OSCE 2012). It is states working together who create
such institutions and such best practices are crucial to preventive action, but they depend on implementation by individual
actors, states, and people. Thus it is difficult to separate the
collective from the individual agent. When a state of the UN
mediates, the collective contribution is authorization to act,
including threats and promising the cases of non-compliance
and compliance. But the actual agent of mediation is the
individual(s) authorized to carry the message and engage in
the crucial exercise of persuasion.

The mandate is capital; the persuasive skills are crucial. It was Secretary-General Kofi Annan – even without
authorization – who convinced Saddam Hussein in the first
rounds to allow in inspectors (by another name); it was Alvaro
de Soto in the name of the UN who persuaded Salvadoran
authorities and guerrillas to come to a peace agreement; it was
Finnish former President Martti Ahtisaari, with the authorization of his own organization, the Conflict Management
Institute (CMI), who convinced Acehnese and Indonesian
leaders to settle their conflict. On the other hand, it was de
Soto who resigned as Special Representative of the [UN]
Secretary-General (SRSG) to the Palestine conflict because
of an inadequate mandate and Ahtisaari who failed to convince the Kosovar not to declare independence because of
the mandate (of his own formulation) given to him by the EU
and NATO. Examples are endless of the need for collective
standards and individual interaction to work in harmony for
prevention to be effective.

The following presentation will identify measures that
states themselves can take to prevent serious conflicts from
arising and then from getting out of control. These measures

include structural barriers that inhibit action and set up attitudinal change. But it is primarily addressed to outside agencies that can help states and other conflicting groups take actions to prevent, resolve without escalation, and de-escalate when necessary if they are not inclined to do so on their own. The UN Security Council is a cumbersome organization for taking action and delivering clear and appropriate mandates, and other coalitions of the willing and IGOs may be more capable of taking action (Touval 1994; Hampson & Malone 2002). It should be noted that there is a real place for NGOs as well. They can be most helpful in identifying and helping to legitimize best practices, in gaining entry and dealing unofficially with conflicting parties, and in keeping attention and implementation on track when official agencies have lost interest after an agreement has been signed. The most important counsel in such cases is respect and coordination: each agency has its role, their contributions should be recognized, but all actions should be coordinated so that they support each other and avoid the trap of shopping and outbidding among third parties. Other remarks on agency will be made where appropriate in the course of the following analyses.

Security Conflict

It is especially in regard to the prevention of conflict over state security that the World Order operates. Were it not so, the anarchy of the state system would be expressed in characteristic wars and aggressions as in the European (and particularly Italian) scene during the Middle Ages and Renaissance. Yet, as in other conflict settings examined below, the number of escalated and violent conflicts is minimal compared with the possibilities of threats to the security of one state posed by another. Perhaps nothing better than the international (and regional) security system illustrates the contention that situations endemically prone to conflict are nonetheless characteristically prevented from escalation. Exceptions are exceptions. It may be suggested that nothing more complicated than cost explains the phenomenon; aggression is expensive, increasingly so, and the results are not worth it, a common explanation for similar social behavior. But there is more to it than that. Conflicts over state security have been prevented by the evolution of structures and understandings operating under the basic mechanism of international politics, the ethos of reciprocity; each member will act in a certain way because it expects the others to act that same way, or will avoid acting in a certain way because it expects the others to retaliate (Zartman & Touval 2010). In the Cold War, reciprocity covered cost as the deterrent effect of Mutually Assured Destruction (MAD) (popularly termed the Balance of Terror), with lesser understandings negotiated under its shadow as the occasion arose. The record illustrates the conflict prevention capabilities of even the loosest set of behavioral standards and expectations, even among the most powerful adversaries.

Following the repeatedly catastrophic results of alliances as an attempt to set up behavioral rules for a system of World Order, a comprehensive system as a universal alliance for preventing global conflicts was established in San Francisco in 1945 in the UN Charter, which was strong in procedural principles, although often lacking in details. These principles were institutionalized in the United Nations and then in a gradually created network of other international organizations, including the 1975 Helsinki Agreements' Principles and Organization. Collective security was to replace collective defense; instead of relying on temporary, competing alliances to hold a rising power in check, the new system depended on the entire international community of states turning against one of its members to put it in its place if it should get out of order and cause conflict (Haas 1968). Before it could be tested and developed by much application, the system was pushed aside by the emergence of the superpower competition and a return to alliances during the Cold War. The two blocs proceeded to enlist the largest number of allies possible into their camps, leaving another third of the world non-aligned. The development of norms for the prevention of direct conflict escalation between the USA and the USSR proceeded through tests of the emerging system in the Berlin blockade in 1948–9 where the two blocs were contiguous, the Hungarian rebellion of 1956 where they were not, and the Cuban missile crises of 1964 where one bloc impinged on the other. Each case confirmed the understanding not to challenge the territorial status quo and to pull back from direct conflict. Regime change failed in the first two cases and was eschewed in the third, and the system emerged strengthened as a result. Deterred by cost, the principals worked out their relations in such a way to prevent their state security conflicts from escalating out of hand.

The spread of colonial liberation from NATO members raised new opportunities for conflict over old and new state security. Rapidly, by 1960 the right of former colonies to achieve independence was accepted, and expressed in UNGAr154. As a result, much conflict was prevented by a change in notions of appropriate behavior, and only a few colonies (Algeria, Angola, Mozambique, Portuguese Guinea, South West Africa [Namibia], Zimbabwe, and Vietnam) had to fight for independence. In Africa, the Cold War dimension of the anti-colonial struggle was laid to rest for the moment in the "Congo Convention" of 1961, a tacit understanding that Africa would be part of the Free World economically but non-aligned politically, preventing competing blocs from attempting to take over new territories and change regimes. Either bloc was expected to support its allies and its bloc area from an attack by the other, and so the reciprocal dissuasion of Mutual Assured

Deterrence to prevent escalation was extended to the Third World as well. The preventive norms were broken by the US in Vietnam, 1964–73, and the preventive "truce" in Africa by the USSR in 1974 with the introduction of Soviet and Cuban troops into Ethiopia (following regime change) and Angola, opening up a new period of uncertainty over the prevention of further escalation in the Third World. In all three cases, war was not prevented but its extension beyond the immediate theater was.

Turning to the most dangerous element of conflict between the two superpowers, the international community led by the Nuclear Weapon States (NWS), unable (after a few tries) to find agreement on banning the atomic bomb that was its own prevention measure, negotiated the Non-Proliferation Treaty (NPT) of 1970, an agreement to freeze competition from any new nuclear powers. The USA and USSR then turned for the next decade and beyond to arms limitation measures for the NWS, resulting in the 1972 Strategic Arms Limitation Talks (SALT I), then the 1979 SALT II, the 1987 Intermediate Nuclear Forces (INF) agreement, the 1991 Strategic Arms Reduction Treaty (START) I, the 2002 Strategic Offensive Reduction Treaty (SORT), and eventually the 2010 New START (Melamud et al. 2014). New Nuclear Weapons Capable States (NWCS) (India, Pakistan, Israel, then North Korea) operated with greater uncertainty under their own MAD deterrence to prevent escalation of their conflicts into nuclear confrontation.

Under this umbrella, minor encounters between the US and the USSR, such as naval incidents in the Mediterranean or cooperation as in the Mideast during the 1967 and 1973 wars or negotiations over Korean denuclearization after 1989, were used to build up conflict prevention procedures of coexistence (Kanet & Kolodziej 1991). The evolving system of World Order received its first formal expression in the

West ("from Vladivostok to Vancouver") in the 1975 Helsinki Principles, which recognized the Soviet bloc's territorial status quo in exchange for a formalization of human rights norms, and established the Conference on Security and Cooperation in Europe (CSCE), later to become an Organization (OSCE). An understanding of the World Order as prevention of direct conflict took more time and conflict to be worked out with the other nuclear power, China, after the experience of the Korean War 1950–4 (unsuccessful in regime change) and the Vietnam War 1964–73 (with regime change). The US hastened to establish relations with China and has been remarkably successful in promoting behavior to avoid direct conflict over the China–Taiwan dispute.

The collapse of the Soviet Union rendered this understanding of the World Order more uncertain. Conventions on acceptable behavior that had prevented conflicts from erupting and escalating in previous decades fell with the collapse of the bipolar order. Nothing prevented Iraq from invading Kuwait in 1992; Saddam Hussein expected Russian support as under the previous regime, but instead he met a US-led UN-authorized military response, but with no regime change, as indication of a "New World Order." The regime change came a decade later with another US-led but ambiguously authorized attack and occupation of Iraq. But a new world disorder was sown by the al-Qaeda attack on the US in 2001, returned by an UN-authorized coalition and occupation of Afghanistan, home of al-Qaeda. Military assistance was used to provide national self-determination from Serbia (but without regime change) for Bosnia-Herzegovina in 1993 by NATO with UN authorization, and for Kosovo in 1998 by a coalition of the willing without UN authorization, and to assist a regime change uprising in Libya in 2011 by NATO with UN authorization but mission creep. Direct military intervention without UN authorization was used by Russia to detach puppet states of Abkhazia and South Ossetia from Georgia in 2008 and Crimea from Ukraine in 2014. Under the circumstances of the second decade of the new millennium, the structure, agents, and norms for conflict prevention are very uncertain, and World Order is reeling. Contrary to the previous era, the West, emboldened by its Cold War victory, has appeared as the revolutionary (pro-regime change) power and the loose ad hoc coalition of the BRICS nations (Brazil, Russia, India, China, South Africa) has protested as the status quo pro-sovereignty group, until Russia then returned to good old nineteenth-century conquest of neighboring territories. It is hard to see how the so-called Islamic State of the Khalifat (known as ISIS or Da'esh) fits into this idea of World Order.

It is perhaps striking that in a matter so marked by naked power as state security conflicts over the past half century, there were clear if evolving regimes that governed behaviors and expectations and at the same time were consolidated by occasional tests of a high magnitude (Avenhaus et al. 2002). As in other issue areas, the exceptional cases have been exceptional because of the widespread prevention of escalation and violence that has occurred in general (Goldstein 2011). Despite some striking exceptions and the challenges they pose, the system of World Order has operated with clear principles and structures to prevent endemic escalation and habitual breach of accepted behavior.

In sum, security conflicts are routinely prevented by some standard structures and understandings that are basic to World Order.

- Over the long term: a preventive system of structures and understandings has been created and recreated as configurations evolve, based on such components as cost and reciprocity;

- In the medium/short run: when exceptions arise to challenge the preventive effects of institutions and attitudes, the system closes around them like a foreign body, and institutional and individual states' diplomatic intervention has worked to help the parties climb down from the slopes of escalation to manage, if not resolve, the conflict.

If this has worked in many cases, the goal of improved prevention requires the mechanisms to be strengthened and the holes to be plugged. Since the World Order mechanism depends on tightening do-don't structures and attitudes, and providing alternative avenues for managing and resolving the legitimate concerns and conflicts, international community responses should be regularized and reinforced. This means more responsive, responsible, and rigorous action by members of the UN Security Council. It means states realizing that reducing conflict escalation is in their common interests. And where minority blockage serves narrow breaches of World Order, it means facilitating means of response by legitimizing and activating coalitions of the willing when established institutional structures and consensual attitudes fail.

Territorial Conflict

Territorial conflicts over the lines between two states and over the territory that the lines enclose have been the major source of conflict and violence for millennia (Holsti 1991; Vasquez 2010). The subject has a tremendous potential for conflict, and yet the actual number of new or salient disputes has diminished considerably since World War II (Frederick 2012). Despite the fact that the phrase "neighborly relations" suggests that neighborliness is the epitome of conflictlessness, any body's first line of conflict is with its neighbor, in urban and rural communities as on continents; "My neighbor is my enemy; my neighbor's neighbor is my friend," wrote Kautilya (1960 [−320]: 293) in fourth-century BC India, giving a locational dimension to the even older adage, "My enemy's enemy is my friend." Often the border dispute is almost an excuse, a tip of the iceberg of a collection of pent-up, emotional grievances or the most visible manifestation of a rivalry of rank and relation. Yet of the 250 land boundaries in the world at the beginning of the twenty-first century, only a dozen are the subject of active hostilities and perhaps a similar number are at worst latent (Diehl 1998; Nordquist 2001; Vasquez & Valeriano 2009).[1]

The summary answer to the decline in border disputes is that by and large, states have learned to live in their skin by acceptance of a number of historical and geographic criteria and by tinkering at the margins. New boundary disputes are in steep decline and those that remain are low in significance. Over history, states have used both human and physical geographical features to determine their natural limits, augmented by past military (not always violent) and diplomatic efforts to define their exact lines. Boundaries off in the wilderness or up across mountain tops have a greater potential for stability than boundaries running through inhabited areas. Where there are no physical features handy on which to hang a boundary, the bounded states draw straight lines (geometric boundaries) which are even more stable because of their agreed artificiality. What is perhaps striking is that the military and diplomatic results have come to be accepted and are not the subject of repeated efforts of the same kind in new eras of power and relations after they had been established. This is true even when the borders are touted – however artificially – as "artificial," as in Africa. All borders are artificial, in that they separate human beings and call them "me" and "non-me." Stable borders, as in much of the world, have come to be adopted as "nationalized," by diplomacy, history and social accommodation. Socially, politically, and economically, populations have increasingly come to terms with the idea that where they are determines who they are.

Territory and boundaries are the subject of international agreements based on domestic political considerations, a mixture that accounts for their large potential for conflict and also for the recognized standard of firm agreements. The obvious fact that any boundary dispute necessarily affects both sides and creates a costly situation for both of them opens an incentive for joint interest in conflict prevention, weighed against the comparative value to both sides of their claims. Major border changes become unthinkable because they are undoable, as a result of the counterweight of the neighbor and the international opprobrium for unilateral changes, but minor rectifications become possible when in the interests of both sides of the border. Occasionally even accepted skins cause inconvenience (such as Geneva's bifurcation between France and Switzerland or Kaliningrad's separation from the rest of Russia or Iquitos' isolation from the rest of Peru). When the inconvenience has become too great, the neighbors negotiate rectifications to accommodate changing riverbeds or grazing patterns or even winding roads (as between the US and Mexico, between Mali and Mauritania, and between Congo and Zambia, respectively). World Order allows for such rectifications as an amicable alternative to escalated conflict.

Such acceptance is facilitated by specific practices in addition to rectification, such as demarcation and reglementation. Demarcation, the physical marking of delimited (agreed on paper) borders, is an important measure that has consolidated boundaries and prevented conflict. Borders tangibly indicated are easier to accept than lines that are hard to see on the ground. Algeria's insistence on demarcation solidified its border with Tunisia, which had long been in dispute, and its borders with other neighbors (except Morocco, where delimitation is agreed to but demarcation has been interrupted by conflict). The measure is particularly important in regard to new states. The complement to demarcation is reglementation. A border regime that allows traffic across it under specified and reasonable conditions works to prevent conflict from escalating out of the countless incidents that occur over lines separating people. Particularly in traffic corridors and populated areas, borders disrupt normal human intercourse that needs to be governed appropriately to minimize conflict. Even where neighbors have good relations, border incidents require management by a mutually satisfactory border regime to prevent escalation. Conflict prevention requires minimizing inevitable minor disputes so that the outbreak of resulting major conflict can be prevented. These measures of attention to the potential for escalation are powerful tools of prevention, and they have lessons for further prevention in the rarer instances of remaining border conflict.

Where states are unable to learn to like their given skins by themselves, external structures of World Order for conflict prevention are available to aid in social learning (Nordquist 2001). States need to be urged to come to terms with their skin, even if it does not fit their dreams. Permanent or ad hoc multilateral institutions assist conflicting states to find solutions for their dispute without escalation and so prevent continuing and even worsening conflict. Sometimes it takes so long for institutions' attention to produce results that it stretches the notion of prevention but illustrates the value of persistence. To prevent impending war, three states of the Hemisphere – Argentina, Brazil, and the US – helped Ecuador and Peru come to agreement on a status quo border line in 1936; renewed war in 1941 revived mediation to establish a demilitarized zone, and the following year a new peace and border protocol was mediated by the three states plus Chile; when fighting again broke out in 1953, 1977–8, 1981, and 1995, multilateral mediation rose to the level of the Organization of American States (OAS) and then back to the four guaranteeing states who finally produced an end to "Latin America's last border conflict" in 1998 by settling a newly discovered piece of mountain jungle that occasioned the last war (Simmons 1999, 2005; Nordquist 2001). The case was just one of the 22 boundary cases since the late 1800s that Latin American states submitted to peer-state arbitration (ten times more frequently than other continents' use of arbitration). The most important international institution of World Order for the settlement of border disputes has been the International Court of Justice (ICJ), whose intervention has usually been accepted and decisive in preventing conflict escalation. The ICJ has no bias and no interest in the disputes, whereas mediated prevention – especially in Latin America – is very often suspect to one party or the other. The great achievement has been the willingness of states to submit their disputes to the ICJ where they are assured of a favorable judgment.

The other type of territorial dispute concerns claims over whole pieces of land beyond simple disputes over lines. The same statistics obtain: over 400 pairs of states are next to each other and perhaps only 45 harbor territorial covetings. Of course, contiguity alone does not establish a prima facie potential for conflict as it does in regard to boundaries; in addition, a state must have a specific reason to claim another's territory. A more relevant statistic would indicate how many states have ethnic population overhang, how many occupy another's natural resources, how many sit on another's holy land, and so on, referring to the main causes of covetousness – statistics nearly impossible to acquire without long disputes over the statistics themselves. They would show, however, that the potential for territorial conflict has been prevented from leading to war in most instances. A few conflicts, from Sudetenland to Kivu, have been pursued rather than prevented in the name of protecting oppressed minorities that are related to a bordering population. As relations between Rwanda and its neighbors show, tribal overhang can serve as a too-convenient justification for interference for a neighboring state, particularly where citizenship has been denied longtime settlers. Suffice it to note that many states' ethnic or national majorities have a minority component in a neighbor's population, rely on energy or raw material resources from a neighbor, and some even contain sites or lands that are significant in their neighbor's history and mythology, without any of these constituting a cause for conflict. How do they do it? How is conflict prevented in such cases?

Again, the summary answer is that open intercourse that allows the neighbors access to lands of importance to them prevents conflict over the details of ownership, or, put otherwise, responsible ownership that meets the substantive concerns of neighbors minimizes the occasions for conflict (Ayissi 2001). As in the case of territorial lines, the longer the management of territorial relations has been done with responsibility and concern for both sides' interests, as long as conflict prevention has been practiced when tested, the more routinized prevention becomes. As in any relation, routines can be broken and broken habits are often harder to reinstate than they originally were to establish, so that prevention must be a subject of constant attention rather than a historical assumption.

Preventing eruption of territorial conflict based on national overhang draws its inspiration from such historical practices. If minority populations are allowed open contact with their majority neighbors and are allowed to maintain practices of their national identity, the formal distinctions of state citizenship can gradually become acceptable; the two demands must be kept in a delicate balance, so that minorities can be themselves within their "host" country in order not to provide a reason for the neighbor to seek to unite their territory with the land of their "home" folks. The limits of the balance are shown in the contemporary cases of Kosovo and Cyprus. Since its independence in 2008, Kosovo has sought to reduce conflict with its former owner, Serbia, by allowing various levels of self-government and self-expression to its Kosovar Serbs, as long as they do not contest their membership in Kosovo and as long as Serbia drops its claim on Serb-inhabited regions. The European Union (EU) urges Serbia to accept its separation from Kosovo, using the incentive of EU membership if it does so (among other conditions), to prevent continuing conflict that can escalate through incidents to violence. On the other hand, because the government of (southern) Cyprus has not been able to recognize sufficient self-government and expression to the Turkish community and the land it occupies, nearby Turkey has felt justified in occupying (protecting) and all-but-annexing the Turkish Republic of Northern Cyprus (TRNC) for some 40 years; the conflict has indeed been managed during this time by UN peace-keeping forces (UNFICYP), removing the pressure for settlement, but the prospect of EU membership for Cyprus in 2004 without settlement of the territorial question removed an incentive for settlement. There is plenty of space between the two countries' type of self-government demanded by and offered to their minority populations and the incentives for prevention offered by an international institution through which to find a solution.

Even sacred territories – as in Kosovo, Israel, India, possibly Ukraine – may not be as much of a different matter as may appear. In a few areas, one national religious group's sacred shrines are found in another state's territory and are cited as the basis for claims on that territory. To be sure, the claims are strident, but in the last analysis, prevention of conflict may be a matter of access – even privileged access – rather than ownership, or rather enough ownership to secure privileged access rather than the symbolic value of total possession. The key to conflict prevention is balanced and respectful dosage. Somewhat miraculously, Christian access to the holy sites of Israel and Palestine has been maintained despite lack of sovereignty, as has Muslim access to the Noble Sanctuary (Temple Mount) in Jerusalem, and when conflict has erupted it is because balance and respect are not preserved. Prevention of conflict requires both a general formula adapted to the case, and also continuing attention to its maintenance, World Order in a small and delicate instance.

Resources were once a frequent cause for territorial conquest; they are currently more commonly a matter for commercial competition. States want to have assured supplies of raw materials by commercial means and not direct possession. Potential conflicts have been mediated by market competition rather than military conquest. States and companies make commercial contracts, build production, develop economies of use, and create substitutes. On a few signal occasions – Angola in the 1980s, Kuwait in 1992, Iraq in 2003, Sudan in 2012, Ukraine in 2014 – oil and gas can become a stake of the conflict itself. In such cases the methods of prevention address the nature and means of the conflict but are not particularly effective in dealing with the object itself. Similar considerations govern conflicts over lootable materials such as diamonds, coltan, timber, and gold in rebel areas. Major international legal and commercial efforts are expended over the control of export markets for such "blood goods" as a means of dampening the resources of conflict groups; the rules of World Order are tightened to deprive violent groups of the use of resources.

Sometimes it takes a rather high level of conflict before the territorial claims can finally be buried in a settlement. The explanation lies in the fact that the costs of repeated escalations and of the consequences of prolonged bad relations outweigh the value of the claimed territory, but that this balance sheet takes time and – like any arithmetic – repeated exercises to sink in. The calculation is easier to make when the object of covetousness is a material resource rather than populations. Two examples from Africa illustrate the effect. A series of small wars in inhospitable territories over limited resources between Mali and Burkina Faso (1963, 1975, 1985) and between Nigeria and Cameroon (1963–7, 1995–8) finally ended in a settlement, by the ICJ in 1986 and 2002, respectively, and by direct (and repeated) negotiation confirming the settlement in 2008. The examples show the cost of unprevented conflict and the contribution of repeated conflict costs to the final prevention of further conflict on the issue, and the assistance of an institution of international order in preventing further violence and conflict. After four decades of independence, Africa, like other areas, has learned that territorial claims are not worth the cost and the opprobrium, and prevention is a matter of painful learning. It took Latin America over a century and a half to learn the same lesson in prevention, as seen in the territorial conflict between Ecuador and Peru.

The situation is similar concerning the conflict potential of basic goods such as water, already in short supply in countries of the Middle East, North Africa, and South Asia. Many internal bodies of water, both flowing and stable, have become the subject of local treaties that make up an international system of water regimes and institutions to provide the guidelines for preventing and settling conflict over the riparian water systems (Zawahri & Gerlak 2009). As a few examples among many, conflict was prevented by the Aral Basin Agreement of 1991, the Zambezi River System Action Plan (ZACPLAN) of 1987, and the Okavango River Basin Water Agreement of 1994, which were negotiated to avoid disputes in their region foreseeable if a regime were not to be provided (FAO 1987; Trolldalen 1992; Elhance 1996a, 1996b).

When conditions change, conflict is bound to appear and the parties rise to devise an agreement that forestalls conflict escalation. Nile and Mekong basin countries, parties to longstanding agreements of 1929 and 1959, and 1995 respectively, entered a period of instability at the turn of the century when upstream countries sought a redistribution of the water and built dams of their own that raised conflict with the downstream countries – Egypt and Sudan, and China, Laos, Cambodia, Thailand, and Vietnam, respectively; lengthy negotiations have been underway to prevent conflict escalation (Waterbury 1979; NBI 2015; Postel 2015). India and Pakistan, in re-escalated conflict over overuse and dam construction beyond what the 1960 Indus Waters agreement was designed to handle, revived difficult negotiations to restore a mutually satisfactory water regime. "History bears witness to the fact that cooperation, not conflict, is the most logical response to transboundary water management issues," judged Pakistani Environment Minister Afridi (Bagla 2010). The Caspian Sea became the subject of conflict with violent moments after 1991 when the original signatories of an agreement on its regime, the USSR and Iran, were joined as littoral states by three other former members of the USSR – Azerbaijan, Kazakhstan, and Turkmenistan. Although a formal new regime on the lake/sea was unattainable over the following quarter century, deft diplomatic and maritime maneuvering provided some practical understandings over access to the oil and gas deposits of the region. Under the pressure of necessity, parties in areas of potential conflict over the use of common water resources work out their own order to regulate and prevent conflict, revising as necessary when change or conflict appears. For the most part, as with territorial relations, countries learn to live with their maritime neighbors, and after occasional ruffled feathers and rattled arms, they settle down again to the status quo, the incidents shelved and the conflict prevented. Worse is not worth it.

In sum, habits, institutions, and costs have discouraged territorial claims on land and sea in modern times, against a historical record of territorial covetousness as the major cause of war (Vasquez & Valeriano 2009). States have become used to their skins and their neighbors, established rules and bodies provide standard ways of handling situations of potential conflict and for dealing with those conflicts that do become activated, and material and reputational costs work to prevent those less frequent behaviors that break through the systems of World Order. Prevention is made possible when land claims are reframed into population welfare, and state control is mitigated by respect for minorities. A history of humane attention to implementation also helps. Perhaps the most insightful lessons come from the cases where the conflict has been redefined and constructed in terms of real issues related to population welfare rather than symbolic issues of possession and sovereignty. The shift accompanies the rise in human security alongside state security in evolving international relations.

In sum, territorial conflicts are routinely prevented by some standard practices and expectations that contribute to the system of World Order.

- In the long term: "political learning" as boundaries become "nationalized" and states learn to live with their skin.
- In the medium/short run: conflicting boundary demands, not worth the cost of war, are handled through negotiation.
- In the short run: boundaries are adjusted and boundary regimes maintained to avoid inconveniences and incidents.

Such measures have been largely successful, although recent events, notably of 2014, show that the success of prevention is not total and established habits can be suddenly upset. Indeed, it is both the widespread shock over the Russian expansion into Crimea and the threat to the rest of

Ukraine, as well as the lassitude over Israeli expansion into conquered Palestinian territory, that brings home the need for firmer structures and stronger attitudes for prevention. Particular attention is needed after new states and new boundaries have been established; where nations have not yet had the time to learn to live in their new shapes, added efforts and reasserted principles, with sanctions to bring home the lesson of cost, are required to accelerate the learning process, to avoid the Eritrean and South Sudanese experience. At the same time, in territorial disputes over great divides between blocs and culture, it is well to recall useful historical devices such as neutral zones, buffer states, demilitarized corridors, and bridging arrangements that attenuate the friction and decrease the challenge that creates conflict.

Ethnic Conflicts

As territorial conflicts diminish in salience, ethnic conflicts have risen in current importance (Themnér & Wallensteen 2014).[2] Yet the numbers of these conflicts, too, pale against the literally innumerable ethnic groups that could contest their status and claim the right to rule themselves in sovereignty. Ethnic sources of territorial conflict through claims upon states by neighboring nations have already been examined; the focus here is on conflicts arising from claims within states by internal "nations." The first concerns a conflict between states, the second a conflict inside states, with different measures of prevention applying as a result. In the first, the conflict focuses on territory, whereas in the second territory is incidental to population. In reality the two often overlap, with secessionists seeking external allies in their fight for independence and annexers seeking internal support. However, in fact, until the Russian border ventures, no secessionist movement had then turned to annexation by its cousin-neighbor, although a few decolonization movements have joined a neighboring state upon attaining independence.

The precepts and practices of World Order operate differently in regard to ethnic conflicts than to territorial disputes. The basic notion is that the sovereign state is the guarantor of order and the manager of conflicts within its boundaries; even the new doctrines of R2P begin with that principle as its first pillar (Zartman 1995; Evans 2008; Ban 2010). As a result, international principles are not friendly to internal ethnic conflicts. The closest they come to the subject is through the right of national self-determination, which merely puts off resolution of the conflict to a prior determination of the "self" that claims that right, usually through the use of violence, and which is itself in conflict with the principle of territorial integrity. However, ethnic relations are handled by most states most of the time well short of the threshold of self-determination.

Given the potential for conflict far greater than the number of actual incidents, what are people – and states – doing right? There are two elements to the answer: conflict is prevented by lowering exaggerated ethnic awareness and by assuring unhindered access to political and economic participation. Inclusionary societies prevent ethnic conflict. Most national communities in the world fit into their state more or less comfortably, probably with some loss of their separate identities as assimilation occurs in a modernizing world.[3] Most such groups make a compromise between their identity and assimilation pressures, and as long as their condition is deemed acceptable, conflict in other than isolated cases is prevented by avoidance. Separate human cultural species are gradually disappearing, along with other, biological species, and cultural groups have a greater power of resistance than biological taxa. Although many separate components of population diversity are weakening and disappearing, global or even national homogenization takes a long time, and the process itself can give rise to increased national or ethnic consciousness as a defensive reaction, as groups formerly tolerated feel their existence threatened by assimilation pressures. What ethnic communities want is recognition and the ability to be themselves and "do their own thing"; if this is actively denied, they will fight for it, and the need is made more pointed by its repression, or simply ignoring. The current Islamist movement with al-Qaeda in the lead is a particularly striking example of a reaction against assimilation in a globalized form, particularly in its socio-cultural manifestations, itself as global in scale as the threat to its existence to which it responds. Ironically, as identity conflict turns global, the Islamist awakening turns inward and is riven by internal divisions, between Sunnis and Shi'a, that undercut its existential reaction.

In many countries, the composition of the population tends to be rather stable, giving communities time to become used to their place in society and their compromise between identity and assimilation, and thus preventing potential or latent conflicts from becoming more serious. However, population movements in some other countries contain the ingredients for possible deep challenges for prevention, and even stable relations contain their own conflict dynamics that set the stage for the exercise of preventive responsibilities. Research findings indicate that highly multi-ethnic (i.e. many groups without a majority) and essentially single-ethnic countries (such as Tanzania and Tunisia, respectively) tend toward stability, whereas pluri-ethnic situations (i.e. a few groups) with a dominant ethnic group (such as Rwanda, Sri Lanka, Cyprus, and Bolivia) foster accentuated ethnic awareness and are the most conflict-prone (Collier & Hoeffler 2000; Elbadawi & Sambanis 2000; Sambanis 2002; Arnson & Zartman 2005; Collier et al. 2013). Studies also show that ethnic groups that share in active civic associations tend to be immune from inter-ethnic violence, whereas separated ethnic communities are most likely to have violent relations, and groups that share neighborhood routines are less so (Varshney 2003).

Further study indicates that within this situation, relations among groups tend toward conflict if one group is heavily favored in the distribution of benefits or if another group's access is hindered by selectivity and repression, particularly when deprivations within the society become targeted on the community and become discrimination (Arnson & Zartman 2005). Social inequality and comparative deprivation break down social values, such as trust and support (Kawachi et al. 1997; Kawachi & Subramanian 2008). Such perceptions generate a dynamic where the powerful in-group fears retribution for its repressive policies, making it both particularly susceptible to fear mongering and prone to co-opt state structures for purposes of self-defense – a deadly combination. It is important to remember that ethnic conflict carried to the point of mass killings and genocide is essentially a reaction of high awareness perceived as defensive (Zartman et al. 2012). The majority group concocts a fear of the minority and acts to defend itself against the perceived existential threat, even when there is no objective danger. The Nazis justified their efforts to exterminate the Jews by the perceived threat that the Jews posed to Aryan society; the Hutu *génocidaires* justified their attempt to exterminate Tutsi by the expectation that, otherwise, the Tutsi would exterminate them.

This dynamic takes the form of a security dilemma, operating even in conditions short of genocide. One group takes measures to assure its security against a perceived threat from another, which in turn causes the other to raise its own group awareness and take similar measures to protect its security, thus lessening the security of the first group and causing it to take further security measures, and so on (Posen 1993). The result is territorialization, when a community gives a spatial dimension to its group awareness and congregates in an identifiable space that then becomes a tangible element in its identity, so that conflict for greater self-defense and self-determination is fostered (Toft 2003; Vasquez 2010). Such concentration may be an accident of history or may be deliberate, but it contributes to the development of a "rounding the wagons" attitude and a physical separation from the rest of the population. When it takes on symbolic value it becomes a barrier to integration. Such actions render the population vulnerable to the organization efforts of political entrepreneurs who seize on an opportunity to promote revolt. The record shows that political entrepreneurs for repressive groups who make disproportionate gains through economic appropriation or political violence acquire habits that lead to sharpened identity conflicts (Toch 1965; Staub 1989: ch 5; Crawford & Lipschutz 1999; Tilly 2003: 31–41). Both head the values of access and accommodation in the wrong direction, and make them more difficult to promote.

To these situations a range of structural approaches is employed to prevent activation of passive conflict and to foster integration when communities become restive (Gurr 1993; Ayissi 2001). Structures that assure access provide unhindered participation in the management of affairs, their own and the larger society's. Successfully integrating states seek to guarantee access for the people of the community, involving national unity, non-discrimination and expressions of being "created equal . . . endowed by their Creator with certain inalienable Rights . . . [of] Life, Liberty and the pursuit of Happiness," in the terms of the American Declaration of Independence, or "Liberty, Equality and Fraternity" as expressed by the French Revolution, or "Dignity, Justice, Bread, and Citizenship" in the slogans of the Arab Spring. Job opportunities, location of schools, open communications, and voting rights need be equally and easily available.

When full integration is not possible, accommodation may be used as the reverse of access, involving an emphasis on positive aspects associated with the community's identity and well-being that are at the same time contributory to the general welfare of the whole population. As long as the ethnic group can find "its spokesmen" in government and more broadly in society, it can feel part of the whole, even when it feels part of itself. Accommodation in its most organized form is power-sharing, where each ethnic community is guaranteed its portion of government (Lijphart 1977); the downside of power-sharing is the solidification of ethnic group membership and identity, on which it depends, to the detriment of integration and assimilation. The prize phrase of the twenty-first century seems to be "ethnic diversity" rather than assimilation, although ethnic diversity tends to reify the diverse divisions and identities, presaging ethnic awareness and conflict. In a sense, this aspect balances assimilation with multiculturalism and pluralism. It includes not only a glorification of community identity but also a promotion of community prosperity, so that the community does not feel left out of either the cultural or the material benefits of being in the home state. When communities feel barriers of discrimination, employment opportunities, educational access, language promotion, and electoral facilities may require extra measures and affirmative action to prevent feelings that fuel conflict. "Separate but equal" in schooling has been outlawed in the US as an unconstitutional oxymoron, but attempts to mix either become very complicated or are decided by demographic patterns that load heavily for one race or ethnic group compared to others. Recognition of the place of Breton, Tamazigh, French, and German languages constituted steps in dampening conflict in France, Morocco, Quebec, and northern Italy, respectively. Measures must be taken carefully, lest the antidote for discrimination involve reverse discrimination until the negative imbalance is redressed. As noted, rebalancing measures begin with structural improvements, with general attitudinal changes following behind.

These general measures have had their particular applications in various states over time and go far to account for the innumerable communities throughout the world who are able to maintain some form of their identity with some form of comfort within their states and therefore prevent possibly passive conflict from reaching into activity. It is important to emphasize that these conditions are continually in movement and in need of continual re-evaluation. Complacency with a given formula for prevention can lead to its wearing out. "Normal politics" in a functioning democracy offers the best prevention for ethnic conflict, followed close after by an attentive authoritative rule, also practicing normal politics. The distinction is that democracy is flexible and has the internal, inherent means to meet new situations, and authoritative rule dies with the ruler and is a tough act to follow. The American system has rolled with a number of punches in the postwar period and righted itself, whereas Felix Houphouet-Boigny's stability in the Ivory Coast died convulsively with him in coups and conflicts after 1999. There is no doubt that the greatest goad to ethnic conflict is perceived discrimination; whether perceptions are correct or not, they can always be exploited, expanded, and evidenced. Discrimination becomes rooted deep in the mind on both sides, even when tangible conditions are improved, but structural improvements are the *sine qua non* for changing attitudinal perceptions. The cycle is vicious, however, and attitude changes among key leaders are necessary to create the structural conditions that foster broader attitudinal changes. The importance for American race relations of the *Brown vs Board of Education* decision of the US Supreme Court in 1954 ending separate but equal education is illustrative of all these aspects.

In sum, many potential ethnic conflicts are prevented by some standard mechanisms.

- In the long term: "political learning" recognizes that the practice of inclusion as a political system and compensatory inclusion when necessary is the soundest insurance against ethnic conflict.
- In the medium/short run: rising existential cycles are prevented by remedial inclusionary negotiations, including temporary separation measures as a step to direct integration.
- In the short run: conflicting demands and grievances, not worth the cost of repression, are negotiated to provide greater self-determination.

The recently increased salience of ethnic and other identity conflicts underscores the need to rethink the usual structures and attitudes for their prevention (Zartman et al. 2012). Identity conflict hides behind the mask of sovereignty and so is harder for established prevention mechanisms to get to. While the developed world in general has learned to share and to live with its multiple identities, the rest of the world is becoming increasingly aware of single-focus identities, especially ethnic and religious, and has not wanted anyone to get in the way of their newly asserted being. When these individual identities become groups and then movements, they overrun attempts at calm and compromise. Learning, inclusion, and self-determination take on new meanings against new odds, as the developing world takes up residence in the developed countries to disrupt established patterns of identity. There is no easy answer to their success, except a continuing quiet insistence that we can all be ourselves (and in the modern world, our plural selves) without impinging on the ability of others to do the same. Conflict prevention hangs on reinforcing that tolerance.

The First Line of Prevention

This chapter has emphasized the importance of established structures and behaviors as the first line of prevention in a system of World Order. They have provided standards for handling categories of conflict situations as an explanation for the widespread absence of conflict in many ostensibly conflict-prone situations. The discussion emphasizes the effectiveness of general principles in the prevention of conflict, large as well as small, and also the use of negotiation and other conflict management and even resolution means to fill in the gaps where the global standards of behavior fall short. Furthermore, conflicts that fall between the cracks of a prevention regime do arise, either because the situation is idiosyncratic (as all situations are) or because the parties have been able to ignore the constraints of the regime, the norms nonetheless provide guidelines for conflict prevention measures to take in individual cases.

States, groups and individuals have for the most part learned to live with their security, territorial, and ethnic situation and handle their problems as they arise. It is notable, in view of the following chapter, that this has occurred because of the prevalence of attitudes that condone conventional behavior and condemn deviation, much more than because of structures of prevention. When a state feels impelled to contravene the system of World Order, physical intervention by the UN Security Council, a coalition of the willing, or a regional organization is slow in coming and is even more exceptional than the breach. But opprobrium and normative judgment is more ready to be deployed and is powerful as a preventive deterrent (Finnemore & Sikkink 1998).

All the while recognizing these effects, the attitudes and structures that produce them must continually be exercised, strengthened, and expanded. Unconventional exceptions will always appear when a party thinks it is worthwhile to break the established rules of behavior. This will occur particularly when the structure of the global or regional system changes, shaking the established World (or regional) Order and opening opportunities for unconventional behavior. It is especially at such moments that the habits of preventive behavior need to be reasserted. This recognition sets the stage for discussions of specific types of preventive measures in the next chapter.

CHAPTER THREE

Norms for Long-term Prevention

The previous chapter has divided conflicts vertically into issue areas and shown that conflict prevention is common and effective. But for conflicts that escape standard prevention practices, it is better to focus on methods of prevention at particular, horizontal stages of the conflict's evolution. Conflict prevention in search of best practices must begin at a distance from the ultimate outbreak of violence or its warning signs and look for broadly held attitudes that serve as standards for prevention and management in various types of conflict situations. Prevention cannot wait to swing into action until the conflict situation has escalated to crisis and broken out in violence; it must start in the early stages to operate effectively to break the course of the conflict. One cannot seek to have prevented World War I by simply arresting Gavrilo Princip before he could shoot the Austro-Hungarian archduke on June 28, 1914, or World War II by having British Prime Minister Neville Chamberlain stand up more forcefully to Hitler at Munich in 1938. The atrocity prevention literature often begins its attention on the eve of the genocide, whereas attention needs to be alerted at the beginning of heightened ethnic consciousness (Bellamy 2011; Zartman et al. 2012).

Standard attitudes and norms about the proper way to handle different types of conflict are components of the World Order system and provide powerful consensual guidelines for appropriate behavior, both for the conflicting parties and for would-be preventers in the early stages of conflict. They can be particularly helpful in separating normal from deviant and dangerous types of conflict. For it must be remembered that conflict is often normal and even useful, seeking and expecting to find standard ways of resolution at the very beginning of the activation phase before much escalation has begun. The best way to prevent escalation and violence is to channel the conflict from the beginning into established, normal standards for handling the conflict issue.

Thus, the first stage in prevention, as shown in figure 1, is the early activation of normative constraints or regimes that create attitudes and rules for behavior in different issue areas (for a similar organization, see Leatherman et al. 1999; Sriram & Wermester 2003). The international community of states, collectively and individually, needs to lay a solid groundwork for prevention by bringing conflicting parties to a recognition of relevant norms and by building and strengthening appropriate regimes for behavior. The second stage or mid-term gestation prevention involves process mechanisms for stopping the conflict in mid-course by developing a sequence of preventive actions by both the conflicting parties and concerned third parties. In the third phase or "early-late" pre-crisis prevention, rapid action is needed to interrupt, separate, and integrate the conflicted parties before it is too late.[1] In the late, post-crisis phases, if prevention has failed to avert violence, it must still find measures to address both old attitudes and new structures for concluding the conflict, implementing the outcome and handling its courses and consequences to prevent conflict relapse and recurrence, lest it happen again, as past conflict is a reliable predictor of renewed conflict within five years (Collier et al. 2003). Thus the stages of prevention reflecting levels of immediacy move from broad attitudes of the international community, to mechanisms for preventing the developing conflict by both third parties and conflicting parties, to emergency methods by third parties to pull back the conflicters from a violent explosion, and finally back to the international community for measures to ensure implementation and prevent recurrence. Attitudes and structures of prevention operate together as the mind and bones of the World Order of prevention.

This evolution is offered as more helpful and accurate than the categorization often used that calls early prevention structural and later phases operational (Holl 1997). Early resort to norms and standards is not the same thing as searching for root causes, often termed structural analysis, which is much like going back to Genesis, absolving present actors of their mistakes. Root causes are generally so broad as to be the cause of any- if not everything, so far from the conflict manifestation that they afford little insight into means of prevention (and after Genesis 2 it was too late anyhow). Instead, norms and attitudes apply to given conflict issues as they start their escalation from early activity toward violence. Socio-economic development is not conflict prevention, nor does poverty cause conflict, even though the two – like many other things – can be related as distant generations. What is needed is general guidelines for handling conflict as it moves into the low-active phase, by helping parties know what to do when the earliest signs of conflict appear on the surface.

Prevention begins at the beginning of conflict, with the attitudes that people and states hold about what is permissible behavior and what is not. It is rooted most fundamentally in the establishment of normative structures and standards that are designed to inhibit the rise of activated conflict from the beginning. The broadest way of approaching conflict situations is to lay the groundwork for prevention by establishing appropriate norms for both stable and conflict-resolving relations in conflict-susceptible situations. Where norms for behavior can be established, they constitute standards for dealing with conflict issues, for channeling conflict, and for making escalation unthinkable. They address types of conflict situations and indicate appropriate standards and behaviors for dealing with them. They can be informal as well as formal laws, treaties, and conventions, usually beginning as the first and then given more institutionalized structure (Blechman & Finlay 2012). When accepted standards of behavior are in place, they can be used as generic prescriptions for states to deal healthily with their own challenges and problems and as model diagnoses for third parties to assist them in achieving appropriate responses – in fact, as guides for Pillars I and II of R2P, i.e. for states to act responsibly to care for their own citizens and for those of other states to help them responsibly in this endeavor. It is here that early prevention can begin, with the construction of international regimes[2] – principles, norms, rules, expectations, procedures, and programs that govern the interactions of actors in specific issue areas for dealing with situations likely to lead to conflict escalation (Krasner 1983; Levy et al. 1995; Hasenclever et al. 1997; Spector and Zartman 2003).

The purpose of this chapter is to discuss the importance of such norms and regimes, more or less well developed as the formulation of standard attitudes, in the long-term prevention of conflict escalation and violence, and to indicate how they can be further developed and improved. Norms indicate that "This is the way it is to be done (or not done)," and they carry with them the implication that "the international community will not countenance its being done in any other way," thus raising the cost of infraction, authorizing counter-action, and working to make the unthinkable undoable (Adler-Nissen 2014). "This/It" is a general, principled indication but at the same time a clear direction, applicable to broad types of situations that give rise to conflict on particular issues.

Norms are one thing; their interpretation and application are another. Regimes are neither enforceable nor self-enforcing;

they are not legislation that outlaws conflict or its escalation. There is no assurance in human society that such norms, any more than any others, will be followed perfectly. They will be broken on occasion, and to make such infractions exceptional and prevention effective, the norm breakers need to be brought to order by the international community and the norm reaffirmed.[3] The purpose of regimes is to articulate attitudes and create habits, practices, expectations, and standards against which behavior can be judged and toward which it can be guided. Norms identify and highlight issues, serve as the basis for data and studies, call for policy consideration and strategies. The rise of human rights attention under President Jimmy Carter and its gradual, continuing development into a loose body of concerns and constraints on general foreign policy behaviors is an ongoing example.

International regimes are live behavioral rules; they evolve and can be changed, adjusted and refined to deal better with the situation to which they are applicable (Spector & Zartman 2003). Existing regimes need implementation by the international community, reinforcement in practice, adjustment to contextual changes, and refinement. That only comes with usage, so the action of prevention starting with basic mechanisms reinforces those mechanisms, strengthening the general norms as well as their application for prevention. Regimes help prevention in three ways. First, they guide and restrain states' own behavior, legitimizing actions designed to achieve and maintain their own good functioning. Second, they provide standards and practices by which states can be held accountable, offered assistance, and subjected to pressure by others acting as commentators, mediators, arbitrators, judges, and enforcers. Third, they provide both a rationale for collective action by the international community and a charter for institutional goals and programs. By no coincidence, these three ways correspond to the three pillars of R2P, itself a set of norms basic to dealing with international conflict, referred to above and to be discussed further below.

Regimes are formed by the international community, including the UN agencies and organs, especially the General Assembly, and in global conferences often mandated by the General Assembly. At most, UN bodies set standards for states to enforce. Action and enforcement depend on the states, acting individually or as Security Council and General Assembly and regional organization members. States can make regime norms part of their policy, or, more permanently, part of their laws, their constitutions, their civil society, and their education systems. But norms also grow up informally, and may not yet be ready for UN specification and institutionalization. In many situations, NGOs are also the agent of regime application and even enforcement through their powers of information and publicity. A number of broad sources of conflict previously identified lend themselves to such regime-building and have already been the subject of some effort. These issue areas include *territorial integrity, weapons of mass destruction, ethnic relations, environmental protection, human rights, population displacement, democratization,* and *good governance.* The list is rather comprehensive.

Territorial Integrity

Faced with a historical record of territorial wars and a tripling of the number of independent states in the world, all of which pointed to a new world of territorial conflicts after World War II, the international community has taken measures to bring international boundaries and territorial uncertainty under control (Henehan & Vasquez 2006). Basic to the prevention of territorial conflict is the establishment of norms declaring the sanctity of boundaries that encircle territory and hold it in place. The resulting international regime of territorial integrity has made significant boundary changes unthinkable universally and also more specifically in many regions of the world. In rare cases when the unthinkable behavior has occurred, the rest of the region refers to the regime in its efforts to prevent continuing and further conflict. Territorial integrity is a cornerstone of the current system of World Order; the regime is not hole-proof but it is powerful in preventing conflict. It is there to be used, and tightened.

Territorial integrity is covered by relatively clear and official norms, which are occasionally transgressed, incidents made all the more striking by their exceptionality. The UN statements on the subject are straightforward: up front, among the first principles of the Charter (chap. I, art 4), member states are bound to refrain "from the threat or use of force against the territorial integrity or political independence of any state." Territorial conquest is thereby declared illegitimate (Zacher 2001). The international community went to war in 1991 to enforce that norm in Kuwait. While the exceptional cases of Russian and Israeli aggression and occupation stand out as failures of prevention, it is notable that even in these cases international recognition has been widely withheld, serving as a deterrent if other states would be inclined to act the same way. The situation illustrates the authority of the norm as an element inhibiting Israeli annexation of the other occupied territories besides Golan, and Russia thinking twice before annexing Transnistria, Abkhazia, South Ossetia, or other parts of Ukraine besides Crimea, and presumably also preventing Armenia from laying direct claim to Nagorno-Karabakh. Similarly, no state but Turkey has recognized the Turkish Republic of Northern Cyprus; even Kosovo has been blocked from full EU relations by the lack of recognition by five EU members. Difficulty in securing recognition as a state has greatly aided the preventive efforts of mediators to achieve a satisfaction of demands for national self-determination short of independence in Aceh in Indonesia, Bangsamoro in the Philippines, Chiapas in Mexico, Zanzibar in Tanzania, Casamance in Senegal, and Kurdistan in Iraq and Syria, and earlier in Biafra in Nigeria.

Regionally, norms have become accepted, initially tacitly and then even formally, rendering boundary conflict illegitimate and recognizing the fact that it is no longer worthwhile. New membership in the EU requires that the state must have settled any territorial disputes it may have had with other members. The only breach in the requirement is in regard to Cyprus in 2004, when the dispute-free precondition to its membership that could have forced an end to its conflict was removed. Membership in the Organization of African Unity (OAU) and its successor African Union (AU) involves recognition of colonially inherited boundaries (reservations from the beginning were noted by Morocco and Somalia, and practiced later by a few other states who disagreed where the colonially inherited boundaries actually were). When Uganda's Idi Amin declared in 1978 that a more "African" boundary with Tanzania was the Kagera river rather than a straight line, the other members of the OAU denounced him and neighboring Tanzania was literally up in arms. Members of the Organization of American States (OAS) have applauded the 1998 mediated Peru-Ecuador border settlement as the last of Latin America's significant border conflicts, although some minor disputes remain and others may be dormant. Thus not only are norms in place to prevent conflict but they have been put to work in relatively recent times, and the work continues on their application. For border conflicts that slip through the regional regimes, there are more specific precedents and applications at the hands of the ICJ, where the norms have been formalized into justiciable international law and the conflicts have tended to find resolution. Of the 16 formally de-escalated border conflicts after World War II, a third were settled by the ICJ (only one judgment was rejected by the parties) and the rest by negotiation.

Beyond these clear principles, the norm of territorial integrity becomes more ambiguous. It has been questioned in situations where ownership of a defined territorial unit is contested, and where it runs up against the norm of national (actually, state) self-determination – which is trumps? The first question, addressed indirectly by the ruling in 1974 by the ICJ on the Western Sahara, is answered by expressions of the will of the contested territory's population, presumably by referendum. The norm still awaits application in Kashmir after over 60 years. The second question presents the horns on which the question of Nagorno-Karabakh is hung, when the two conflicting norms – territorial integrity and self-determination – are cited by the two sides, Azerbaijan and Armenia, respectively. The cases illustrate the power and limitation of norms – not absolutely observed rules for behavior but authoritative guiding referents, clear in their statement yet contestable by another norm in detailed application. The regime of territorial integrity does not absolutely prevent conflict (in fact, it introduces conflict at a more detailed level) but it serves as a guide for efforts at conflict prevention, effectively working to inhibit new territorial conflict.

The picture is even less clear in regard to maritime claims (Conca 2005). The UN Law of the Sea has provided a sound, specific normative basis for the delimitation of sovereignty over the waters around land, including islands, in a notable case of formal regime creation (or revision) to prevent conflict. Its provisions range from clear statements, such as on territorial waters and exclusive economic zones (EEZs), to more general provisions for dispute settlement. The norm, like any law, also provides the material for conflict in cases where the rough configuration of geography does not fit the neat and clear specifications of the law. Granted, it only gives general elements for larger questions of interpretation and application, presumably left to the parties to negotiate or adjudicate. Where its regime is not directly applicable to prevent conflict, a reframing of the issue from ownership to usufruct can serve as a key to prevention.

Thus, maritime disputes are often matters of fishing and mining, where considerations of access and ownership form the possibilities for conflict prevention. The Law of the Sea conference was unable to prevent fishing disputes between the UK and Iceland but directed the parties to negotiate an agreement directly in its spirit, which they did in 1996, trading expanded Icelandic sovereign limits against special waivers for British fishers at special times. Despite disagreement over a regime provided in the North Atlantic Fisheries Organization agreement, Spain and Canada were able to find an agreement in direct negotiations (increased EU quotas in exchange for tightened enforcement) to prevent further conflict escalation in 1995. The East and South China, Aegean, and Caspian Seas are up for grabs without adequate guidance except for the power of the claimants. Not just the maritime territory but the applicability of World Order norms are contested by the claimants, a conflict-prone situation that has already reached occasional armed escalation in all these areas (Valencia, Van Dyke & Ludwig 1997; Djalal & Townsend-Gault 1999; Dutton 2007, 2009, 2010; Gao & Jia 2013; Faure 2014).

In such touchy situations, new norms to handle unintended accidents take a bite into the area of prevention, and show how a small but important regime of mutual interest – even though non-binding – can be extended. Such a situation is found in the Western Pacific's 2000 Code for Unalerted Encounters at Sea (CUES), ASEAN's 2002 Declaration on the Conduct of Parties in the South China Sea Disputes, and the International Maritime Organization's Regulations for Preventing Collisions at Sea (COLREGS), which have been combined by the Western Pacific Naval Symposium, after a decade of discussion and in the very midst of China's South China Sea expansion, into a 2014 Code for Unplanned Encounters at Sea that can be used as a model for other maritime regions for the coordination of conflict prevention (Faure 2014; Wright & Schoff 2014). Prevention can also be accomplished by reframing, shifting the conflict from ownership to the use of maritime resources and even to mixed sovereignty, as the Law of the Sea itself does on seabed resources (Sebenius 1984; Friedheim 1993). Where a norm is not clear, it is nonetheless open to creative use by the ultimate resort of prevention: diplomatic negotiation.

Elements of the territorial regime to prevent conflict can be formal and informal:

- Recognition of the illegitimacy of territorial conquest.
- Development of more detailed regimes to handle other types of conflict.
- Clarification of regime overlaps.
- Negotiation of flexible formulas in conflict situations not covered by formal regime norms, including substitution of usufruct for ownership.

In sum, the acceptance of the norm of territorial integrity and boundary stability is available for the prevention of much territorial conflict and for the lowered level of territorial disputes. When potential conflicts appear, they are either covered by specific provisions of formal or looser regimes or are facilitated in their resolution by applicable precedents and practices for the prevention of conflict escalation. In both cases, of interpretation and practice, the norm is further developed and strengthened. But the norm of territorial integrity also bears further development for greater guidance in difficult cases. The conflicts between national self-determination (examined below) and territorial integrity, and between freedom of navigation and exploitation and sovereign maritime extension, and the means of fully preventing territorial aggression are all areas for normative development in order to flesh out the relevant issue area of World Order.

Weapons of Mass Destruction (WMD)

Intense efforts have been devoted to creating a preventive regime for the issue area occupied by weapons of mass destruction (WMD or ABC – atomic, biological, and chemical – weapons), with still some way to go on both coverage and implementation (Garcia 2011). Although the original Baruch and Gromyko Plans for banning all nuclear weapons never got very far, all subsequent efforts at arms limitation have included total elimination as the final (if distant) goal. In the interim, the core of the functioning regime is the Non-Proliferation Treaty (NPT) of 1970, whereby nuclear weapons are the exclusive domain of the five nuclear weapons states (NWS). That status and the limitation of nuclear power for peaceful purposes is the subject of a regime of on-site inspections (OSI) by the International Atomic Energy Agency (IAEA). Whereas President Kennedy (1960) saw 15 to 20 nuclear states by the end of the century, in fact there are even now only nine (even though one or more are now straining at the door).

Yet the NPT is a leaky regime. An additional category of nuclear-capable weapons states (NCWS) comprises those who are armed with nuclear weapons but "illegally" – India, Pakistan, Israel, and most recently North Korea. Whereas North Korea has joined the NCWS without a reaction other than interrupted negotiations within the Six-Party Talks, Iran, pressing at the same gate, has met serious sanctions and more threats; both countries live under a fear of induced regime change. A treaty to close another loophole by controlling all fissile materials (FMCT) is being discussed, but the

Nuclear Suppliers Group, Nuclear Power Plant and Reactor Exporters' Principles of Conduct (NuPOC), Proliferation Security Initiative, and Global Partnership against the Spread of Weapons and Materials of Mass Destruction are functioning informal elements of the regime. If Iran succeeds in joining the NCWS, Saudi Arabia and others in the region are next in line, and a further bulwark of prevention will have been breached. A treaty to complement the NPT by banning all nuclear weapons testing (CTBT) was adopted in 1996 but has not yet been sufficiently ratified to go into force; yet the Comprehensive Test Ban Treaty Organization (CTBTO) is nonetheless in limited operation (Melamud et al. 2014). The regime needs tightening.

Where efforts to close loopholes in the global regime are still needed, some groups of states have set up regional regimes for nuclear weapons-free zones (NWFZ) (Finlay 2014). The Antarctic Treaty of 1959 bans all military activity including nuclear weapons in the southern continent. Latin America declared itself a NWFZ in 1967 in the Treaty of Tlatelolco, with an Agency for the Prohibition of Nuclear Weapons in Latin America (OPANAL) to monitor compliance; the South Pacific and Southwest Asia established similar nuclear-free zones in the Treaty of Rarotonga in 1985 and the Treaty of Bangkok in 1997, respectively, and the states of the African Union (AU) made Africa a nuclear-free zone in 1996 in the Treaty of Pelindaba; Central Asia became a NWFZ in 2009. As a result, states within these areas that already had advanced into nuclear capability or were engaged in arms races to gain such capability, such as Argentina, Brazil and Chile, Australia and Indonesia, Iraq, South Korea, Taiwan, Ukraine, Kazakhstan, South Africa and Libya, renounced their plans and weapons, in some case because of material inducements but in general because of a worldwide ethos of prevention in nuclear matters. The Outer Space Treaty of 1967 and the Sea-Bed Treaty of 1972 also ban nuclear weapons from above and below the surface of the earth. These provisions tighten the regime geographically, but the areas of most intense conflict – notably Europe and Asia – are still not covered by the global nuclear norms. This dimension too needs more preventive work.

There are other and older WMD regimes that are clearly stated and universally adopted; while they have not prevented a very occasional breach, the reaction to such behavior has been almost universally condemnatory. The 1975 Biological Weapons Convention has been effective in preventing an area of conflict escalation. The prohibition of mustard gas after World War I has turned into the 1997 Treaty on the Prohibition of Chemical Weapons, most recently signed by Syria after it had breached the regime several times (and then continued to do so). The norm operates as a strong prevention measure but breaches of the norm are punished only by disapproval, nothing stronger, as the Iraqi infraction in 1988 and the Syrian infractions in 2013–15 show. Perhaps stronger punishments would lower the number of infractions even further.

- Norms for the prevention of WMD have generally been quite effective.
- WMD regimes have increased over the past half century.
- Stronger enforcement and punishments are needed to tighten the norms.

The WMD regime is a good example of a normative alignment of attitudes with some institutional structure behind it (Garcia & Herz 2014). It has been remarkably effective in controlling WMD use of all kinds and in eliminating nuclear arms among most countries and many regions of the world. Nonetheless, a few countries have plowed their way through the net of norms. They cite the example given by the NWS themselves as an excuse, but they offer their own behavior as an example for even more norm breakers. The regime has been widely useful for the prevention of conflict escalation but the challenge of further tightening is daunting.

Ethnic Relations

Ethnic relations constitute a subject of increasing importance and changing norms, as the ages of nationalism in the nineteenth century and then of social consciousness in the twentieth give way to an age of subnationalisms in the late twentieth and early twenty-first centuries. Since well before the nation-state was invented (usually dated with the French Revolution), ethnic groups conquered other ethnic groups, establishing the right to rule them under the conqueror's god, as accepted as a norm in the Peace of Westphalia in 1648. Whatever preventive effect this norm had, it was formally challenged in the aftermath of World War I with the very restricted introduction of the notion of national self-determination (NSD) (Cobban 1944), which recognized the right of certain ethnic and national groups to claim independence.[4] Certain identified national groups in Europe were promised independence with the breakup of specific (Russian, Austro-Hungarian, Ottoman) empires, a right denied to non-European parts of the Ottoman Empire and to other European (specifically British, French, Spanish, and Portuguese) colonies elsewhere, particularly in Africa and Asia. It was only after World War II that the norm was extended to these latter territories (Gordon 1971). There were major problems in this conflict prevention measure. It justified further conflict in its name, when colonial powers were slow in implementing it. It left open the identification of a nation and it did not specify how the right could be claimed, thus opening a new if further refined source of conflict. Further, it referred only to "blue water" colonialism, i.e., that exercised by states from one continent across the waters like the Portuguese in Angola, and excluded "brown land" colonialism, exercised by one state over a nation within, like the Ethiopians over the Ogadenis. In addition, it opened up but specifically excluded any right of self-determination of national minorities with the national subject to the first self-determination.

The justifying basis of this evolving norm was the assumption that ethnic homogeneity was the best system for preventing conflict, seen as inter-ethnic. This assumption came to be bypassed and overruled by the standard of state self-determination, which joins the issue area of state integrity with that of ethnic self-determination. The basis for secession recognized as legitimate is the existence of a preconstituted administrative unit (such as Bosnia or Southern Sudan) rather than an ethnic community (such as Bosnian Serbs or Croats, or Southern Sudanese including Abyei Dinka). The new implication is that states should be multi-ethnic and that legitimacy and stability are achieved by ethnic groups living together and sharing governing responsibilities, rather than by ethnic homogeneity, as was the tendency a century before. Thus the issue of boundary redrawing, with all its additional conflicts, was obviated, at least by definition: the preconstituted unit's boundaries were to be unquestioningly inherited. Identity is to be focused on the state rather than the nation, and ethnic diversity is counted a virtue, the best situation for preventing ethnic conflict. Since in reality state self-determination is driven by the desire of the dominant ethnic group to rule itself, the result is often a pluri-ethnic situation with a dominant ethnic group, pointed out earlier as the most conflict-prone situation (such as Albanian-dominated Kosovo with its Serb minority, or Macedonian-dominated Macedonia with its Albanian minority, or Tigrean-dominated Ethiopia with an Oromo minority, or Hutu-dominated Rwanda with a Tutsi minority, or *a fortiori* a Tutsi-dominated Rwanda with a Hutu majority).

However, the debate is still open on the extent and meaning of self-determination required for the norm to be met (Shehadi 1993). Self-determination can take many forms (UNGAr 1541 (XV), 2625 (XXV)). The softest form is autonomy within the state, referred to as internal self-determination (Wolff & Yakinthou 2012). It has worked, when presented with imagination, patience, and persistence. The five sisters of autonomy in Italy – Sardinia, Alto Adige, Val d'Aosta, Venezia Giulia, Sicily – have been effective in preventing escalation in touchy conflict areas. Confronted with separatist nationalisms in Euskadi and Catalonia, Spain created a state of 17 regions of various degrees of autonomy and dynamic provisions to meet various degrees of demands; violent conflict and secession have been managed, shakily, to date (in 2014, ETA was officially disbanded in Euskedi but Catalonia unofficially voted for independence). The Philippines have been confronted with an indigenous revolt in Mindanao for decades, long led by the secessionist Moro National Liberation Front (MNLF). After a succession of repress-and-negotiate policies depending on the tenor of the government, another group, the Moro Islamic Liberation Front (MILF) took up the struggle and signed a framework agreement reduced to autonomy in 2012 and a comprehensive agreement in 2014 providing for an autonomous Bangsamoro (Moro Nation). The Islamic Liberation Army (GAM) fought for decades for independence in the old Sultanate of Aceh in western Sumatra. After Indonesia switched to a democratic system, negotiations for something less than independence began under successive mediations, but it took a massive tsunami and the skillful intervention of former Finnish President Martti Ahtisaari in 2005 to produce an autonomy agreement labeled "self-government." Prevention to lower the means for self-determination usually also requires lowering the sights and rights, by making national communities more content with their situation, and meeting them halfway by increasing their protection and assurance, under the often successful reasoning that if they can have all but the most symbolic advantages of self-government without violence, the conflict can be resolved. This is the core of preventive measures at any stage of the potential conflict, whether to keep conflict passive or to limit its activity.

An agreement is an important first step but not enough; conflict prevention is an ongoing job, even when the summit of violence seems to have been passed. Such agreements are only conflict management beginnings, awaiting implementation to become conflict resolution. The Spanish and Italian autonomies have already illustrated the need for careful tending. Aceh and Mindanao face the same requirements; earlier "autonomy" collapsed in 2005 and 1996, respectively, because of insincere implementation. Autonomy in Chiapas was betrayed by the Mexican government in 2003. Rulers often claim that autonomy only sets up the blueprint for secession but in fact the reverse is true: it is revocation of autonomy that leaves communities with a frustrated taste of what they had and makes them push for secession so that no one can take away their effective autonomy again; populations of Biafra, Timor Leste, Kosovo, Zanzibar, Eritrea, Somaliland, Bangladesh, Nagorno-Karabakh, Aden, South Sudan, Casamance, and Chiapas have felt the effect. Autonomy once installed needs to be pursued loyally to be an effective prevention of re-escalation. A solid example of correcting weakness in autonomy arrangements so as to assure population satisfaction and conflict prevention is found in the successive stages of handling mounting ethnic conflict in postwar Alto Adige (South Tyrol) in northern Italy. Immediately after World War II, in 1948, the region was given autonomy to preserve its German (Austrian) cultural distinctiveness, but economic attention did not follow and Italian immigration lessened the autonomy provisions. Violence followed in the 1960s. The autonomy statute was revised in 1972 to grant greater advantages and protection to the German minority and the region has prospered, for the benefit of all, and further violence has been prevented (Gurr 1993).

However, some claim that ethnic conflicts can be prevented only by the achievement of sovereignty as a "human need," and therefore presumably that prevention is achieved by early independence (Azar 1990; Burton 1990, 1996; Kaufman 1996). While the record shows this to be obviously wrong as a generality, there are cases where the conflict has so embittered the ethnic rebels that even autonomy under the government is not trusted and not possible, as in Eritrea, Timor Leste, South Sudan, Bangladesh, and Kosovo. Nothing in the norms indicates how to recognize preemptively the right to break away from a state or how to grasp that right other than by violence, always with varying degrees of help from outside, as Biafra, Bangladesh, Eritrea, South Sudan, the pieces of Yugoslavia, and Crimea have all shown. The most successful cases, the separation of Czechoslovakia, the USSR, and parts of Yugoslavia, remain the exceptions that prove the possibility of a Velvet Divorce, under particularly attentive preventive conditions (Hopmann 2001). Perhaps earlier attempts to prevent the ultimate stage of conflict by pressing for greater accommodation on the part of the government could have ended violence earlier with a more integrative result, as others' autonomy outcomes have suggested. Prevention in these cases can only focus on accepting the inevitable and accomplishing the secession without the violence that is usually required for such an important political action.

Prevention of the most egregious instances of ethnic conflict, genocide and mass murder, is addressed by a regime indicating appropriate concerns and policy responses, overlapping and predating some of the other regimes already

mentioned. While widely accepted now, the regime of genocide prevention was developed painstakingly and only due
to the tireless efforts of key individuals who made it their
cause. The ultimate crime of ethnic violence was named by
Raphael Lemkin (1944), a Polish Jew, who devoted his life to
the fight to obtain its recognition and condemnation (Schaller
& Zimmerer 2009). In 1946, the General Assembly unanimously passed a resolution condemning genocide, and with
the 1948 Convention on the Prevention and Punishment of
the Crime of Genocide the term was officially defined and the
practice banned. The US Congress ratified the Convention
only in 1988, largely due to the efforts of Senator William
Proxmire of Wisconsin who took up the crusade in 1967
and made a speech every day on the floor of the Senate for
19 years, totaling 3,211 speeches. The connection of the term
with a responsibility to act has made its use extremely controversial. In 1994, the US referred to events in Rwanda as "acts
of genocide," in 1999 it cited "deliberate, systematic efforts at
genocide" in Kosovo, and in 2004 it controversially employed
the unqualified term "genocide" in regard to Darfur.

The debate over the existence of genocide in Darfur and Syria
is not just a lexical exercise. It concerns the existence of conditions requiring and legitimizing specific policy responses, so
that the distinction between genocide, mass killing, crimes
against humanity, and war crimes necessarily ends up being
political semantics that hinders effective preventive and
responsive action (Evans 2008; Hamburg 2010). The US in
2014 contested that the Syrian government's killing of more of
than 170,000 of its people in the civil war was genocide, forget-
ting that "mass killing" and "crimes against humanity" are also
a trigger for R2P. Even where norms of intervention have been
authorized, their application is eschewed. The Western countries long pulled back from any type of intervention in Syria,
authorized under R2P to prevent mass killing if not outright

genocide, until it was too late. They have observed a unilateral prohibition of arms deliveries, applied to themselves, while Russia, Iran, and China defend the right of the Syrian government to do anything it wants with its population and their right to send it arms, under the blanket of non-interference in internal affairs and with the goal of preventing Islamist takeover (which their policy actually worked to encourage). Yet Russia intervenes in other states' affairs under the pretense of protecting its own ethnic populations abroad.

Preventing genocide and other mass killings requires concern over the first signs of identity conflicts, or it will be too late for intervention to be effective (Zartman et al. 2012). It is possible to monitor ethnic relations for dangerous developments in early stages of ethnic conflict. High reliance on group identity, open wounds and recent scars, protective regroupings creating security dilemmas, exclusionary policies, ethnic scapegoating and demonizing, mutually reinforcing vertical and horizontal social cleavages, group-based feelings of helplessness and negative identity, in-group/out-group relations, pent-up feelings of discrimination and injustice, and uncritical acceptance of authority combine to provide the most significant warning signals of impending identity-group conflict with potential for genocide (Staub 1989; Koenigsberg 2009; on security dilemmas, Posen 1993). Violent ethnic conflict is generally preceded by the spread and adoption of myths and narratives demonizing a target group, which then serve to justify extreme measures against it. When such purposeful demonization occurs, it is a clear warning sign of discrimination, repression and eventually of attempts to eliminate the targeted group. Radio Mille Collines in Rwanda before the 1994 genocide is the well-known example. Spiraling recriminations between Armenians and Azerbaijani neighbors in the early 1990s and mid-2010s and hate broadcasts in Ivory Coast in the late 1990s are less well-known cases, and there are others. Such activities can be jammed as part of cyber-warfare, again best conducted under specific authorization by the Security Council or a regional organization. But since they almost always involve the government as the repressor rather than as protector of minorities, they require an alert international community and insistent intrusive measures to enforce norms.

In striking cases, the refusal to follow preventive norms has led to long and bloody conflicts. In Sudan, the dominant group in the North, which was in charge of government, regarded the Southerners as inferior and even considered them slaves (*'abid*). It took a quarter century of violent conflict for the Southerners to finally gain autonomy in 1972, which was then cancelled in the following decade, and another quarter century of conflict to achieve – in the 2005 Comprehensive Peace Agreement at least – equally shared participation in national government and self-government in local affairs. However, proportional power-sharing did not satisfy the Southerners, who seceded six years later, by agreement, but merely transformed the former civil war into an international war and added an internal civil war in South Sudan. Normative standards of equality and autonomy, fought for by visionary Southern leader John Garang, inspired the costly struggle against cultural if not fully physical genocide. In Sri Lanka, denial of equal access to government, employment, and education led the Tamils to launch a political protest in the 1970s and then a bloody terrorist rebellion in the 1990s, ultimately crushed by an equally bloody response in 2010; renewed discriminatory treatment of the Tamils in a victor's peace, instead of an effort at reconciliation, promises a return, rather than prevention, of protest and rebellion. The norm was operative in its absence, making conflict continuing and inevitable. Where the "normal politics" of a government–citizen contract is not present for all, internal conflict or external intervention is usually necessary to bring about change.

Yet there are no indices or general norms for sound ethnic relations to serve as the basis for a full preventive regime. Despite the mandate and work of the UN Committee on the Elimination of Racial Discrimination (CERD) and the OSCE Office of the High Commissioner for Human Rights (OHCHR), there is presently no accountability mechanism for sound ethnic relations other than the threat of identity conflict if they are ignored, the very threat that ethnic diversity standards would seek to prevent. Policymakers have called for "mutually agreed indicators [of impending atrocities] to be applied consistently across relevant office and agencies," similar to the Homeland Security color-coded terror alert system (Thaler 2010). The publication of an index of ethnic concentration in individual state government positions, along with ethnic data in various human rights reports, would provide both useful standards and an initial basis for early warning. Such an index, like the Freedom House or other ratings on degrees of freedom, would not be an official trigger for action but would increase transparency and provide early "yellow" or "red" lights, helpful both domestically in the target country and internationally as calls for corrective policies. But it would throw a spotlight on the otherwise sleeping dog, and over-accentuate the very awareness that may be best avoided.

The 1969 International Convention on the Elimination of All Forms of Racial Discrimination is the first step toward the creation of norms for preventing ethnic conflict that can be subjected to spotlight publicity, aid conditionality, and even muscular mediation backed by sanctions in extreme cases. Like any tools, standards must be used carefully and put into the right hands, again a matter of definition. Attention to the need for healthy ethnic relations can be useful for evaluating stability and conditioning development when used by distant funding sources. World Bank programs were criticized for not heeding expert advice about the dangers of skewing benefits for the majority Hutu ruling group in Rwanda in the early 1980s, foreseeing the Tutsi reaction that finally overthrew the government but not before the genocide could take place (Lemarchand 1982; Uvin 1998; Anderlini & Nyheim 1999).

Exemplary cases showing the application of measures for healthy ethnic relations are found in various national practices, although they also show that referent data must be kept up to date. In Morocco, Algeria, and Niger, informal allocation of "Berber seats" in government, and mention of Amazigh history, culture, and language in the constitutions and in school programs has worked to prevent feelings of exclusion and reduce inter-ethnic conflict. EU members have revised their often discordant history texts; Israel has too, whereas its Arab neighbors keep denying its existence and blaming its aggression. Consociational provisions have brought at least the management of identity conflict in Northern Ireland and have been proposed for Cyprus, until the time comes when hostile identities can be softened. In the US, France, Bolivia, Peru, and Venezuela, open competition and robust electoral participation have brought indigenous and minority leaders to power. Constitutional protection of minority rights provides a strong standard and reference point for prevention and settlement of ethnic disputes (Baldwin et al. 2007). Projects that engage different groups working together until they find their pride in accomplishments rather than ascriptive differences constitute a major preventive direction worthy of adoption (Varshney 2003).

Often, society itself contains its own norms and procedures for preventing the spread of kin and ethnic disputes, developed and implanted over centuries of practice to manage conflicts. Blood money (*diya*) in Sudan and other African countries, ombudsmen (*du-nku*) in West Africa, and traditional Arab reconciliation processes (*sulha*) are time-proven conflict management mechanisms that have modern use-fulness (Zartman 2003). In North Kivu in Congo, the 2008 Goma peace agreement and the Amani peace process attempted to provide local ethnic participation, although implementation lagged and then was jeopardized by escalated violence (Autesserre 2008; van Tongeren 2013). In response to a 1994 chieftancy conflict in Konkomba-Nanumba terri-tory in Ghana, an Accord on Peace and Reconciliation was signed in 1996 which, following another dispute in 2002, led to the establishment of a Northern Peace Council in 2004 and a National Peace Council in 2006, which then in 2008 mediated a conflict management agreement using traditional principles (Nuamah 2008; Bombande 2007). Traditional practices can be used more frequently and refined for con-temporary applicability; they can also be combined into larger regimes for wide areas as the basis for more coordinated normative development.

Despite the absence of a firm regime on sound ethnic rela-tions, many helpful elements are in place nonetheless, as guidelines for prevention in order to limit ethnic conflict:

- Protect local minority identities while building an overarch-ing state-nation identity.
- Promote inclusion and avoid excluding minorities from the exercise of power and its benefits.
- Hear grievances without stigmatizing and provide mech-anisms for handling them even if not satisfying them completely.
- Develop education systems to overcome prejudice and focus on similarities among groups.
- Undertake joint projects and cooperative endeavors cutting across ethnic groups.
- Use traditional practices to restore the broken tissue of society.

An international regime for conflict prevention in ethnic relations is far from being in place but pieces are available or discernible (Chandra & Wilkinson 2008). Ethnic relations are extremely impervious to external attempts at preventing conflict, so that effective norms come best from inside and below, to be gathered together at various levels and extended over larger areas, geographic and functional. Academic research on causes of conflict and conditions of stability also help feed the search for what works.

Environmental Protection

The world today is plastered with uncoordinated normative practices and agreements to prevent conflict both with and over nature, leaving huge holes and gaps where nature unmastered poses conflict material to humankind. The traditional farmer learned over centuries of experience to come to terms with nature; modern society is still in conflict with nature and trying to tame it, and is also in conflict over nature, as it fights over non-renewable resources and raw materials. International, local (or even personal) efforts are focused on controlling environmental damage that the present world is causing to the future world and on protecting non-renewable materials that the present world can insure for sustainable development. Warning systems on seismic activity are not yet at the point of being able to prevent earthquakes and tsunamis, but in the absence of direct prevention they prevent losses by protecting humans against the effects of quakes. Prevention of hurricanes, tornadoes, and drought is far beyond human capabilities, and so prevention efforts turn to still inadequate protection against their effects. Scientific modeling of the dynamics of a forest fire is of increasing help in preventing its spread, although uncertainty still exists about the conditions that favor forest fires in the first place and the measures to take against them. The beginnings of a climate change regime are indeed present, but still voluntary and insufficient. The Montreal Ozone Treaty of 1989 stands as uniting ideological and interest communities into an effective measure. But the 1992 Framework Convention on Climate Change (FCCC) had only a facultative 1997 Kyoto Protocol as its next step, and new approaches are being sought. In the face of the inability of the international and local communities to agree on adequate measures of prevention of climate change, efforts are turning to protection from the unprevented effects.

Droughts, earthquakes, and typhoons are natural disasters, but famine, building collapse, and relief failures are man-made. Prevention of conflict arising from natural disasters means preparedness, much as it does for ethnic conflicts. Whereas the international response to the 1992 drought in Mozambique helped prevent escalation of the internal conflict, droughts in the Horn of Africa in 1973 and 1974 where preparations were absent contributed to the overthrow of the Ethiopian Emperor and the Ogaden War. Adaptation Science, the United Nations Development Program (UNDP), and the Drylands Development Paradigm are developing best practices and new standards for meeting climate change risks (Reynolds et al. 2007; Moss et al. 2013) and the UN's Office for the Coordination of Humanitarian Affairs (OCHA) monitors and evaluates conditions in conflict areas for natural disaster effects as well.

At the same time, resource conflicts are becoming more likely as rising populations raise demands for limited or even dwindling resources. Norms to protect natural resources are widespread but still inadequate, notably to protect tropical forests and to prevent desertification, as in the Permanent Interstate Committee for Drought Control in the Sahel (CILSS). Rules to protect endangered stocks and species in turn engender conflict among those who would use them. The

Convention on International Trade in Endangered Species of Wild Fauna and Flora (CITES) provides norms for the protection of wildlife but at the same time is the source of conflict (violent among people as well as toward animals and fish) over the terms of the protective regime as well as the interruption of traditional life sources. Quotas protect fish and wildlife against overfishing and hunting in order to prevent depletion of the species and preserve stocks for reproduction and harvesting. Sharing and regulating water rights and reframing ownership conflicts as usufruct have already been mentioned.

- Prevention of conflict with and over nature requires far-sighted cooperation and difficult changes in established behaviors.
- Establishment of norms governing specific situations demands coordination of separate and joint interests.
- Further commitment to enforcement and to deepening commonly beneficial cooperation is needed.

In the absence of any firm regime, some norms are coming into acceptance to provide building blocks for a future set of best practices in dealing with conflicts with and over nature. Despite stalemate over regulations governing the reduction of global warming or the division of transboundary waters, norms covering responsibility for infractions are informally in place, such as "polluter pays" in transboundary pollution or upstream responsibility in transboundary water flows or the precautionary principle (Bodansky 1995). Like any norm or law, these still leave details in question, such as "Which polluter – past or present?" or "How much responsibility – to supply, to share, to compensate, or to be penalized?" (Zawahri & Gerlak 2009). The importance of developing such norms for conflict prevention is enormous, as natural disasters affect more and more people and natural resources are in restricted supply in the face of increasing demand.

Human Rights

Human rights constitute a large area for regime-building, essentially preventive in nature. They are covered by a very explicit and detailed regime of preventive norms in the monumental statement contained in the Universal Declaration of Human Rights, adopted by the General Assembly in 1948, and the International Covenants on Civil and Political Rights and on Economic, Social and Cultural Rights. More specifically, they are monitored vigorously by the UN and regional organizations' treaty bodies and mechanisms and by NGOs such as Human Rights Leagues, Amnesty International, and Human Rights Watch groups, among many others. The regime is also strengthened by statements and activities related to its many components. An example of the latter is the Convention against Torture which has worked its way through the UN until adoption by the General Assembly in December 1984, monitored by the Committee against Torture and other bodies, advanced by a strong campaign of Amnesty International, and strengthened by additional instruments of which the Optional Protocol adopted in December 2002 is only the latest (Korula 2003).

Human rights campaigns have had some effects both in direct prevention and in the ensuing accountability and punishment that is designed to prevent indirectly by shaking the culture of impunity (Risse et al. 2013). They have been the reason for the creation of international tribunals, from Nazi Germany to Rwanda and Yugoslavia, Sierra Leone, and finally Iraq itself and the indictments before the ICC of leaders from these countries and Sudan and Kenya. More indirectly, but perhaps more effectively in the direction of prevention, human rights pressure has resulted in states' policy changes, such as the liberation of political prisoners, the creation of domestic human rights leagues, and finally the establishment of truth and reconciliation bodies such as the Equity and Reconciliation Commission in Morocco.

Human rights norms run from very specific injunctions to broad attitudinal orientations for conflict prevention, none unbreached but all serving as powerful norms for states to adopt or dodge:

- Ban on torture and incarceration of political prisoners;
- Limitation of conflict damage to civilian populations;
- Observance of the rule of law;
- Right to fair trial;
- Equal access to development, education, and other benefits of citizenship;
- End to culture of impunity.

Building respect for human rights is slow but despoiling them is usually deadly for the offending state, even if the judgment day may be long in coming. Humanitarian issues have been used as justification for direct intervention, in Iraqi Kurdistan, Somalia, Kosovo, Afghanistan, and finally Iraq itself. None of these actions have been without debate and many debates have gone on without action, despite a rather well-codified human rights regime; none have prevented identity conflicts and violence in these cases, locking the barn door after them instead. There are many places where human rights prevention measures have been ignored and identity groups persecuted, but these same norms have at least served to provoke red-faced denials and justify international outcries and action, however inadequate. Every case of defiance, however much of an exception to observance of the norms, strengthens the counter-norm of impunity. Yet the aspiration is that the demonstration and deterrent effect of retribution after the fact in these cases will defeat a culture of impunity and dissuade leaders from reproducing the action in other cases. Protecting and promoting human rights also serves to entrench a human rights culture around the world and not just as a part of Western civilization, so that that culture in turn can be more powerful in preventing violence and its effects.

Human rights abuse is an ill to be prevented in its own right but it is also an ingredient in conflict prevention. Human rights abuses are the symptoms of conflict and the means of pursuing it. Prevention of human rights abuses and, more positively, promotion of human rights limit the excesses of conflict and encourage greater attention to the welfare of a state's population (the focus of Pillar 1 in the R2P). Broadly, human rights encompass the right to exist and the right to protest (or, more neutrally, to participate), within the limits – as with all rights – of the rights of others to do the same. If such rights would seem to protect conflict, they also work to keep its expression within limits and encourage its resolution.

Population Displacement

Like human rights, population displacement, either between states as refugees or within states as internally displaced persons (IDPs), is the subject of complementary and well-developed regimes that serve as the basis for the prevention of abuses to displaced populations. Even though they govern situations that result from failed primary prevention and are subject only to secondary prevention, they are considered here among a review of conflict prevention norms because they work to reduce further conflict by preventing escalation. States are enjoined to follow the norms and help others to do so; prevention is advanced by making use of the institutionalized standards and strengthening them with material and policy support. The refugee regime under the 1951 Convention relating to the Status of Refugees and the UNHCR covers the rights to refuge (asylum), and to resettle, return, and remain, and IDPs are covered in a set of Guiding Principles on Internal Displacement (Deng & Cohen 1998), backed by the indefatigable promotion by the Assistant Secretary-General Francis Deng and his successors.

Although these norms and standards are unevenly applied, have no mechanism of accountability, and do not serve to prevent the causes of the original displacement, they are broadly accepted and form the basis for preventing, however imperfectly, the repercussions of violence and persecution on often innocent populations. Internally and internationally, displaced populations are usually either the direct targets of repression or the indirect victims of violent conflict. They are subjects of ethnic cleansing, often as a prelude or part of genocide, and the regimes are present to guide efforts to deal with these symptoms, even if not their causes. Both the UNHCR and the Office of the Representative of the Secretary-General on IDPs under the Guiding Principles have emphasized prevention.

The regime provides guidelines for the prevention of the worst effects, still applied insufficiently. This is particularly important in an age of large migrations from conflict areas and more broadly from developing to developed countries. In Vietnam in the 1970s, Haiti in the early 1990s, and North Africa in the 2010s, desperate populations fled persecution and poverty, packed in unseaworthy boats, and their plight as refugees attracted international attention and intervention. Dissidence in Syria, Congo, Rwanda, Colombia, and North Korea, among many others, has created major refugee and displacement problems, and serious problems of immigration have conflicted US and European relations with Latin America and Africa, respectively. Conflicts have generally been prevented from escalating by the use of careful diplomacy, often with great effort. In 1988, tens of thousands of Iraqi Kurds streamed into Turkey, finally triggering US and world condemnation of Saddam Hussein's Kurdish extermination efforts; after 2011, tens of thousands of Syrian Kurds and Sunnis streamed into Turkey, Lebanon, and Jordan with only limited humanitarian attention. Around Darfur in the 2000s, targeted populations fled to internal displacement camps and to international refuge in Chad and Central Africa, triggering greater – but insufficient – international concern by the norms established in the population displacement regimes. Because the IDP regime concerns preventive measures often dependent on the government causing the displacement, as well as rebel groups, application remains patchy. International aid workers were left in a quandary when Rwanda's genocidaires sought protection in eastern Congo in 1994. Political entrepreneurs in identity conflicts will continue to displace populations without fear of prevention, punishment, or accountability until deep damage is done.

The development of the IDP norms provides a particularly instructive insight into the growth and strength of regimes. Although not the subject of UNSC action, the Principles were the result of an innovative non-government practice, sponsorship by a few states (Norway and Austria), an effort to fill in grey areas in existing law, and persistent personal attention by a UN official. Two decades later the Principles were cited in national and regional court decisions, adopted by 11 states of the African Great Lakes region in 2006, codified by 20 African states in their domestic law, and finally adopted by the 53 members of the AU in the Kampala Convention, binding them to take concrete measures to improve IDP conditions (Cohen 2011). At the same time, two campaigns along the same lines of operation were begun to extend the principles to cover displacement because of natural disaster and climate change and to extend the right to non-refoulement to mean the right to remain in asylum, and then a third extending the entire concept to imply the right not to be dis-placed (Stavropoulou 2010; Morel et al. 2012). These efforts marked a regime on the move, strengthening its power of prevention.

Preventive norms in dealing with displaced persons and ref-ugees dictate humane treatment and early efforts to mitigate their condition:

- IDPs and refugees deserve humane protection away from home and a return home free from persecution as soon as possible.
- If return to their homes is not possible, resettlement and refuge should be provided expeditiously.

The regime covering the prevention of abuses of refugees and displaced populations involves protective norms to deal with the results of conflicts that have already broken out but do little (other than assigning responsibilities) to prevent the cause. The operative regimes outline the appropriate treat-ment to be accorded to the refugees and the displaced, leaving the element of accountability still missing for host coun-tries and especially for home countries. On the other hand, collective NGO and state pressure has led to the inclusion of obligations in binding treaties and domestic legislation. Responsibility for refugees, displacement, and ethnic cleans-ing lies most with the home country actions and policies in contravention of the first pillar of the R2P trilogy, that a state is responsible for its people, as discussed below. The regime exists and can be used for prevention of further conflict, but an effective regime means that a state be held morally and legally accountable to follow the norms and financially accountable for their infraction. In the meanwhile, the pressure of fellow states in the international community has shown a notable degree of effectiveness in reducing the causes and results of conflict.

Democratization

Democratization is a process of informed selection and accountability of governors, designed to prevent conflict escalation to violence through its ability to handle and balance the pressing needs and demands of its electorate. Current analysis – perhaps mixed with a bit of faith – holds that societies are best governed by a healthy and functioning relationship between governors and governed, with regular occasions for the governed to hold the governors accountable for their stewardship and both to choose freely and to repent of their previous choice, under conditions of "normal politics," although normal politics might take some locally bred form other than standard democracy (Zartman 1996). Such an open society is less likely to generate fears and repression of citizen groups, and hence conflict, than a closed, controlled society, and is a regime that contains mechanisms for prevention, management, resolution, and transformation of citizens' conflicts. Democracy has a number of identifying characteristics:

- Free and fair selection of candidates;
- Free and fair registering of votes;
- Free right to organize and participate;
- Institutionalized practices and procedures for governance;
- Free availability of information and discussion of issues; and
- Neutral protection of the law.

Elections themselves are a classic example of a conflict management mechanism; they by no means remove the conflict between candidates and their parties, but they replace its violent expression with one accepted as authoritative (with a little help from the courts, also accepted as authoritative). While democratization and its component election process can easily side-track into demagogy and partisan conflict, an assurance of repeated occasions of accountability can help curb extremes. Publication of such standards and reference to them by governments and NGOs in their operations reinforce the norms, and specific activities serve to put them into effect.

While each of these activities can stand on its own rights and norms, they are strengthened in turn by reference to a common set of standards, functioning as part of the overall regime. Thus, election monitoring makes most sense as part of a regime of democratization rather than as a discrete activity, as do programs in training the judiciary and strengthening the rule of law or in promoting responsible journalism and the role of the media. The international community, including UN agencies, has not yet formalized a code of conduct for democracy,[5] and it will not do so as long as the members cannot agree on its definition and measures or adopt its practices themselves. Individual authors and NGOs have worked on a number of draft norms that are helpful, even if not authoritative, and are part of the regime-building process (Harris & Reilly 1998).

When not followed by the conflicted country as a set of standards to prevent escalation, democratization norms also serve as policy guidelines for interveners, operating either directly or from a distance through pressures and incentives, as in R2P Pillars 2 and 3. The Community of Democracies, established in Warsaw in 2000, has developed a series of collective actions against the erosion of democracy (Albright & Geremek 2003). Perhaps the most (although not totally) successful use of the norm is the OAS and AU policy of non-recognition of military coups that overthrow elected governments, through the 1992 Washington Protocol for the OAS and the 1999 Algiers and the 2000 Lomé Declarations and the Constitutive Act for the AU. Imperfect practice has helped the norm grow; when the unrecognized coup in Mauritania in 2008 was then followed by elections that the coup's leader won, the AU extended the norm to ban such practices as well. Norm-based interventions by the Economic Community of West African States (ECOWAS) and then the African Union (AU) tried to bring democratization back to Ivory Coast after 2000, with little effect, until abuses were so blatant in 2010 that foreign intervention by France became justified, enforcing the respect of election as a conflict management mechanism.

Democratic standards provided the basis for pressure from states and the international financial institutions (IFIs) to prevent and manage conflict through the conduct of free and fair multiparty elections in Cameroon in the mid-1990s, in Peru in 2000, in Kenya in 1997, 2008 and 2012, in Ivory Coast in 2010, and in Zimbabwe in 2012 (with less effective results). They justified the US intervention in the Philippines in early 1986 to prevent the escalation of conflict; and would have served just as well to justify a decertification of the Liberian elections of the previous year and to legitimize active pressures to support a freer election process in Serbia in 1996 or Zimbabwe in 2008, thereby arguably preventing the subsequent decade of vicious conflict (Zartman 1995; Mutwol 2009; Vucović 2015a). Earlier attention to resolving the real problems of majority domination in Rwanda and Burundi, as are being addressed after the fact, would have gone far to prevent their genocides, just as even framework provisions for the West (Darfur) and East (Beja) in the 2005 Comprehensive Peace Agreement between the North and South in Sudan would arguably have worked against continued conflict there. Where taken, actions went far to prevent the escalation of identity conflicts; where not taken, the inaction preceded preventable failures and targeted group killings.

Pro-active interventions to create democracy are more

controversial as a means to prevent and manage conflict, considering that early stages of democratization are the most conflict-ridden. The intervention of a coalition of the willing to protect targeted ethnic groups from genocide and to establish conditions for democratization in Iraq after 2003 brought in an elected government but also identity-group conflict. In Kosovo in 1998 such intervention brought in more successful elections and democracy. UN-authorized interventions brought democratization along with independence to Namibia in 1988, and Timor Leste after 1999, successfully preventing further violence in the first case but merely moving violence from interstate to intrastate in the second. International ostracism for systematic non-democratic practices, coupled with internal protest, was eventually effective in bringing democracy to Spain after 1975, Eastern Europe after 1989, and South Africa after 1990, is working ever so slowly on Burma, but has been stymied in Zimbabwe and Ethiopia.

Democracy is a system of conflict management and resolution to prevent conflict from being settled by violence, but the process of installing and enforcing the regime of democratization is itself a source of conflict. The passage from authoritarian to democratic rule is pocked with conflict, not only over the direction of the course but over the steps on the way (O'Donnell & Schmitter 1986; Zartman 2015). There are no norms for democratic transition. Large challenges to norms for prevention of conflict connected with democratization are presented when whole areas with similar experience suddenly aspire to new practices of governance, as occurred in Eastern Europe and the Near Abroad beginning in 1990 and in the Arab World beginning with the Arab Spring of 2011. The overthrow of the Old Order is a process of sudden change and conflict that inevitably brings disorder. It is followed by a popular longing for any order at all and by an opportunity for the elites of the Old Order to capitalize on their experience of governing to return to power. Or when a formerly controlled population is suddenly opened to electoral competition, political parties gravitate to the ready clientele of their ethic constituencies instead of moving on to cross-cutting interest or issue coalitions, and the situation returns to the ethnic conflict that the authoritarian rule repressed.

The best that can be done to prevent conflict during transition to democracy is for the population and outside supporters to insist on the norms of democratization – identified above – even when the result is only a lame process. Both the colored revolutions of the Near Abroad and the Arab Spring have shown that even free and fair elections do not democracy make and that the heritage of authoritarian experience, repression of political organizations, distrust of political organization and politics in general, and ideological conditioning work against sudden democratization as a manager of conflict. Yet, selectively and unevenly, the process moves ahead, taking time, patience, and assistance. Internally, it takes forward-looking statesmen to avoid instability and identity-based parties; externally, public encouragement or criticism and international training are the only ready means to intervene in domestic politics to create a more stable situation, but, as the above examples show, they are not likely to be enough in severe cases.

Democracy is a system for the management of conflict, but it does not guarantee good governance, only a chance to rectify bad governance (Zartman 1996). Thus it is filled with conflict. The norms for its operation are designed to prevent that conflict from escalating to violence. Current (and continuing) active discussion of the necessary conditions for the operation of a democratic system helps build a system of norms that are helpful to reducing the conflicts occasioned by democratization itself as well as by its use to handle other conflicts.

Good Governance

Good governance was one of the first subjects to be treated by political analysts (Plato, Aristotle, al-Farabi, Kautilya, Shahnameh) but it is only beginning to be the subject of specific, modern norms and expectations. People know what good governance is and governments know that people know, even though a consensual book of normative principles is still in the making. Governments, both democratic and authoritarian, either listen to the people or they sit on them, but they are eventually accountable to them for performance, more immediately under the first type of government than under the second. Prevention depends on comparing the conduct with the standards, and doing something about it. Thus the enforcement of the norms of good governance ideally returns to the democratization regime. Adherence to the norms of a good governance regime, however implicit, prevents normal conflict from escalation out of hand.

Good governance has also been the subject of norms created under the auspices of the IFIs (Lateef 1990, 1991). While a regime has not been devised that would eliminate poverty, the structural adjustment guidelines are designed to prevent the economic irresponsibility that can lead directly to deprivation, discrimination, and conflict. This issue area is an instance where the regime has not simply grown but has changed course dramatically over the years, as different standards have evolved for appropriate policies to prevent poverty. At the same time, other international bodies have taken up a range of socio-economic performance measures to monitor governance and conflict prevention, such as the African Peer Review Mechanism of the AU's New Partnership for Africa's Development (NEPAD).

Much has been written about the importance of institutionalization for good governance, and within it the rule of law, or formal norms for the performance of institutions (if not an institution in and of itself) (North 1990). Despite or because of this enlarged attention, there is no agreement on the norms of institutionalization. But there is agreement on the importance of routinized procedures, consensually established and surveyed by accountability mechanisms, providing equal protection and redress, embodying both permanent principles and revisable applications, and their implications for conflict prevention. Institutionalization works to prevent the rise of conflict and also the means (institutions) by which conflicts can be handled to prevent their escalation.

An impediment to good governance, corruption, is also the subject of a robust regime to prevent abuses associated with domestic conflict. Standards and monitoring by international NGOs such as Transparency International and Global Integrity and their many local branches shine a powerful light of publicity on corruption as a source of underdevelopment and conflict (Abed & Gupta 2002; Spector 2005, 2008, 2009). Its most important preventive function is to highlight the insides of offending states, which in turn serves to empower citizen recourse to the courts, domestic opposition and, more broadly, world public opinion. Such attention then finds its way into external states' practices, as in the US Foreign Corporate Practices Act provisions against side payments in business dealings abroad as at home, even where adherence to such norms puts the US corporation at a disadvantage compared to unprincipled foreign competition. Ample indirect interventions, such as USAID training programs against corruption, find their justification under the umbrella of the good governance regime (Spector 2008, 2009). Further enforcement of the regime's principles depends on domestic legislation and effective court systems, items contained in the standards of the regime itself.

Even in the absence of an authoritative work on good

governance practices, some basic norms are evident to prevent conflict from escalating beyond the reach of normal politics (Kaufmann 2003; Grindle 2005):

- Keep communications open between governors and governed;
- Consider public officials as public servants, not private entrepreneurs;
- Maintain and observe institutionalization;
- Ensure the rule of law;
- Mediate conflicts equitably between demand-bearing groups;
- Consider the security and welfare of the people to be the prime task;
- Install strict controls on corruption;
- Keep income and spending in balance.

Responsibility to Protect

Responsibility to Protect (R2P) constitutes a new and dramatically evolving regime established to deal preventively with escalating conflicts. While it is formally limited to conflicts leading to genocide, war crimes, ethnic cleansing, and crimes against humanity, it opens the door to much wider applications and ways of thinking. It serves as an appropriate transition after the regimes discussed above because it constitutes a radical change in the normative consideration of sovereignty, in which the details of extent and application still remain to be worked out, and it shows how new norms are set up, expanded, and limited. The norm is debated and developed as it is being applied and contested (Evans 2008; Cunliffe 2011).[6]

The film of its development is instructive in the creation of norms and regimes. In a statement of the *UN Agenda for*

Peace, remarkable for a report to sovereign states, Boutros Ghali (1992a: 44) noted that, despite the fundamental UN position on state sovereignty and integrity, "the time of absolute and exclusive sovereignty, however, has passed; its theory was never matched by reality. It is the task of leaders of States today to understand this and to find a balance between the needs of good internal governance and the requirements of an ever more interdependent world." The subject was also addressed in the mid-1990s by academic analysis within non-governmental research organizations. From its inception in the late 1980s, the Brookings Africa Project led by Francis Deng synergized with the work of Olusegun Obasanjo's Africa Leadership Forum (1991) that had resulted in the 1991 Kampala Document's declaration that "domestic conditions constituting a threat to personal and collective security and gross violations of human rights lie beyond the protection of sovereignty" (Deng & Zartman 2002: 165). The Brookings Africa Project's research program culminated in a final collective work, *Sovereignty as Responsibility: Conflict Management in Africa* (Deng et al. 1996); rather than a protection for the state, sovereignty was viewed as a responsibility for the protection of the state's people, to be exercised by the state and shared by other states if the primary state did not perform its own duties for the welfare of its people, foreshadowing the three pillars of responsibility to protect later adopted by the UN. Under the inspiration of David Hamburg, the Carnegie Corporation's Commission on Preventing Deadly Conflict sponsored a broad collection of investigations into prevention, culminating in Jane Holl's (1997) *Preventing Deadly Conflict* and other studies by Jentleson (2000) and Zartman (2003). The US Institute of Peace also published a strategic toolkit and analysis for conflict prevention by Michael Lund (1996), *Preventing Violent Conflicts: A Strategy for Preventive Diplomacy*. Notable attempts from Scandinavia to address the questions of measures and mandates were the Norwegian Institute of International Affairs study (Ginifer et al. 1999) and the Swedish Initiative (Sweden 1997, 1999) launched under Jan Eliasson to focus and energize Swedish and eventually EU policy to develop a culture of prevention (Svensson & Wallensteen 2010). As a result of these initiatives, the G-8 (2000) foreign ministers meeting in Japan produced the *G-8 Miyazaki Initiative for Conflict Prevention* that laid out a strategy of "chronological comprehensiveness," and covered structural prevention, early and late prevention, and post-conflict peace building.

The various paths of attention came together in the Canadian-sponsored International Commission on Intervention and State Sovereignty (ICISS) (Evans and Sahnoun 2001, I, xii–xiii, 22–7, 47–69), whose report *The Responsibility to Protect*, declared, in bold type, that "prevention is the single most important dimension of the responsibility to protect." Prevention is divided into structural or root-cause prevention and direct (operational) or conflict prevention. The report states that although "the primary responsibility for the protection of its people lies with the state itself, . . . where a population is suffering serious harm, as a result of internal war, insurgency, repression or state failure, and the state in question is unwilling or unable to halt or avert it, the principle of non-intervention yields to the international responsibility to protect" (Evans and Sahnoun 2001, I, xi).

These concerns then found their place in the report of the Secretary-General's High-level Panel on Threats, Challenges and Change (2004), unanimously adopted by the General Assembly at the 2005 World Summit.[7] The agreement establishes a norm to supersede the Westphalian notion of the sanctity of state sovereignty, but at the same time, it limits the bounds of such actions by defining a hierarchy of action and actors for intervention, circumscribed by a just cause threshold, precautionary and operational principles, and proper authority. Direct intervention is justified only in extreme cases of human rights abuses, and UN and peaceful action are to be the first recourse. "The international community, through the United Nations, also has the obligation to use diplomatic, humanitarian, and other peaceful means, including under Chapters VI and VIII of the Charter to help protect populations from genocide, war crimes, ethnic cleansing, and crimes against humanity. In this context, we recognize our shared responsibility to take collective action, in a timely and decisive manner, through the Security Council under Chapter VII of the UN Charter and in co-operation with relevant regional organizations, should peaceful means be inadequate and national authorities be unwilling or unable to protect their populations."

Elaboration of the principle continued in the report, "Implementing the Responsibility to Protect," of Secretary-General Ban Ki-moon (2009) to the General Assembly (much the work of his Special Advisor on the Responsibility to Protect, Edward Luck). It developed the preventive sequence associated with the three R2P pillars: protection responsibilities of the state, assistance and capacity-building responsibilities of the international community, and timely and decisive responses of the international community when the first two pillars fail. The three pillars of the doctrine serve to reinforce each other: the threat to intervene (Pillar 3) can influence states to ask for friendly help while still in charge instead (Pillar 2), and the danger of needing to ask can act as an incentive to handle the conflict alone (Pillar 1), where states (and people) operate most comfortably.

Second pillar examples of prevention are, by their nature, less splashy than those of the third pillar, and they are harder to undertake at a distance from the purported stage of violence. It is delicate to warn a government that it is handling its ethnic relations badly and if it continues it will run into trouble. Reportedly, US diplomats warned then-Presidents Zine Labadine ben Ali in Tunisia and Hosni Mubarek in 2011 and Mohammed Morsi in 2013 in Egypt that their tenure was threatened by the Arab Spring revolts (urging ben Ali to leave, Morsi to negotiate, and, initially, Mubarek to hang on), in order to prevent violence and state collapse. The Special Representative of the (UN) Secretary-General (SRSG) in Yemen, Jamal ben Omar, worked assiduously with the political forces emerging from conflict to hold the 2012–14 National Dialogue stipulated in the 2012 Sanaa conflict management agreements, in order to prevent a return to internal war and to bring about a genuine conflict resolution. His quiet efforts were typical of those of many similar SRSGs assisting governmental and political forces to prevent conflict escalations. While France intervened militarily in its former colonies of Ivory Coast, Mali, and Central African Republic in 2012–14, it also worked with the governments to prevent a return to violence and to establish an effective and responsible rule. Faced with clear indications of a deeper slide into violence and dissidence at the hands of the Revolutionary Armed Front of Colombia (FARC) and United Self-Defense Forces (AUC), the US instigated its Plan Colombia to prevent operations of the drug trade that fed both groups.

Much more subtle Pillar 2 cooperation is more frequent and less visible. Preventive action need not be crisis politics. US, German, and other NGOs work abroad to promote democracy and train political parties in effective representation in order to prevent conflict from finding satisfaction in politics and moving to violence. Development aid programs prevent the economics of rising expectations from turning into rebellions of falling satisfactions.

But prevention may also have to enter into the mechanics of the conflict to be effective and not just exert pressure and emit counsel from the outside. Third Pillar intervention is highly risky, even if necessary at times, and it is often difficult to know when the ensuing responsibility stops. The NATO action in Libya in 2011 was a preventive intervention under duress to save not only the mounting resistance but above all the population of eastern Libya from the extermination that Qaddafi promised them (Theiss 2015); Qaddafi was defeated, but once the National Transitional Council handed over power to the newly elected People's General Council, governance fell to fractionated militias and out of the hands of any national coordination (Mezran & Alunni 2015). The poor shape of Libya two years after the preventive intervention was used as a conclusive argument against similar intervention in Syria, but the lack of a firm policy in support of the resistance in Syria ("letting them work it out by themselves") clearly created a situation where the regime could kill (including using gas) hundreds of thousands of its own people in a conflict that was not prevented. US diplomatic intervention in the Bosnian War at Dayton in 1993 prevented the continuing massacres of the civilian population (and UN peacekeepers), but military intervention by NATO was required three years later to prevent continued killing in the Kosovar War (Zartman 2005). Yet the Dayton Accords have at best managed, but not resolved, the conflict in Bosnia-Herzegovina, while recognition and reconciliation in Kosovo have gradually moved ahead.

Long-Term Norms and Regimes

In general, norms gathered into international regimes provide only the most basic and incomplete standards and guidelines for the prevention of conflict and its escalation. Not all such norms and regimes are examined here, only arguably the most significant. As "codes of conduct," they are works in progress. However, what is striking is not their inadequacy but the number and extent of issue areas into which they tread. If their spirit and standards were internalized in political and social (and economic) systems, much conflict would be prevented, and their guidelines would offer general wisdom on how to handle what remains. There needs to be greater awareness of and familiarity with the available standards and regimes, a committed effort to strengthen and improve them, and an active resolve to ratify the many such statements of principles that are now languishing in signature-only status.

There also needs to be more work on sharpening regimes and deepening their application. Most regimes discussed are still in a loose stage, their coverage imprecise and facultative, with more loopholes than tight prevention. In the case of ethnic relations, for example, the guideline is "inclusiveness," but it is not clear what this means in detail. The debate over democratization, good governance, and even human rights is raging and imprecise. For all the specificity of guidelines and principles on refugees and IDPs, practice depends largely on the enormous efforts of persuasion deployed by the UN High Commissioner on Refugees and the Assistant Secretary-General for Displaced Persons. Many regimes, reaching the stage of international agreements, remain unratified by major powers. These are all areas where more work is required if norms and regimes are to achieve maximum effectiveness for conflict prevention and resolution and make their required contribution to World Order.

Furthermore, it is not enough to observe the preventive effects that have resulted from current norms and regimes as guidance for action. Norms need enforcement, in an anarchic system of World Order where there is no central enforcing agency. It is the nature of the current and foreseeable system that enforcement is left up to the members of the international community, through the shaming of deviants and the exemplary behavior of others. But enforcement also requires dissuasion, correction, and punishment, in the tough World Order where a sense of membership in the international community is trumped by assertions of national pride and interest. The opposite of international norms and regimes is idiosyncratic individual behavior and a culture of impunity, which must be made costly if there is to be order in World Order. Prevention defied needs to be redone, as was accomplished directly by military counter-action in Kuwait under President Bush senior in 1993 or indirectly by economic measures in Ukraine under President Obama in 2014, so that future prevention can be reasserted. Such extreme action does not apply literally to all the norms and regimes discussed, but the principle that deviance must have its costs is universally applicable, even if variable according to the case. Bad governance, authoritarianism, ethnic exclusion, and environmental despoiling all have their inherent costs. In some cases, external imposition of costs may also be needed, if conflict prevention is to work.

Prevention too is not without cost. The provision of norms and regimes can also have negative side effects or externalities that reduce their benefits. Fiscal responsibility required by the IFIs also means cutting or requiring payments for social programs in health, education, and welfare, often discriminatorily. Good governance means picking and choosing among equally insistent – if not equally justified – demands for attention. Human rights and democratization norms, and standards for handling ethnic minorities (and majorities) can be destabilizing, at least in the short run, and can impose additional operating costs on the government. Executive accountability measures have led indicted rulers and rebels to be more, not less, resistant to their responsibilities. Were such standards of behavior unambiguously beneficial, they would be easier to adopt. The point is less that there is no perfection in this world than that even accepted standards for prevention require fine-tuning, consensus-building, policy choices, and costs for their benefits that make prevention debatable and resistance natural. The contemporary world continues to search for appropriate definitions, thresholds, and actions involved in the responsibility to prevent.

It might seem that the matter of regimes is lofty and ano-dyne compared with the brutal and dirty processes of conflict, escalation, and violence. Enumerating the highest standards of socio-political relations might appear to be an agenda for angels when what is needed is advice for dealing with devils. But without such standards, action for curing sick societies becomes ad hoc and contradictory, lacking justification and coordination. As consensual methods of problem-solving, regimes coordinate and facilitate the generic prevention of conflict and its escalation. While universal in their stand-ards and coverage, they are applicable individually to specific situations in need of diagnosis and prescriptions. But under-standing broad categories of conflict conditions is not enough and prevention cannot stay at that level. Prevention must look more specifically at conflicts in the next stages, as activated conflicts that break through the net of normative prevention start to escalate, in an "early-early" gestation period.

CHAPTER FOUR

Mechanisms of Mid-term Prevention

As conflicts begin to emerge from their passive state, take shape, and gather steam, the dynamics of the conflict process require the attention of conflicting and observing parties alike if they are to prevent intensification to violence. These dynamics should be the first order of attention for agencies and parties concerned about prevention, even if they are involved in the conflict. When norms and regimes are not adequate to assure prevention through reflexes governing issue areas, prevention moves closer to the event and "early-early" process mechanisms are needed (Zartman 1991; Evans 1994; van de Stoel 1994). Here attention shifts from universal principles of behavior and focuses on the courses of the particular conflict. These dynamics constitute "things to think about and start doing something with" as the conflict starts to move out of its passive shell and head toward activity and eventually violence if not properly handled, as illustrated in figure 1. At this stage, prevention works directly on the attitudes of interested parties toward the evolution of the situation, without the time to develop structures.

The prime focus of gestation prevention is to make the parties to the impending conflict think of the costs of their actions, before they become locked into a dangerous policy, and to manage the process to avoid escalation. They should be brought to recognize the dynamics inherent in the conflict which can carry them away in helpful or in harmful directions. While the conflicting parties may not be persuaded to change their goals, they can be encouraged to look for other ways to accomplish them, for example in cooperation rather than in conflict with another party. F.W. de Klerk in South Africa, Charles de Gaulle in regard to French African colonies, Richard Nixon in regard to the Panama Canal, the Acehnese and Moros in regard to self-government – all took a second look at what they *really* wanted and found ways to achieve it through cooperation instead of conflict; the previous course was seen as simply too risky, too costly, or too dangerous. "Early-early" mechanisms of conflict prevention start with ways of gaining entry into the thinking process of the conflicting parties to introduce new appreciations of the situation and new calculations. The dynamic – that is, moving and changing – aspects of gestating conflict present opportunities or traps, to be seized, avoided, or controlled. Such guidelines concern *awareness, escalation, stalemates, ripening,* and *institutions of resolution.*

Awareness

Parties must be aware of what they are getting into, whether as those conducting the conflict or as others affected by its conduct. There is no area of a diplomatic activity where the Boy Scout virtue of "Be Prepared" is more urgent than in prevention. Early awareness means a combination of looking, seeing, and acting, an alertness to scan the horizon for potential conflicts, an ability to identify available warning signals, and a willingness to consider preventive action. Early awareness is not an obvious response. It is hung between the two notions of activism and of noninvolvement, whose importance differs in different societies. In popular cultures, maxims such as "An ounce of prevention is worth a pound of cure," "A stitch in time saves nine," "Better safe than sorry," "Forewarned is forearmed," "Be there in a minute," and "Plan ahead" (the last letter scrunched against the margin) vie with "Never trouble trouble till trouble troubles you," "Don't go looking for trouble," "Sufficient unto the day is the evil thereof," "Let sleeping dogs lie," "Discretion is the better part of valor," "Out of sight, out of mind," and a recent addition, "If it ain't broke, don't fix it." The balance between the two views is often a cultural matter. For example, in the first list, all but the last proverb come from an English tradition, whereas in the second list the first four come from fatalistic or traditionalistic strands in American culture, Negro spirituals, and Judaic tradition. It is this ambivalence that is probably the most basic expression of the difficulties that dog preventive action.

Early awareness also involves an analytical understanding of the possibility of prevention, an awareness that not only is a conflict looming but that something can be done about it. As with any negotiation, sound diagnosis is the basis of any strategy. This means wandering through a field of uncertainties in an effort to make it tilt in the direction of management and resolution (Kahneman & Tversky 1995). Diagnosis begins by gathering information on the current and impending situation and analysis of the dangers inherent in it, followed by consideration of measures to deal with the conflict, to remove its causes, allay its effects, limit the chance of accidents or motivated incidents, and replace its dangerous dynamic with a more beneficial one, and a more than shortsighted calculation of costs and benefits. The Latin American countries became aware of the problem that a nuclear arms race within their midst might pose for their own relations, sowing conflict by means of preventing it. But, alerted by the Cuban Missile Crisis, they saw a way of providing a blanket prevention of the problem, instead of small bilateral measures. As a result, within five years after the crisis, they agreed to establish a nuclear-free zone for the whole continent, in the Tlatelolco Agreement. People long knew there were dangers of a nuclear accident. But, galvanized by the 1986 Chernobyl disaster and the fallout over a wide swath of countries, they moved the same year to negotiate a Convention on Early Notification of Nuclear Accidents at Vienna.

Often both conflicting and third parties may shrug off the impending conflict as unimportant and costless. Preventive awareness hangs heavily on a clear understanding of the costs of conflict and the harm to parties and bystanders that its pursuit is likely to entail. It is well established that prevention is cost-efficient, much less costly than conflict (Cortright 1997; Brown & Rosecrance 1999; Skaperdas et al. 2009). Violence brings heavy losses in life and treasure, but it also carries significant opportunity costs, blocking plans for positive enhancement of development and welfare. The Colombian government under Juan Manuel Santos entered into a committed policy to prevent the continuation of the conflict with the FARC (Revolutionary Armed Forces of Colombia) in the mid-2010s because the conflict impeded hopes and plans for economic development. But not only does conflict impose costs on the parties involved; it also brings costs to third parties, both directly and in their relations with the parties to the conflict. Bystanders are impelled to mediate and prevent above all because the conflict is costly for them. The guarantor states became involved in mediating the Peru–Ecuador border dispute in the 1990s and the US and EU became involved in mediating the Morocco–Spain island dispute in 2002 for that very reason.

As much as awareness poses a problem for parties sliding toward conflict, it poses an even larger challenge for third parties who could be preventers. The obstacles to awareness have been laid out at the beginning of this book. Third parties have to overcome all sorts of valid reasons not to act, until it is too late. The United States was urged by the Secretaries of State and Defense in mid-2011 to give concrete support short of "boots on the ground" to the nationalist resistance in the Free Syrian Army (FSA) against the murderous regime of Bashar al-Assad, but the president turned down the advice and sent bandages for casualties and non-violent resistance advisors instead, for the reason that uncertainties were involved. By 2013, the FSA had nearly died for lack of sustenance, and the two sides to pick from were the al-Qaeda allies – the Nusra Front and the Islamic State of Iraq and [Greater] Syria (ISIS) – and the Assad regime, former enemy, eventually chosen as the lesser evil. More positively, both the Carter and the Reagan administrations were aware of the problems that a low-level conflict in South West Africa (eventually Namibia) could pose both for southern African relations and for US–Soviet relations. While the Carter administration picked up only the South African half of the problem, with no results, and the Reagan administration took on both the South African and the Angolan parts of the conflict, and resolved it, both were aware of the growing conflict, its tractability, and its potential for resolution, resulting in a major preventive effort (Zartman 1989; Crocker 1993).

Awareness must be especially alert to situations of change. Gradual or sudden changes can lead to new or worsened conflict, creating disputes where they did not exist before, upsetting patterns where people "knew their place." For example, demographic changes can be destabilizing, even when they are gradual (but people suddenly realize that they are occurring). If such effects can impact populations with relatively stable composition, migration and more rapid internal changes in a population bring inherent dangers of conflict and instability. Demographic changes tend to enlarge less endowed groups in a society, who trade off advancement for children. Whereas political pacts based on population proportions can create conditions of stability and prevent continually conflictual challenges, they come to be called into question

when proportions change, with highly conflicting consequences. The population census of 1932 was the basis of the
Lebanese Pact of 1943 that prevented conflict for decades but
was no longer accurate three decades later (and therefore dared
not be repeated) as the shift in the proportions of Christian
Maronites, Sunni Muslims and Shi'i Muslims was not
reflected in the distribution of political offices. Negotiations
for an end to the Troubles in Northern Ireland culminating
in the Good Friday Agreement of 1998 were influenced by
the fact that Catholics were likely to become a majority in
the near future. Negotiations over the future of Israel in the
former Palestine Mandate are influenced by the rising Arab
population, by the demographic impact of the right of return,
and also by the higher birthrate among Sephardic than among
Ashkenazi Jews. The increasing proportion of Muslim North
Africans and Turks among the citizenry of Europe, notably
in France, Belgium, Germany, and Austria, has a significant
impact on the electoral politics and foreign policies of the host
countries. Centralizing power and policy in the consolidating
states of Thailand and Burma in the late twentieth century has
led to neglect of the diverse ethnic regions and thence to the
rise of regional protests and demands for greater autonomy
in the early twenty-first century (Fuller 2014). Governments
need to keep up with changes in their populations in order to
prevent conflict, but they also need to take care of the parts of
the population that have lost benefits in the process.

An important dynamic, referred to as the J-curve effect (the
graphic image is not very obvious), has a powerful impact
in accounting for distributional changes that induce conflict
(Davies 1962; Gurr 1970). It indicates that it is not poor conditions or even envy of others (comparative or interpersonal
deprivation) that creates rebellion but the more mobile effect
of relative deprivation, where realizations are judged in relation to expectations (relative or intrapersonal deprivation).

When groups have enjoyed some benefits, especially if conditions are on the upswing, a noticeable drop in welfare causes
frustration: Rising expectations interrupted by falling satisfactions create conflict-proneness. Nothing assumes that the
initial expectations were justified, which adds to the delicacy
of prevention measures. Tamils, usually Christian, in Sri
Lanka were favored by colonization in their privileged access
to education and government service, even though a minority. Independence in 1948 brought the Buddhist Singhalese
majority to power, relieving the Tamils of their privileged
position in society. Several generational waves rose in ever-
escalating protest against the situation in 1958, 1977, 1981,
1983, and 1987 until 2009, when the murderously violent
Liberation Tigers of Tamil Eelam (LTTE) were exterminated
and many Tamil civilians with them. Sudden changes in food
subsidies as a result of economic structural adjustment but
unexplained by the government invariably trigger "IMF riots"
and even violent conflict as in Tunisia in 1984, Senegal in
1986, Argentina in 2001, among others. The economic and
employment grievances preceding the Arab Spring were rendered dynamic by a rise in youth unemployment at the same
time as economies were growing over the first decade of 2000
(Cincotta 2008/2009; Larémont 2014). Awareness of this
effect can lead to modifying measures, lowering expectations,
and justifying policy statements that can attenuate the danger
of conflict.

As another element of being prepared, it is predictable
that divorced states will return to violent conflict soon after
independence if they are separated by disputed borders.
New states for the most part accept the skin in which they
were born, being preoccupied with consolidating the internal conditions of independence. But when that boundary is
ill-defined, violent conflict is predictable as a continuation of
the independence struggle. The Sand Wars of Somalia with

Ethiopia and Morocco with Algeria in 1963 occurred over a boundary that simply did not exist, even on paper. The vicious Eritrean–Ethiopian war in 1998–2000 over a little neglected piece of border was absolutely foreseeable, if not preventable, as were the 2011 border (and other) war after South Sudan broke away from (North) Sudan and the 1974 border (and other) war between North and (South) Cyprus. Commentators noted each of these problems beforehand; the states ignored them, or positioned themselves for the impending conflict. But as Palestinian independence before boundary consolidation would predictably bring war with Israel, the unresolved state of the boundaries is used as an excuse to prevent Palestinian statehood. In all these and similar cases of new states with uncertain boundaries, prevention came only very late, to prevent further violence, after World Order practices broke down, and it was left to costly wars to show that military means to change the border were unavailing. The border (and larger) dispute between Ethiopia and Eritrea that burst into flames in 1998 was preceded by clear signs of a problem; in fact the independence agreement for Eritrea indicated that the border needed to be clarified.

Conflicts can be softened by developing an awareness of alternative ways of conceiving or defining the conflict so as to reduce the distributive element and bring out elements of common interest (Kriesberg & Dayton 2012). Consideration of similar conflicts and situations and their solutions can open up attitudes toward the underlying problems; efforts to bring out parties' real interests rather than simply conflicting positions can lead to a productive reframing of the problem in such a way that those involved can see positive-sum outcomes and problem-solving possibilities. The Moro Islamic Liberation Front (MILF) and the Philippine government came to a peace agreement in 2014 when they saw a common interest in fighting underdevelopment in Mindanao rather than fighting each other. India and Pakistan stopped fighting over the Indus and other rivers in 1960 when they saw that they could assure steady supply of water for themselves with an agreement, which has held ever since despite recent challenges and despite the otherwise hostile relations between the two neighbors. Finding such alternative frames and perceptions is a challenge to creative thinking and is part of the process of changing attitudes toward the conflict. These are the standard components of reframing an integrative perception of a conflict (Walton & McKersie 1965; Tversky & Kahneman 1981; Bazerman & Neale 1992; Pruitt & Carnevale 1993; Spector 1994). They are the key to a supportive mood that is crucial in sustaining the subsequent efforts, one that continually keeps hope alive for a peaceful and beneficial solution. Thereafter, the conflict prevention effort can be considered to be in march, pursued like any negotiation, persuasion, or de-escalation process, as will be developed in later sections.

Awareness leading to preventive action takes specific, interlocked steps, for the conflicting parties as well as potentially helpful third parties:

- Perception of the signs of impending conflict;
- Identification of the costs and dangers that the conflict poses;
- Study of predictable effects and of possible destabilizing changes;
- Conception of alternative conflict forms to meet given or reframed interests of the parties;
- Examination of the possibility of prevention, management, and resolution;
- Comparison of similar conflicts and outcomes.

The obstacles to awareness in the "early-early" phase of conflict are often both trivial and enormous, so it takes a major step of statesmanship on the part of both the conflicting and the observing parties to separate the two and take preventive action. Parties to the impending conflict must see the dangers way down the line on their current path and see and take measures to avert them before the conflict is in flames. Third parties must see the opportunity to put out the smoke before it becomes fire, even though they themselves are not parties to the conflict. Yet prevention at this stage is less difficult – or at least poses different challenges – than when the fire breaks out. Creative awareness is the key to the fork in the road from normal conflict to either positive, preventive resolution or costly, inexorable escalation into eventual violence.

De-escalation

Escalation is the process of moving from passive to active conflict and then of pursuing active conflict into violence; de-escalation is winding down the conflict, often by countering or undoing the steps of the original escalation. Escalation raises the stakes of the conflict, because more is now involved and the parties have more to climb down from to settle it, making prevention increasingly difficult. Parties escalate for various reasons, some of them rational, in the sense of being appropriate to a goal, and some of them emotional or even out of control, dysfunctional in terms of the ostensible goal. They escalate conflict in order to win but also for many other reasons – in order not to lose, to stay in the conflict or bring about negotiations, to cover investments and sunk costs, to show strength, to gain support, against the opponent or simply for oneself, at home or abroad, to seize an advantage or target of opportunity to use now or later, and even for affective reasons, to feel like a king, to reward oneself, because "I deserve it," or to feel like a dragon-slayer, to punish the other, because "he deserves it" (Zartman & Faure 2005). De-escalation involves first identifying the reasons for escalation, to be able to counter them effectively.

Escalation is often thought of only as stepped increases in the means of pursuing a conflict – first politics and then violence (Ikle 1971: 39; George et al. 1971; Leatherman et al. 1999: 74–7), but it can take place along many other dimensions as well, each of which complicates the challenge of prevention and the search for a solution. Escalation of ends means adding related demands to cover the initial demand; for example, a party that wants grievances redressed, then wants power-sharing to insure that grievances are removed, then wants to take over government entirely, as in the evolution of nationalist movements (Brown et al. 1964). Escalation of space involves adding unrelated issues; for example, hostage-takers add the additional demand for extra resources such as money or weapons to their original demand for freeing political prisoners (Hayes et al. 2003). Escalation of price refers to increasing tradeoffs asymmetrically (tracking): for instance, a union initially on strike for a raise now includes the strike costs in its new requirements for a settlement (Raskin 1987). Escalation of parties adds players to the conflict, as in the build-up of opposing alliances before the two World Wars or in the Cold War. Escalation of images is demonizing, where the opponent may be considered an obstacle, then an opponent, then an enemy, then a force of evil, as occurred during the Cold War, but also during the security dilemma that characterizes escalating ethnic conflicts, as discussed earlier (White 1984; Whyte 1986; Posen 1993). Escalation of risk means increasing dangerous uncertainties; for example, increasingly conflictual actions or tactics by one party can raise the danger that the other increase its demands, then refuse to talk, then take unilateral action, or simply can increase the chances that the other will take unilateral action directly (Avenhaus & Sjöstedt 2009). Escalation of costs increases the parties' outlays and deprivations, since maintaining the conflict requires greater and greater expenditures and increasingly blocks other actions, as occurred in the Vietnam War for the US and in the Western Sahara where Mauritanian participation in four years of war bankrupted the country and finally felled the government (Zartman 1989). Finally, escalation of commitment means increasingly firm resolution not to go back but to continue escalating, keeping on raising the ante once engaged (Brockner & Rubin 1985; Meerts 2005). Again, effective de-escalation depends on identification of the dimensions of escalation and pulling them apart for separate treatment.

Escalation is inherent in conflict and is required for the pursuit of conflict to the point of prevailing, but the curse of escalation is entrapment, which raises commitment along with costs. "In for a penny, in for a pound" and "If at first you don't succeed, try, try again" are bits of folk wisdom that lead into the vortex of entrapment. Escalation is a reciprocal spiral: escalation along any dimension brings escalation along other dimensions by the escalator, and invites counter-escalation by the other party along any dimension in response (Pruitt & Kim 2004). The first is called transitive, the second intransitive, as a voluntary action pulls in an involuntary response. Handling transitive escalation involves changing conflicting parties' policies and actions, whereas blocking intransitive escalation means holding back a runaway process. There is an inherent tendency for escalation to proceed on its own, dragging the parties along and making decisions for them, engulfing them in unintended and inescapable consequences. In between transitive decisions and intransitive pressures lies a whole minefield of "inappropriate" or "irrational" decisions fed by judgmental and perceptual biases, producing an intransitive effect even though specific decisions are involved (Ebbesen & Konečni 1980; Bazerman 1994; for a discussion of why parties might *not* escalate, see also Ikle 1971: 40).

Together, these two types of bias produce competitive irrationality, one of the most common phenomena associated with escalation.

Perceptional bias functions as a selective filter to maintain commitment to a course of action, leading the decision-maker to seek out only the information serving this commitment. Escalation is exacerbated when consequences of a decision are unclear, especially in the long term (Janis 1972; Rubin & Brockner 1975; Schwenk 1986; Bowen 1987; Staw & Ross 1987). Judgmental bias driven by losses from the original investment in escalation is the most common cause of further escalation. The parties engage in an activity that is irrational in terms of possible outcomes, as illustrated by the dollar auction game (Shubik 1971; Rubin 1981); they keep on bidding beyond the intrinsic cost of the item in the hope that the other will abandon. The desire to win takes on a life of its own, functioning as an additional motivation to pursue escalation (Bazerman 1984; Meerts 2005). This translates directly into entrapment but also into related phenomena such as overcommitment, or the inability to escape from escalation because of engagement to followers, and lock-in or personal entanglement through self-fulfilling prophecies, rationalizing (cognitive dissonance), demonizing, and selective perception. Countering entrapment is a challenge, for it means halting and reversing a powerful dynamic; escalating parties need to be called to their senses and brought face to face with the ever-rising costs without benefits. Decision-makers and their entourage do not want to admit to having made an initial mistake or to having missed or underestimated later consequences. Cognitive dissonance can produce escalation; once a course of action has been decided, negative feedback regarded as dissonant is rationalized away, and the party escalates, thinking that the next step is necessary to reach the goal and avoid the dissonance (Festinger 1957).

Escalation constitutes a dynamic barrier to conflict pre-vention that works against the preventer, which means that prevention needs to know how to handle it and how to turn its dynamics in a de-escalating direction. Careful diagnosis of the situation, considering its evolution, and of the opponent(s), considering their past tactics, performs the functions of early awareness for de-escalation. Understanding of the dynamics of escalation, as just laid out, is the posture of active monitor-ing as the conflict begins to emerge, in order either to forestall escalation itself to prevent increasing conflict, to slow it down to prevent it from getting out of hand and running away, or to turn it around to begin de-escalation. Escalation prevention invokes basic strategies of negotiation or mediation, depend-ing on the nature of the agent. Parties should continually consider how to disengage, even if they have no intention of doing so at the moment, in order to insure against entrap-ment. "How do I get out of this mess?" "Are there alternatives to more and more, to getting in deeper and deeper?" and "Are there other ways of getting a similar result with greater certainty?" are always relevant questions.

Strategies should also include clear indication to the other side of the costs and consequences of continued escalation in order to help the other side start thinking of the same ques-tions. Part of this may be threat or bluff but in any case it is important for the parties to walk up the stairs with their eyes open. However, the measures to prevent the other party from continuing the escalation must not be so challenging as to constitute a cause for further counter-escalation. Such meas-ures can be divided into "escalations to raise" and "escalations to call"; the first keeps the climbing going but the latter indi-cates that the outbidding stops here. Thus, in the 1962 Cuban Missile Crisis, the US maintained the pressure of the quaran-tine, maintaining but reducing its perimeter and boarding a non-Russian ship, both escalation to call measures. The issue was capital in the escalating crises of the mid-2010s, notably in Syria and Ukraine, where Western responses to escalation of the conflicts were timid and measured, for fear of exciting further counter-escalation, which then came anyhow. Measures to prevent the spread of conflict may need to be robust at the beginning, to avoid testing and creeping escalation.

If escalation is already taking place, it is important to prevent it from taking off on its own (intransitive) and impelling the parties to follow. The parties themselves need to observe these warnings but they cannot be relied on to be impartial observers at the same time as being committed tacticians; a third-party preventer has an indicated role. This means, again, having and conveying an accurate awareness and understanding of the forces being unleashed by the conflict, its costs and consequences, and the capabilities, credibility, and intentions of each side, including their limitations. Each escalator needs to judge the expected effect of the move: what does it take to make the other stop and consider alternative courses of action? And does prevention of conflict require merely stopping the escalation process, or actually backing down, undoing the gains to date? Again, the 2014–15 Ukrainian crisis is a case in point.

But, contrary to popular belief, escalation does not always preclude management and resolution; it often actually invites negotiation, under proper conditions, as will be analyzed in greater detail in the following section. Preventers and parties alike should look for negotiation opportunities despite or because of recent escalations, examining the parties' reactions to the situation produced at any round, notably the type of stalemate, as will be discussed in the next section. Parties should be encouraged to take a rest and study the situation: there is an opportunity for one or more of the parties on their own or with the gentle help of a third party to introduce new elements that can help prevent further conflict and reverse its direction. Revised perceptions of the stakes, construction of decommitting formulas, emphasis on an attracting focal point, reframing of the issues, and introduction of a new concept of justice and fairness are all tactics that can take advantage of the moment of de-escalation. There are some specific indicators that preventers should look for that help define escalations that can lead to de-escalations (Zartman & de Soto 2010):

- Signs of escalation costs' becoming too heavy to bear, as happened at the end of the Cold War or between Israel and Hamas in the early 2000s.
- Signs of escalations to call as in the first Iran–Iraq war, of shortfalls in escalations to raise as in the El Salvador rebellion, or of either party's inability to escalate further as in the Western Saharan dispute in the 2000s.
- Signs of second thoughts caused by threatened escalations, again as in the first Iran–Iraq war or the Ukrainian crisis.
- Signs of alternative focal points and positive outcomes to distract from the escalation process, as in the oil discovery off the coast of Cyprus in the mid-2010s.
- Signs of a common adversary's entering the escalation, as in the Israeli–Palestinian conflict on the rise of Hamas in the early 1990s.
- Signs of the escalators' search for third-party intervention or distraction from their conflict by third-party bait, as in the US aid offer to bring about the second Sinai disengagement in 1974 or the initial EU precondition (later withdrawn) of conflict resolution for Cyprus's entry.

Prevention faces the powerful dynamics of escalation and the compelling suction of entrapment at every stage of mounting conflict, lower at the beginning of a conflict, rising as the conflict escalates. All the elements discussed go into the production of escalation (transitive or intransitive), which goes on until the parties reach the point of capitulation or the buffer of fatigue (Smoker 1964). That process is a strong reason for early efforts at prevention, before the full dynamic effect sets in motion. Prevention needs to respond flexibly as the conflict rises from its inactive stage and to seize whatever opportunities it can for de-escalation. These preventive mechanisms are available to the parties as well, but they are likely to be so busy escalating that they need some help to focus on achieving their goals by alternative paths. Third parties need to look for weak points and hesitations in the escalation process that they can utilize to reverse its course.

Stalemate

Escalation is a dynamic situation that moves parties to victory/defeat or stalemate/stagnation. Stalemate, however, is a resting point that can be a promising sign that sets up parties to consider accommodation as well as to desperate attempts to burst out. If the parties come to the realization that they cannot win and that further escalation at an acceptable price cannot put them over the top, they are impelled either to hunker down at some level to stay in the game (and continue to block the opponent's efforts to win), or to turn from unilateral to bi(multi)lateral efforts to prevent further conflict through resolution. The choice between the two paths depends on whether the stalemate is sustainable or is painful. Sustainable conflicts, often termed frozen or intractable, are particularly dangerous because they are – counterintuitively – so unstable. Parties stuck in intractable conflicts are just waiting for a shift in fortunes that will enable them to prevail. These situations come in many forms that pose different opportunities for prevention.

One can be called an S5 situation – soft, stable, self-serving stalemate (Zartman 2005b; Kress & Szechtman 2009). In an S5, a rebellion seeking to overthrow the state finds itself in control of a part of its territory, comfortable in its pseudo-governmental role yet blocked from its ultimate goal, while the government is comfortably in control of the rest of the territory and busy doing all the other things a state does. The conflict may – often by this fact – develop an ethnic dimension tied to the territory but that is not a necessary characteristic. The continued civil wars after independence between the Revolutionary Nationalist Movement (Renamo) and the Front for the Liberation of Mozambique (FreLiMo) government and between the Popular Movement for the Liberation of Angola (MPLA) government and the National Union for the Total Independence of Angola (UNITA) gradually developed an ethnic nature between northern and southern tribes, respectively in each case. The radical rebellion of the Revolutionary Armed Forces of Colombia (FARC) evolved into control of large tracts in southern Colombia, which it governed as a pseudo-state, frustrated in its goal of governing the whole Colombian state. Often in such cases, the rebellion, in search of resources to keep itself alive, becomes hooked on its sources, which then become its ends rather than its means. The FARC's drugs, Savimbi's UNITA's gold in Angola, Foday Sankoh's drugs and diamonds in Sierra Leone were all resources that kept their S5 situations alive. This is an unhappily stable situation, and prevention of continuation or escalation depends on breaking its self-serving stability.

A further variation on this situation may be termed the Default Impasse, where the stalemate is neither stable nor self-serving and is maintained only because the alternative is much worse to each side, a true Prisoner's Dilemma. Unfortunately, this stalemate is unstable since, unlike the mutually hurting stalemate (MHS) or the S5 situation, the parties are tempted to try to revert to escalation if the occasion presents itself, but they fear more the attempt of the other side to do so than they do the continuing, bearable impasse, thus keeping them unstably stalemated. In this situation, the best prevention is not to disturb the delicate instability, lest it lead one of the parties to fear a tip away from their interests and try to escalate for advantage. The situations in the Western Sahara and Nagorno-Karabakh have all the appearance of stability but the fear that one side will move for an advantage leads the parties to reject all attempts at solution (the conflict being already managed to prevent violence). Often, as in the cited cases, it is an external protector that keeps the impasse from turning sour, and so a preventive de-escalation can only come from the external protector.

Another variation is a "staggered stalemate," which occurs when only one side feels stalemated; it cannot escalate its way out but dare not make any concessions for de-escalation. Then fortunes change, the dynamic continues, but the sides are reversed. This was the history of the Sudanese conflict for over half a century, where the two sides were not stalemated at the same time but unable to eliminate each other. A further variation is the "revisionist blockage," which occurs when one side, the status quo party or "shopkeeper," is already ready to negotiate the conflict but finds no chance for conflict prevention since the other side is a revisionist or "warrior," dedicated only to winning, in violent conflict (Kissinger 1964; Nicholson 1964; Ury 1991). A revised situation and an external mediator are required to bring the parties to prevention and resolution.

Most promising for further conflict prevention is the stalemate that is painful to both parties – the mutually hurting stalemate (MHS), not present in the above types. Such a moment, ripe to begin resolution, must be seized, either by the conflicting parties or through the help of a third party, if a return to open conflict is to be prevented. This condition, paired with a perception that each side believes a way out to be attainable, is termed "conflict ripeness" (Zartman & Berman

1982; Zartman 2000). It is a subjective perception, related to objective conditions only to the extent that they are perceived, and is the necessary but insufficient basis for the opening of attempts to resolve conflict. It does not guarantee a successful outcome; the push of the MHS must be coupled with the pull of a mutually enticing opportunity (MEO) developed by the negotiating parties out of their sense of a way out. The way to an MEO begins with an MHS; there is no other.[1]

There are specific MHS indicators that parties and mediators can seize on to begin the process of preventive negotiation, both objective and subjective, but it must be remembered that there is no MHS unless the parties feel, subjectively, the pain of the objective factors of stalemate (Zartman & de Soto 2010):

Objective signs:
- When parties lack the capacity and will to take measures to escalate, as between Israel and Hamas in 2008 and 2012.
- When financial and casualty losses rise beyond expectations and anticipated gains, as in South West Africa (Namibia) in 1986 and South Africa in 1990.
- When contextual conditions impose hardships on the parties, as in the case of the tsunami in Indonesia in 2005 and the drought in Mozambique in 1990.
- When more tractable leadership comes to power, as with Yitzhak Rabin in Israel in 1992.
- When allies of the parties tire of the conflict, as with the US and UK in regard to Northern Ireland in the 1990s.
- When allies of the parties improve their relations, as with the US and USSR in regard to the South West African conflict in the late 1980s.

Subjective signs:
- When official statements or informed commentators openly acknowledge an MHS, as did Joe Slovo in South

Africa in the early 1990s, or the Armenian and Azerbaijani leaders in 1994 (Mooradian & Druckman 1999), or US and Taleban spokespersons in 2012.
- When parties begin to draw down forces in the conflict area, as with the US in Afghanistan in 2012 or in Vietnam in 1975.

The mutual perception of ripeness requires tending if it is to lead to effective prevention of further escalations and further conflict. The parties probably need help in developing an MEO attractive enough to both of them to begin the decline of the conflict. A ceasefire or similar measure that demotes the conflict from the violent to the political level is a good place to begin but it cannot be expected to hold from the start (Fortna 2004a; Mahieu 2007). Violence, or its threat, may be necessary to remind the parties they are still in an MHS till the end, when the MEO takes over. Violence is often the only money that one or more parties (particularly rebels) has to compel attention to the conflict and to their grievances; they will not voluntarily give it up before any substantive agreement has been reached (Darby 2001, 2006). Furthermore, one may expect a shot of violence as parties get closer to an agreement and jockey for the best bargaining position. Preventers can be helpful in keeping discussions of ceasefire on track as the parties move toward agreement on resolution measures.

There is no better example of the challenge of ripeness than the mid-2010s Syrian civil war, where each of several sides felt they could and indeed must win, and where an initial Western perception was that Bashar al-Assad was worthy only of removal. Then the international community tried to use the United Nations Secretary-General and a multiparty conference to mediate an end to the conflict, but without any attempt to ripen it. Pursuit of ripeness for joint resolution was rejected by any potential third parties except for UN SESG Lakhdar

Brahimi, as well as by the parties to the conflict. Subsequent searches for a mediated joint solution to prevent the massive killing (including by gas) met parties dug into their opposing positions by three years of war. On the other hand, there are more positive examples of ripeness and prevention. The 1992 negotiations to end the rebellion in El Salvador followed objective evidence that the Farabundo Marti Front for National Liberation (FMLN) offensive could penetrate the capital but not hold and the army could not defeat the FMLN, opening the way for mediation by UN SRSG Alvaro de Soto (1999). The same perception in South Africa in 1990 led to a remarkable agreement that changed the nature of the state, led by Nelson Mandela and F.W. de Klerk, without need for a mediator; South African Communist Party leader Joe Slovo said, "The National Party couldn't rule any longer, we couldn't seize power by force. So that means that both sides have to compromise." Many of the successful efforts to prevent further conflict cited in other issue areas – Oslo in 1993, Namibia in 1988, Mindanao in 2013, even Eritrea in 2000 – benefitted from similar moments of ripeness, seized creatively.

The perception of ripeness involves a new attitude toward the conflict, turning from an encounter that each thinks it can win to one whose blockage makes them turn to each other for a solution. Such recalculations of alternatives are facilitated by exogenous events and shocks that occasion and justify a new perception (Kuperman 2015). They can be merely a sharp form of the new calculations or something totally extraneous to conflict. Israelis and Palestinians were impelled to stretch out a hand in Oslo in 1993 because of the appearance of Hamas, a common enemy, on the scene. The sudden appearance of body bags with South African white soldiers in them in 1986 (coupled with some other events) brought home to South Africa the awareness that the stalemate was hurting them. More exogenously, the 2004 tsunami brought

Acehnese and Indonesians to the table to sign an agreement that year (the same earthquake did not bring an end to the war in Sri Lanka). The Chernobyl effect in focusing minds to negotiate the Convention on Early Notification of Nuclear Accidents at Vienna in 1986 is another example. Preventers must be alert to seize on such events to rapidly ripen perceptions, lest their effect pass with time.

Not all stalemates lead to the prevention of further conflict. In the absence of mutual pain or of a firm appreciation of the impasse or in the presence of a high commitment to victory at whatever cost, the natural tendency is to look and wait for a way out in escalation, not in negotiation. The opportunity offered by checked escalation is not self-implementing and remains to be seized, by the parties themselves or through a preventive mediator, but the rising escalation can also produce other types of results. Righteousness for the true believer, revolutionary commitment for the Warrior, and implacable hostility for the embittered enemies are frequent emotional responses to escalation frustrated by mutual blockage, and the expended investment, rising costs, heightened commitment, and accumulated scars that escalation occasions only increase the obdurate reactions. The challenge of prevention is to turn the reaction instead in the direction of de-escalation.

Ripening

If the parties do not feel themselves to be caught in a mutually hurting stalemate that pushes them to begin lowering tensions, they need help in changing their perceptions and attitudes. Ripening is required. Conflicting parties do not look for a way out of a conflict if they think they can win and if the conflict is not hurting them. Therefore to open their minds to pre-crisis prevention, they must be made aware that winning is rare and attempts to win costly. If one or both sides does not have a change of heart by their respective leaderships (probably requiring a change of leadership) that allows them to perceive a path out of conflict, a third party's attentions are required to bring about that perception. This is a primary challenge for external parties who would position themselves to take advantage of the stalemate to begin a mediation and conflict (or escalation) prevention process. Before it can begin the process of helping the conflicting parties find a joint solution, they must be convinced that they need one: for example, that coveted territory cannot be seized and even if it is, the conquest will not be recognized, or that an ethnic group cannot be cleansed and even if it is, it will resurge next door to continue the conflict. Only when the parties' attitudes have been changed can the mediator get to the job of mediating. The mediator's biggest challenge is ripening, before it can ever begin mediating.

Prevention of continuing conflict in this situation can require many angles of persuasion to ripen the parties' perceptions (Zartman & de Soto 2010). The parties have to be made aware of the stalemate in which they are caught by their own efforts and must see it as truly inescapable and painful. Cultivation of the subjective perception can require reference to its objective bases and even the creation of such objective aids to the perception. Thus, the preventing agent may even be required to change some conditions on the ground, in addition to highlighting conditions that do exist. Mediators must also develop an awareness on each side that the other side has a similar perception of a hurting stalemate and feels the need to reach out bilaterally for a jointly crafted solution to prevent further escalation and heightened conflict, preparing in this way for management and solution of the conflict. Only when these mutual perceptions are developed can the preventer then help the conflicting parties turn to a joint effort to give body to the notion of a way out. The biggest challenge is to help inculcate the sense of hurt and stalemate against the dogged pursuit of winning. The fact that pursuit may well be rational and desirable, at least in the eyes of the parties, as discussed in the opening section on challenges, only highlights the size of the task for the mediator.

Most of the cases cited in regard to stalemates that were turned to prevention of further escalation involved the painstaking efforts of a third party working to bring the parties to recognize the pain of the stalemate. Mediators spend more time in ripening than in crafting of an agreeable outcome – an MEO – once the parties' perception is awakened. US Assistant Secretary Chester Crocker spent six of his eight years' tenure in trying to get Angolans and South Africans to feel the need for an agreement to prevent continuing escalation and provide a resolution to their conflict, followed by one year of actually mediating the outcome (Crocker 1993).

Ripening is above all persuasion, enhancing the subjective perception, but it may even require providing some objective evidence as well – or even creating that evidence:

Subjective encouragement:
- By emphasizing costs, highlighting lost opportunities, and comparing difficulties of escalation with the advantages of resolution, as Crocker with the South Africans and Angolans in 1980–6, and Brahimi with Assad in 2013–14.
- By encouraging thinking about creative outcomes and salient solutions, as the guaranteeing states did in the Peru–Ecuador border dispute in 1998.
- By encouraging op-eds, articles, and study groups examining the situation with an eye to providing creative insights and hard calculations, as was done in dialog sessions involving the conflict parties in Liberia in 1993 and in Ivory Coast in 2003.

- By encouraging the parties to think ahead to the consequences of their present course of action heading toward conflict, as Kissinger did with Golda Meir in 1973 and as states and the Intergovernmental Panel on Climate Change (IPCC) are doing in regard to the conflict with nature in global warming.
- By reframing the conflict in manageable or mutually attractive terms, as Lord Caradon did by providing the formula of "territory for security" in the Arab–Israeli dispute in 1967 or the guaranteeing states by proposing development as the main issue in the Peru–Ecuador dispute.

Objective inducement:
- By tightening the hurting stalemate with economic sanctions, as used against Serbia in 1995, Iran in 2013, Russia in 2014, and Israel with blocked loan guarantees in 1991.
- By direct military intervention to freeze the stalemate until the parties felt it, as France did in separating the conflicting parties in Ivory Coast in 2005.

There are fewer cases to cite where ripening succeeded in turning parties from violence in the first place than from preventing conflicts from continuing once violence had occurred; the latter is easier, albeit costlier, because the objective evidence for the hurting stalemate is present, not merely prospective, and the former is harder to prove since costly violence did not (yet) take place. The conflict between the FMLN and the Salvadoran government opened itself to UN mediation in 1990 when, after an FMLN offensive with no prospect of further success, the mediator helped the parties see that neither side could win but both were sustaining unbearable losses. In the Israeli–Palestinian conflict in 2008 over Gaza, an imperfect ceasefire was arrived at between Israel and Hamas when both sides saw they could not prevail but costs were mounting, a realization of ripeness sharpened by Egyptian mediation; the same scenario was repeated in 2012 and 2014. Backed up by examples of political conflicts turning dirty and under the pressure of mounting violence, a series of international mediators, ending with former Secretary-General Kofi Annan, were able to convince the presidential candidates in Kenya in 2008 to negotiate a power-sharing agreement rather than deliver the country into ethnic violence. In sum, negotiators seeking to ripen identity conflicts for prevention need to muster enormous skills of persuasion, but they may also need to affect objective facts on the ground to enhance the subjective perception of ripeness.

Resolution

The ultimate way to prevent a conflict from intensifying is to resolve it. A number of standard practices and institutions offer a way to salvage goals while avoiding costly escalation. Resort to such institutions of prevention requires a change in attitudes, from a belief that a solution can be found only in unilateral efforts to one that sees a solution in cooperation. "Institutions" here does not refer to organizations but to established conflict management practices of prevention, including negotiation, mediation, and adjudication (Zartman 1991, 2009). These practices allow the parties to pursue their conflict non-violently in search of an outcome that satisfies both sides.

Negotiation
The most obvious means for parties to prevent conflict escalation and violence is to negotiate directly with each other to resolve their conflict. There is no better way to prevent violence than for the parties to come together to find a jointly satisfactory solution, under the pain of stalemate or the threat

of escalation. Negotiators seek prevention by devising a mutually enticing opportunity for themselves, crafting a conflict outcome that provides something for both parties, not for goodness' sake, but in order to give each an incentive to keep the agreement from which each party benefits. The parties do not have to gain equally; the allocation of the gains is a matter for further negotiation. Negotiating is "giving something to get something" and the parties come away having established a fair price for the outcome they have received. Positive-sum attitudes reflect its basic nature. The two "somethings" constitute the basic terms of trade, the principle or formula on which the agreement is based.

Formulas are the key to a negotiated solution to a conflict; they provide a common understanding of the problem and its solution or a shared notion of justice to govern an outcome. Once the formula is established, the parties can turn to translating it into the details of the agreement. In mercantilist terms, "If you can't take it, you must buy it," and negotiating details is the process of setting the price. The formula, "Territory for security," contained un UNSC resolution 242 in 1967 was the basis of the Israeli withdrawals from Sinai and the Golan Heights in 1973–4, preventing the continuation of the 1973 October War. The Washington peace treaty of 1979 was the security price that Egypt paid to Israel to get back the Sinai territory. The 1998 Good Friday Agreement in Northern Ireland was based on a "three strands" formula in which the roles of both Britain and Ireland were formalized in the settlement, arms were to be laid down ("decommissioned"), and power shared among the Northern Ireland political parties. In both cases, violence achieved negotiations; negotiation achieved further conflict prevention. Both of these notable examples involved mediation, discussed below, showing that direct negotiations between conflicting parties without third-party facilitation of some degree are rather rare.

Parties can achieve positive sums through concession, compensation, or construction (reframing). Concession means dividing the contested item between the contesting parties. While the result is essentially zero-sum (what one side gains the other loses), losses are balanced by the gain for both sides in ending the conflict. Concessions are most clearly applied to territory but can also be in the form of intangible items. In the Aceh–Indonesia agreement of 2005, Aceh moved from its demand for independence and Indonesia toward its acceptance of autonomy to end up with "self-government" between the two. Compensation refers to an exchange of concessions on different matters, one party "paying for" a favorable outcome in one matter by granting the other party a favorable outcome on another matter. By Homans' Maxim (1961; see also Nash 1950), "the more the items at stake can be divided into goods valued more by one party than they cost to the other and goods valued more by the other party than they cost to the first, the greater the chances of a successful outcome." In the South African negotiations in 1990–4, a rare case of direct, unmediated negotiations to prevent violence, the Black majority gained political power in exchange for the Whites' continued predominance in the economy. Of course, not all stakes are Homans-divisible, still leaving a distribution problem in many cases. In such cases, compensation can be made only by bringing in items external to the original stakes, as side payments.

Construction or reframing refers to a redefinition of the stakes in such a way that both parties can find an interest in the outcome, instead of defining it distributively. The next step in prevention awareness is the reframing of the problem in such a way that those involved can see a positive-sum outcome to the preventive efforts. Reframing is the key to the continuing process and a natural part of awareness of the problem-solving possibilities. This means removing or softening the distributive nature or perception of the problem, and converting it into an integrative problem. Or, if the problem is obstinately distributive, it means seeking an accepted notion of justice to govern the allocation of outcomes. It is unlikely that reframing can totally recast the stakes to the elimination of all distributive concerns over details, but it can provide superordinate goals and a cooperative atmosphere, in addition to redefined stakes, so that distribution becomes less contentious. After 13 years of talks to prevent further violence by resolving the Panama Canal dispute, Panama and the US redefined the zero-sum ownership problem by constructing a formula involving Panamanian ownership and US security, allowing the Canal to function in the interests of both parties. A comprehensive peace agreement was possible in Colombia in 2015 because the FARC felt it was better to pursue its goals by election than by violence and so both sides sought to work out the conditions for democratic non-violent participation in politics for everyone.

If the parties do not enter negotiations with positive-sum attitudes, seeking to prevent further conflict as well as defending their interests, they will continue their conflict in deadlock. Zero-sum perspectives focus on winning at the other party's expense, continuing and escalating the conflict. Zero-sum thinking is accompanied by a perception of the stakes in terms of relative gains, where a party measures its success relative to the position of the other party. The Cold War conflict is a good example of relative-gains thinking and a zero-sum attitude toward the conflict, where it was deemed more important to keep ahead of the adversary than to achieve a particular goal and where the absence of trust between the parties long prevented them from reaching mutually beneficial outcomes of cooperation, attitudes that linger decades after the Cold War. It also is found between Indians and Pakistanis, Israelis and Palestinians, francophilic West Africans and Nigeria, North and South Korea, and many other pairs of adversaries.

The problem with zero-sum encounters is that their unbalanced outcomes leave little prospect of stability and a bad impression on the loser, who looks to improve its relative gains in the next round or elsewhere. If negotiations were a one-shot affair, parties could drive the hardest bargain possible, sign, and run. But preventive diplomacy is the business of managing relations, that is, ongoing ties and contacts, among states. Even if a party feels a need to prevail in a particular diplomatic negotiation, it is under pressure to do so in such a manner that the outcome does not impel the other party above all to seek revenge at some later moment and undo the prevention. "Diplomacy," said Cardinal Richelieu (1947 [1638]), "should aim, not at incidental or opportunistic arrangements, but at creating solid and durable relations."

Mediation
Mediation has been necessary in many prevention approaches at different stages, when the parties were unable to prevent conflict escalation by themselves and needed an agent and catalyst to bring them to work together. Parties in conflict need help. Mediation, like any negotiation, carries with it the implication that there is a perceived legitimate grievance to be resolved and legitimate interests to be protected, and that none of the parties is seeking self-destruction (Rubin 1981; Mitchell & Webb 1988; Bercovitch & Rubin 1992; Zartman & Touval 2007; Bercovitch 2007, 2009; Wiegand 2014; Fixdal 2015). In an internal conflict, mediation will generally be resisted by the government, as it implies that a government cannot handle its own problems, that the rebellious or repressed groups deserve recognition and equal standing before the mediator, and that in the end the only resolving outcome will be a revised political system that accords the rebels a legitimate place in politics. However, the rebels often also reject mediation for fear of its being biased against them, as the FMLN did initially in El

Salvador, SWAPO did in South West Africa (Namibia), and the several rebel groups did in Burundi (Zartman 1995). It is the mediator's job to meet the parties' desires for an end to the conflict in such a way that they do not end up losers.

Such were the challenges to Sant'Egidio (backed by the US, Russia, Portugal, Italy, Zimbabwe, Kenya, and Zambia) and to the US and the UN, who mediated more or less successfully between Renamo and UNITA and the Frelimo and MPLA governments of Mozambique and Angola, in Rome in 1990–2, and in Estoril in 1992, in Lusaka in 1994, and in Luanda in 2001–2, respectively, to overcome post-colonial rebellions. Such too were the challenges to first Libya and then Malaysia and a complicated group of interested states and NGOs who mediated the conflict between the Mindanao Moros and the Philippine government between 1976 and 2014, finally producing a special form of autonomy.

The mode of mediation depends on the obstacle that stands in the way of direct negotiation between the parties. When the obstacle is the inability of the parties to trust and to talk to each other, thereby preventing them from listening to each other and from making concessions without appearing weak or losing face, the mediator can serve as communicator, sometimes termed facilitator. In this situation, mediators simply act as a conduit, opening contacts and carrying messages. They may be required to help the parties understand the meaning of messages through the distorting dust thrown up by the conflict or gather the parties' concessions together into a package, without adding to the content. This role is completely procedural, with no substantive contribution by the mediator, and in its simplest form it is completely passive, only carrying out the parties' orders for the delivery of messages. It was performed by the Vatican in the 1984 Beagle Channel disputes and by the Norwegians in the 1993 Oslo talks. Tact, credibility, trust, wording, and sympathy, mixed in equal doses with accuracy and confidentiality, are necessary character traits of the mediator as communicator.

If the obstacle in the conflict is the inability of the parties to conceive of a solution, they need a mediator in the second mode as formulator. Just as the conflict often inhibits the parties from communicating proposals to each other, it may also block them from even thinking of solutions. Therefore, the mediator as a formulator is needed to provide ideas and persuade the parties to consider them. Not only does the mediator get involved in the substance of the issue, but it must also lean on the parties – albeit in the subtlest ways – to be open to new perceptions of a way out. Successful formulators must be capable of thinking of ways to unblock the thinking of the conflicting parties and to work out imaginative ways to skirt those commitments that constrain them. Agreement to end the conflict in Namibia and Angola in 1988 was reached by the mediator's proposal of "linkage" or compensation – to "purchase" a withdrawal of 50,000 South African troops from Namibia (and its consequent achievement of independence) with the withdrawal of 50,000 Cuban troops from Angola, and vice versa, thus achieving a full realization of both parties' goals.

But if the obstacle is that there is simply not enough on the table to attract the parties toward a positive outcome, the mediator needs to act as a manipulator. Here the mediator assumes the maximum degree of involvement, becoming a party to the solution, even though not to the conflict. As a manipulator, the mediator uses its power to bring the parties to an agreement, pushing and pulling them away from conflict and into resolution. When the obstacle to agreement is the seemingly paltry size of the outcome, the mediator must persuade the parties of its vision of a solution; it must then take measures to make that solution attractive, enhancing its value by adding benefits to its outcome and presenting it in such a way as to overcome imbalances that may have prevented one of the parties from subscribing to it. The mediator may have to go so far as to improve the absolute attractiveness of the resolution by increasing the unattractiveness of continued conflict, which may mean shoring up one side or condemning another, either of which actions strains the appearance of its own neutrality. This is the role of the "full participant," such as American diplomats played in the 1970s Middle East peace process and in the 1990s Northern Ireland negotiations.

Mediation is a triangular relationship. When the mediator operates as a communicator, it operates as a bridge between two contestants, or as a pump on the conduit between them. As a formulator, the mediator assumes a position of greater activity, one from which pressures and messages emanate as well as pass through. As a manipulator, the mediator becomes so active as to call into question the triangular relationship. It may even unite the two adversaries in opposition to the mediator; for example, in the Yemen civil war (1962–70) the two sides resolved their differences in order to oppose Egyptian interference, when Egypt was acting more as an intervener than as a mediator. But the manipulator, by throwing its weight around, threatens and is threatened by the possibility of turning the triangle into a dyad as the US Secretary of State Al Haig did in 1982 in the Falkland Islands dispute. The mediator's threat to side with one party may bring the other party around, for fear that mediation might end and with it any possibilities for a solution. As a threat to the mediator, each party may try to win the mediator over to its own side to increase its chances of winning rather than of having to come to terms. At the same time, of course, each party may regard the mediator with high suspicion as a potential ally of the other side. Although it makes the mediator's job more difficult, suspicion is good because it keeps the mediator honest.

On the parties' side, valid spokespersons for the various parties are required. If the parties are many or the spokespersons are not clearly authorized, the mediator may first have to form coalitions and to designate spokespersons for mediation purposes, necessitating deeper involvement in internal politics and seriously complicating the task. The US at Dayton arranged for Serbian President Slobodan Milošević to speak for the Bosnian Serbs and Croatian President Franjo Tudjman to speak for the Bosnian Croats, but not without complications for the process and subsequent implementation. In Abuja in 2006, the US and Nigeria unwisely picked and pressed some of the rebels to the exclusion of others in an attempt to craft an agreement to end the genocide in Darfur, but the excluded rebels continued the fight, each seeking a better deal than the one originally negotiated (Brooks 2008).

Power – the ability to move a party in an intended direction – is often referred to in mediation as "leverage." Although leverage is the ticket to mediation, mediators tend to remain relatively powerless throughout the exercise, contrary to the common perception. The extent of the mediator's power depends entirely on the parties, whose acceptance of a mediator depends on its likelihood (potential power) of producing an outcome agreeable to both sides. This circular relationship plagues every mediation exercise. Contrary to another common misperception, mediators are rarely "hired" by the parties; instead, they have to sell their services, based on the prospect of their usefulness and success. From the beginning, the mediator's leverage is at the mercy of the contestants. The parties, whose interest is in winning, view mediation as meddling, unless it produces a favorable outcome. They welcome mediation only to the extent that the mediator has leverage over the other party, and they berate the mediator for trying to exert leverage over them.

A mediator has five sources of leverage in working to prevent further conflict: first, persuasion, the ability to portray an alternative future as more favorable than the continuing conflict; second, extraction, the ability to produce an attractive position from each party; third, termination, the ability to withdraw from the mediation; fourth, deprivation, the ability to withhold resources from one side or to shift them to the other; and fifth, gratification, the ability to add resources to the outcome. With every source, however, the effectiveness of the mediator's leverage lies with the parties themselves, a characteristic that makes leverage in mediation difficult to achieve.

- Persuasion shows the value in terms of the parties' own interests of preventing escalation before it goes too far, as Kissinger did in the 1974 disengagement negotiations and President Carter did at Camp David and in preparing the 1979 Washington Treaty.
- Extraction requires formulating a proposal for prevention that is acceptable to one party and attractive to the other, as President Ahtisaari did in 2005 in Aceh.
- Termination, perhaps counterintuitively, is the mediator's willingness to walk away and leave the parties alone face to face with the dangers of escalation, as Senator Mitchell did in the Good Friday talks on Northern Ireland in early 1998 and Secretary Christopher did in the Bosnia talks at Dayton in 1994.
- Deprivation, referring to the customary notion of mediator's "leverage," warns or threatens to worsen the situation of one or both recalcitrant parties, as Secretary Kerry did in warning Israel of isolation and a further intifada if movement in peace talks were not forthcoming in 2014, and Secretary Baker did in 1991 by withholding Israel's loan guarantees.
- Gratification, the opposite of deprivation as carrots are to sticks, provides incentives to parties to engage in

preventive cooperation, as Secretary Kissinger did for both Israel and Egypt in providing a long-term promise of aid for making the second Sinai disengagement possible in 1974.

Of all these, the principal element of leverage is persuasion – the ability of the mediator to reorient the parties' perceptions to the value of prevention. Like any kind of persuasion, the mediator's ability depends on many different referents that are skillfully employed to make conciliation more attractive and continuing conflict less so. These referents may include matters of domestic welfare and political fortunes, risks and costs, prospects of continuing conflict and of moving out of it, reputations, solidity of allies' support, world opinion, and the verdict of history.

The other basic element in leverage is need – the parties' need – for a solution that they cannot achieve by themselves, for additional support in regional or global relations, and for a larger package of payoffs to make a conciliatory outcome more attractive. Perception of this need can be enhanced by the mediator, but it cannot be created out of nothing. Side payments with no relation to the outcome of the conflict are effective only insofar as they respond to an overriding need for a solution that outweighs the deprivation of concessions on the issues of the conflict itself. Parties can be made aware of needs that they did not recognize before, particularly when the chances of assuaging them had seemed out of reach. The provision of Cuban troop withdrawal from Angola, which met South Africa's need for a countervailing reward, led to the South African troop and administration withdrawal from Namibia, yet this need was not formulated during the 1970s rounds of the mediation. Persuasion often depends on perceived need, but then need often depends on persuasion.

Mediation to prevent continuing and escalating conflict is exceptionally difficult in cases when identity takes an ideological form, when the violence takes on a terrorist form, and where the rebels have an independent source of funding that allows them to enjoy their Sherwood Forest existence. For example, it has been hard to find an appropriate mediator in the Colombian, Sri Lankan, Ugandan, Nepalese, Somali or Sierra Leonean conflicts. In Colombia, ideology and the drug trade made the Revolutionary Armed Forces (FARC) and the National Liberation Army (ELN) uninterested in seeking a solution out of talks with the government for decades, and various would-be mediators have found little purchase on the situation, until the mid-2010s when the government of President Santos took on the task directly, witnessed but unmediated. In Sierra Leone, the Revolutionary United Front (RUF) proved unworthy of mediation and broke the Abidjan (1996), Conakry (1997) and Lomé (1999) Agreements made by West African mediators; an end to the conflict was achieved instead by the RUF's defection and British military intervention (Mutwol 2009). In Sri Lanka, the Liberation Tigers of Tamil Eelam (LTTE) joined their enemy, the government, to defeat all attempts at mediation, notably by such well-placed mediators as India and Norway, until the government broke the cooperation and crushed the rebels. In Uganda, a number of well-placed mediators have come close to closing a deal with the Lord's Resistance Army (LRA) but Joseph Kony, its leader, has slipped away from contact and agreement a number of times. In such cases, it is only when the terrorists are worn out and have become fully isolated from a population alienated by their own tactics that they become amenable to a return to civil politics and become susceptible to mediation. Otherwise they must be defeated. Mediation as a means of preventing identity conflict and its escalation into genocide is not merely a matter of making peace; it must be a means of reforming and restoring the political fabric of the state in order to render it a functioning entity again.

These are all elements within the mediation process, but the greatest challenge outside the process concerns spoilers, those political entrepreneurs who are set on conflict as the path to power and want no prevention (Stedman 2000). Since the political entrepreneur, or agent provocateur, is likely to lose his job in the process of prevention, there is certain to be resistance. The opening counter-strategy is to wean weaker spoilers away from the hard core and involve them in the dynamics of the prevention process. But dealing with the spoilers who remain requires a different kind of confrontation, to isolate and neutralize them until they become powerless to undermine or block the ongoing prevention. The best mediation strategy is the "train leaving the station" ploy to form an agreement among a critical mass of parties on both sides of the conflict, and then to urge the would-be spoiler to come on board as the process moves ahead to implementation. This approach worked in South Africa in 1994 and in Burundi in the early 2000s, in two very different conflicts.

These various mechanisms are process elements that can be used, alone or in combination, to defuse a crisis in formation or in escalation. They carry no guarantees and their success depends on skillful diplomacy and persuasion, and on collective support for the state or party chosen to bell the cat. They all need to be backed by a threat alternative as much as possible; nothing looks attractive to parties bent on conflict unless it is coupled with worse alternatives in the absence of compliance. As UN Secretary-General Kofi Annan (1998) said when returning from a successful mediation with Saddam Hussein, "Diplomacy can be effective, but it helps to have a military presence in the region . . . You can do a lot with diplomacy, but with diplomacy backed up by force you can get a lot more done."

Adjudication

The distinguishing characteristic of adjudication (and arbitration) as institutions of conflict resolution is that the parties are bound beforehand to accept the judgment, which is rendered by a third party (Merrills 2011). Treaties and other "political" agreement are legally binding and therefore formally effective as institutions for preventing further conflict, but their terms are set up by the parties, whereas judicial determinations are made by others and binding on the parties who accept the jurisdiction. Whether that makes them more effective institutions for conflict prevention is up for debate. They are unlikely to contain elements of interest, compensation and construction, manipulation, reconciliation, follow-through and many others that embody the creativity of negotiated (including mediated) settlements, but they have often been satisfactory where the parties were hitherto unable to craft their own agreed outcome and needed an authoritative judgment. Almost no ruling of the International Court of Justice (ICJ) has not met compliance (Bilder 2007; Cede 2009). Referral to a judicial or arbitration instance where arguments can be exchanged, as over the Aouzou Strip between Libya and Chad put before the ICJ in 1994 or the Beagle Channel submitted to the Vatican for mediation/arbitration in 1984, allows each party the satisfaction of having its day in court.

Unfortunately perhaps, most international conflicts are not justiciable in the sense that they involve elements not subject to clear legal principles and judgments. Even when norms are clear, they are more likely to serve as political guides than as legal precepts. It is certainly desirable to expand the scope of legal settlements as part of a World Order that seeks to strengthen conflict prevention, working at the edges of prevention. Territorial and maritime disputes have been particularly amenable to adjudication, when the parties have been able to get out from under the weight of power imbalances.

"Early-Early" Conflict Gestation Prevention

The thrust of mid-term or "early-early" gestation prevention is on using the conflict process to help the potentially conflicting parties recalculate their interests and alternatives, building an awareness of the costs of the course of conflict and the possibilities of other paths. These efforts above all work in attitudes and perceptions that are needed if the conflicts are to be handled creatively. Stalemates and escalations in conflict, in the present or in perspective, constitute signals that a second look is advisable before the path of conflict is pursued. Third parties interested in prevention face the same types of calculations as they weigh the prospects of assistance, mediation, and ripening. Like the parties, they can use the conflict process to change their minds about the value of escalating conflict, and reassess the possibility of achieving goals and protecting interests through preventive resolution.

CHAPTER FIVE

Methods of Pre-Crisis Prevention

Crisis prevention is an entirely different matter from long- and mid-term prevention. Parties are now engaged and committed in pursuing conflict even to violence, if they are not there already. Crises are characterized by a rapid turn of events, sparse information, emotional peaks, and short reaction time (George 1983; Brecher 1992, 1996; Brecher & Wilkenfeld 1997). Immediate measures are needed to handle the movement toward a violent outbreak or toward a further worsening of violence against entrenched policies and perceptions. Preventers have to make sure that steps toward management are of a nature to "fall forward" toward resolution, rather than backward toward renewed conflict, and that steps toward resolution also carry the movement further forward to keep that outcome in place. Prevention is involved in each step, to prevent the current stage of conflict from continuing, to prevent it from getting off the track of de-escalation, and to prevent its revival in old or new form later on. The last stage will be the subject of the following section; the first efforts will be dealt with here, but remembering that they too deal not only with the present but also with the future.

Pre-crisis prevention involves three moves and fast and committed action: *interruption*, *separation*, and *integration*. The three are successive, even if overlapping, phases that run throughout the whole period until the crisis has been resolved. In brief, interruption means that the escalatory march of the parties to violence must be arrested. Its transitive and intransitive dynamics must be stopped in their tracks. Then the conflicting parties must be separated, in time and space, given a breathing period to prolong the interruption of the momentum of the escalation, to stop and reflect, but also physically separated to avoid incidents from too close contact. And then, counterintuitively, they need to be brought together, directly or in proximity, to lay things on the table and work out measures of de-escalation, cohabitation, and even restrained cooperation. The parties are most unlikely to do this by themselves. On their own they will keep on marching into the mouth of the crisis. Parties in conflict need help, and a committed third party is needed to produce all three of the required moves.

These preventive moves to head off an impending crisis are only the urgent introduction to a longer effort of the same nature that is required if the crisis is to be wound down more durably. They are immediate, "early late" responses to an impending crisis but they are also the introduction to "late" measures of post-crisis prevention. Interruption presages the introduction of confidence-building measures that serve to preclude repetitions of the crisis. Separation gives the parties autonomy to pursue their interests out of each other's way. Integration is the corrective to separation as parties move toward conflict transformation.

While measures of prevention at this stage in the conflict are often termed operational, as opposed to structural in the early stages, the processes that they involve operate on the proximate structures and attitudes of conflict (Holl 1997). To call them operational makes them simply tools without a larger sense of where they fit in the toolbox. Structural methods change the relations between the conflicting parties by removing or restricting the possibility of pursuing the conflict. Structural policies pursue either separation or integration of the parties as means of preventing the continuation of conflict. Earlier, norms were seen to harmonize attitudes for dealing with issues and situations that had a conflict potential, and at the same time setting standards for dealing with situations that escaped the normal patterns. As crisis looms, there is no time to work on attitudes; rapid change is needed in the structures of conflict. Structural solutions make it impossible for either party to harm the other without harming itself, or to threaten or dominate the other party. Measures of separation reduce fear and prevent conflict by keeping the parties away from each other, whereas measures of integration bring the parties together as groups, working away at that fear and gradually reducing the notion of groupness itself. Structural change can then translate into changed attitudes.

Structural changes require establishing either a higher, neutral authority to guarantee the non-threatening functioning of relations or a system of interlocking interdependence among the parties themselves to ensure that each side's welfare depends on its cooperation with the other. The first change removes supreme authority from the grasp and threat of either of the conflicting identities, whereas the second makes the determination of each party's welfare depend on its own behavior toward the other party. Both structures can support either separation or integration as tools of prevention, but in either case, the more prevention is in the hands of the conflicting parties rather than a third party, the more fragile the structure of prevention will be in the beginning but the more durable in the long run (Walter 2002; Fortna 2004b).

Interruption

The urgent measure in the face of a crisis is to freeze the action to prevent the impending explosion of the conflict into open violence. The sum of the crisis characteristics is the absence of trust and communication between the parties and a need for explanation of motives and fears (Holl 1997: 49). Interruption calls for third-party intervention; parties on the warpath are unlikely to be able to stop on their own. The external intervention has to be swift and pressing, assorted with threatened and warned consequences if ignored. It requires standing in front of the oncoming train to say, "Stop!" The train has momentum, entrapped in its own inertia and fueled by its eager followers. Prevention takes a tough stance.

Interruption can come in many forms, fitted to the crisis. When Abdullah Abdullah challenged the June 2014 results of his run-off against Asraf Ghani in Afghanistan and threatened to form his own government, US Secretary of State John Kerry stepped into the emergency before the Afghan political system could blow itself apart and called for a recount of all ballots, followed by a power-sharing government (that then took a long time to put together). "He saved the situation at the very last moment," said Abdullah. The conflict then transferred to the terms of the recount, but the pressure of the overly eager followers on the two candidates was released for a time. A more complicated situation arose, and over a more extended period of time, when Russian President Vladimir Putin decreed the invasion and annexation of Crimea in February 2014. Secretary Kerry, giving up on Crimea, worked rapidly to interrupt any further aggression, in a meeting in March between foreign ministers in Geneva. A period of testing and parrying filled the interim until the Ukrainian presidential elections, and Russia downplayed the eastern Ukrainian independence referendum in March. Another period of interruption appeared, with the eastern Ukraine ceasefire, but Russia used it to replenish dissidents' armaments. Thereafter came an extended period of "eyeballing" from each side to find out how far the other would go: Was Putin bent on absorbing eastern Ukraine, and more, as he did with Crimea? Were the Western allies willing to impose meaningful sanctions or engage militarily to meet Russian surreptitious involvement? When the sternly threatened sanctions did not appear in July 2014, the Ukrainian government resumed its offensive and Russia resumed sending arms and officers to the dissidents; interruption was again required. This time it was not forthcoming; the West acted as if it did not expect the Russians to push ahead and it was caught with its plans down. The difference between the Afghan and Ukrainian situations was that – in terms previously discussed – a mediator as a formulator was sufficient in the first case because the two parties wanted help out of the impasse (egged on by the extremists among their followers), whereas the second required a mediator as a manipulator, a role the US and the EU eschewed.

As the illustrations show, "Stop!" is usually not enough. The command must be "Stop or else!" As seen in the discussions on stalemate, if the party heading for catastrophe is not blocked and forced to feel the cost of its conduct, it will hurtle on to crash. The preventer must be willing and able to threaten and if necessary impose sufficient costs to make the escalator stop and think. It must be ready to impose the interruption in order to stop the locomotive. At this point, prevention is not a matter of recalling norms or being a helpful facilitator but of threatening credible consequences if the train does not stop. This is what was done in the Cuban Missile Crisis in 1962, the Croat-Bosniac offensive in 1995, the Israeli drive toward Damascus and Cairo in 1973, but not in the Ukraine crisis.

Regularly every few years before 2014, Israel and Hamas faced calls for a ceasefire to interrupt the escalation of their conflict. That finally brought interruption when the ammunition ran out, symbolically, but it was never followed by next steps toward resolution. Interruption, when it comes, must be immediately picked up by the next phases of separation and integration, oxymoronically, at the same time, so that the parties stopped in crisis do not gear up for a new round at a later date. Again, the dribbling crisis over Ukraine should stand as a lesson.

Separation

Once the escalation to a crisis has been interrupted, the first order of business is to separate the parties. Separation is the most obvious structural measure to keep the parties out of each other's hair while allowing space and time for solving issues and developing more harmonious relations. Separation begins as a preventive measure to initiate the process of halting and winding down the escalation of hostility. Measures to pull the parties apart make space to breathe and room to reflect. They can provide physical separation – as withdrawals and cantonments, safe havens, buffer zones, and disengagement – or temporal separation – as a pause or delay in impending escalation, through a prolonged truce or cease-fire – in the midst of a conflict that threatens to escalate. Or they can involve separation of the issues and of the natures of escalation, dealing with immediate concerns immediately and leaving the less explosive or broader issues for handling afterward (Kriesberg & Dayton 2012: 7). They work to interrupt the operation of the security dilemma and the escalation spiral, where the intransitive escalation often carries away any transitive control. The separations could be set up by the original instigators of the conflict having come to their senses, or by a moderate faction that has taken over to lead the conflicting party – rebel group or government – in a more constructive direction, or by an authoritative mediator seizing the initiative to pull the parties apart; referral of the crisis to the UN Security Council can serve to turn interruption into separation if the UNSC members are willing to take solid action. The no-contact zones surrounding the Israeli withdrawal from territories in Golan and Sinai are an example of the first, the

Sinn Féin ceasefire an example of the second, and the French (although not the UNSC) role in the 2003 Linas-Marcoussis agreement among Ivoirians a case of the third.

Such policy change can be triggered by a sense of stalemate and rising costs on one or both sides in the conflict, but if the parties themselves do not take such steps, an external party is needed to help them see the need to do so or simply to impose the measure. Separation needs someone to hold the coats of the parties as they agree to disengage, and to help them then turn separate into more durable institutions of de-escalation, as the Irish ceasefire turned into decommissioning and the Israeli Sinai withdrawal turned into a peace treaty with Egypt. A creative innovation of the Mindanao peace process was a complex international triad of bodies to prevent incidents that might derail the negotiations, which finally came to a comprehensive agreement in February 2014. A coordinating committee of the two forces' representatives on the cessation of hostilities, on alert from local monitoring teams, coordinates movements of the opposing forces and checks ceasefire violations; an ad hoc joint action group of the forces' representatives investigates criminal and break-away activities; and an international monitoring team composed of seven countries' police and military officers, two civilian socio-economic and human rights teams, and an unusual civilian protection component of local and international NGOs, controls incidents to prevent escalation (Hopmann 2014). Such complex measures are needed to make sure that a ceasefire is not simply an occasion for rearming. In the Sri Lankan conflict, the 2008 ceasefire gave both parties the opportunity to rearm for a final assault, which the government won. The 2014 ceasefire in Ukraine was finally cancelled by the government because it allowed Russia to arm the dissidents.

When more serious separation is needed, peace-keeping forces (PKF) can be used preventively to keep the parties apart, either before, during, or after violent conflict. "Early late" prevention can help defuse a situation nearing violence by introducing a tripwire, removing the excuse from either party that they are merely responding to the other's provocation. PKFs provided an unusual example of pre-crisis interposition in Macedonia in 1992–8 as UNPREDEP (United Nations Preventive Deployment Force) and then after 2001 as a NATO mission. Less recognized, there is often a moment within violent conflict when the parties pause, temporarily exhausted, leaving an opportunity for the introduction of separating PKFs before the conflicting parties can regroup, rearm, and pick up the offensive. It is often insisted that the "K" must be taken seriously in PKF mandates, that there must already be a peace to keep and not one to make. But a literal reading can miss the functional purpose of the forces; as seen in eastern Congo, and finally authorized in 2013, interposition forces may have to fight to make room for themselves and play an effective preventive function as "peace-making forces" (PMFs). Preventive deployment of troops is a preemptive for separation (Lund 1996; Holl 1997). A crucial occasion for a PKF in an informal mid-conflict moment of calm in Congo-Brazzaville in 1997 was turned down by the Security Council, which ordered a study of African conflicts instead and the crisis played on. After hostilities, PKFs monitor and, with a proper mandate, enforce the ceasefire. Less often, PKFs are considered as adjuncts to police rather than military forces and yet they could be used where the government does not fulfill its own policing responsibilities (Howard 2007).

Policing with an evenhanded authority is a minimal function of government, and is often all that is needed to prevent hotheads and public passion from bursting into flame. Since riots are frequently the initial step in deeper conflict and violence, escalation can often be checked simply by effective policing, assuming that the government is not the agent of the conflict; when the government is the agency, pressure for it to assume its responsibilities or more invasive measures is needed. Outbursts of civil violence usually involve a determined core of agitators (the political entrepreneurs) and an inflammable mob – the arsonists and the tinder – and the police's job is to separate the two, sending the first group to jail and the second home. Even when government is not the instigator or the tacit cover of violence, the police often remain passive for fear of facing the inflamed crowds with insufficient forces, or of tarnishing a government's human rights record or incurring political costs. Thus adequate police forces dedicated to law and order constitute a basic element of prevention, to be provided by external intervention if not by the state.

Good police are the unsung heroes of prevention, and examples are not common knowledge: negative cases, from Selma (AL) to Watts (CA) to Ferguson (MO), are better known. The management of policing during South Africa's transition from apartheid was a critical element in the process, and there are clear examples of incidents where police leadership was able to move from the (well-earned) stereotype of being the repressive arm of the minority regime, and lead to peaceful resolution of ethnically based confrontations, a transformation also accomplished gradually in Northern Ireland. UN police (CIVPOL) played effective roles in separating the two sides in Cyprus and in assuring free and fair elections in Namibia and Haiti; the constitution of a new National Civilian Police was an important part of the 1992 El Salvador agreement, as it was for the implementation of the 1995 Dayton Agreement on Bosnia-Herzegovina (Hampson 1996; Zoufal 2013).

Separation is the immediate interruption on the road to crisis, but it is also a longer-term stage in preventing further conflict. Temporary separations can be employed transitionally as sanctuaries to work out new relations between conflicting parties and they can also be institutionalized and rendered permanent (Hancock & Mitchell 2007). Spatting couples can take a holiday, together or separately, or they can get a divorce. Separations such as a ceasefire are the essence of conflict prevention and management – moving a conflict from violent to political means of pursuit – rather than actual resolution. But conflict management is a temporary, procedural, and essentially unstable resting stage, carrying with it the implied promise of conflict resolution. The job of prevention then continues into the next phase, to move management of the conflict toward the more substantive prevention by helping the parties deal directly with the perceptions and grievances that occasioned the original conflict and ensuing separation.

But when conflict moves from substantive (grievance) to procedural (governance) issues, where the affected group no longer believes that it can trust government with its fate, separation may turn permanent and functional, as regional self-government, or even independence, to prevent further conflict. The Iraqi Kurds, Puertoricanos, Basques, Southern Sudanese, Zanzibaris, Tatars, South Tyroleans, Québécois, Catalans, and Acehnese were given autonomous self-government (under whatever name) to end their identity conflict and the first five also enjoyed a share in central government power, although in a few cases it did not satisfy them. Forced separation of inter-mingled populations, particularly under harsh conditions, is ethnic cleansing, a form of identity conflict and a low-level form of genocide, depending on the number of deaths the forced migration brings. Although some may see "gentle" ethnic cleansing as a way to restrain and avoid identity conflicts by encouraging population transfers, it is merely a sanitized way of pursuing ethnic conflict (Kaufman 1996).

Further conflict can also be prevented by "representative separation," maintaining the separate corporate identity of the conflicting parties but bringing them together as collaborating groups, to share power in government (Lijphart 1977). Power-sharing is actually a form of separation in that it freezes the identity-group divisions in society and accords them participation in governance only through their representatives, precluding the possibility of gradually erasing the salience of separate identities in politics (Horowitz 1985). Power can be shared executively or legislatively. The first makes the executive a coalition of identity-group representatives, in a consociational form of government (Wolff & Yakinthou 2012). The second can take the form of separate reserved seats, quotas, and assigned roles in legislative bodies, preselected or not, decided by system-wide processes such as general elections. It can also take the form of a bicephalic system, in which the president, directly elected, and the prime minister, based on a parliamentary majority, share (or contest) power, although such cohabitation can lead to stalemate or unstable results (Elgie 2007).

Despite extensive academic discussions, power-sharing has only a few salient examples. Preventive power-sharing among identity groups brought decades of peace to Lebanon, as already noted, before it fell apart owing to demographic and generational changes among the groups; power-sharing between identity groups is also the core of the Good Friday Agreement of 1998 in Northern Ireland, which has gradually been put into place despite criticism for perpetuating identity groups and politics. It is in use in Iraq, giving rise to more violent conflict. It was the key to a special regional settlement in South Tyrol/Alto Adige in Italy in 1969 that has lasted, and a federalized system in Belgium after 1970 that is gradually falling apart. Indeed, any coalition government, from Germany to Tunisia, is a power-sharing exercise among collaborating parties that maintain their separate identity. Along with a ballot recount, Secretary Kerry in July 2014 also proposed a new constitution system for Afghanistan (diametrically opposed to the centralized executive power the US had earlier imposed) involving a separation of powers (dual power) system with a strong executive president counterbalanced by a strong legislative-backed prime minister; despite all the problems of cohabitation seen in France and the US, the bicephalic system at least prevented an authoritarian presidency that caused the crisis. Territorial separation or autonomy has also been adopted to prevent conflict in the US, Spain, and Russia over the entire country, and in Italy for five peripheral territories, and has been considered in Yemen. To work effectively to prevent conflict, power-sharing has to be complemented by an overarching sense of loyalty to the greater system, adaptability to changing power balances, cross-cutting (horizontal) cleavages to counteract identity (vertical) divisions, and a culture of compromise and mutual understanding.

Prevention of crisis requires immediate efforts that can then be translated into longer-term preventive measures:

Immediate measures:
- Separate the parties in time by giving them breathing space through ceasefires or temporary suspension of moves, as the US mediator imposed on the two sides in Bosnia after the Croat-Bosniac offensive in 1995 or the UNSC repeatedly called for in the three Israeli wars with Hamas in Gaza in 2008, 2012, and 2014.
- Separate the parties in space to avoid accidental (or intentional) contact, through demilitarized zones, neutral areas, and force pullback, as was tried, raggedly, in eastern Ukraine, or more directly in the demilitarized zone in Korea.
- Separate the parties by interposition of neutral forces, such as UN peacekeepers in Congo or in Macedonia or on the Green Line in Cyprus (UNFICYP).

Long-term measures:
- Separate hostile parties by neutralized territories or buffer zones, such as Belgium between France and Germany, or Cambodia between Communist and non-Communist territories, or, as proposed, Ukraine between the Eurasian [Russian] Group and the EU.
- Separate restive parties into autonomous self-governing regions, such as Chiapas in Mexico, Tatarstan in Russia, Puerto Rico in the US, and Bangsamoro in the Philippines.

Integration

Integration is the opposite of separation as a structural measure for preventing conflict and its escalation, and yet both are necessary, at the same time (with coordination). From the beginning, it is necessary to get the parties to start talking. Conflict after all means the separation of parties into conflicting sides, so that a basic preventive approach means bringing the parties together to explain their positions and eventually to work together. A strong school of anti-terrorist prevention emphasizes the importance of talking, to break down the demonizing polarization that feeds the conflict and changing attitudes in the process (Faure & Zartman 2010; Zartman & Faure 2010). Integration as a preventive strategy involves most immediately the establishment of structures and opportunities for communication between conflicting parties, and then, ultimately, of structures of integrating cooperation and governance. Since integration is overcoming separation, the conflicting parties will probably need external help in its initiation and accomplishment.

More than separation, integration is a process; it has to be initiated, pursued, and maintained if conflict is to be effectively prevented. Integration involves intensified communication and cooperation between parties to clarify their interests (as opposed to simply their positions), to bring them out of crisis, and eventually to enable them to formulate a joint agenda for dealing with crisis issues. Even when the answer to the 2014 Afghan post-election crisis was separation of powers, it also required integration of the separate and competing branches of government – executive and legislative – into a working system if effective governance was to be the result. Thus, the crisis went through the three structures – interruption, separation, and integration – rapidly and almost simultaneously, with a long aftermath to working out the relationship on the job. A crisis in December 2014 in the Colombian peace talks brought suspension, secret communications, and then resumption of talks; a crisis at the same time during ratification of the Philippine Comprehensive Peace agreement brought denials of direct involvement of the sides, reaffirmation of the supervision process, and careful resumption of the ratification process. Both cases showed forms of interruption, separation, and (re)integration.

Communication for a constructive consideration of the elements of the conflict constitutes an attempt to deal coolly with them before they sharpen into violence (or afterward in reconstruction). Dialog is called for as the final act before the crisis breaks, the ultimate moment of ripeness between states nose-to-nose, as over eastern Ukraine in April 2014 (which was then ignored). As this imperfect example shows, communication is crucial to convey intentions and to find out what the other side is after. After decades of non-communication, the US and its five partners opened negotiations with Iran in which the parties could explain to each other what they really wanted in regard to Iranian nuclear capabilities; the cloud of the third of a century of suspicion made the communication extremely difficult. One of the best examples is the Oslo dialog, which spent much time on the two sides explaining to each other why they hurt and how each made the other hurt;

they were then able to take a deep breath and plunge into the future, on the basis of a better understanding of the past. SRSG Ahmedou Ould Abdallah sprang into action in Burundi in 1994, alerting and consulting interested parties to head off an imitative reaction to events in Rwanda where the shooting down of the president's plane triggered the genocide. World diplomatic and economic pressure against the apartheid regime in South Africa brought the government to open a dialog with its opponent, the ANC, and shape a new political system in South Africa before widespread violence broke out.

The conflicting groups may not easily agree to sit down together, so a firm and helpful conciliator may be needed. Any external intervention is bound to be seen by considered authorities as an indication that they cannot correctly handle their own affairs. The first step is for the external party to achieve welcoming entry into the impending conflict (Crocker et al. 1999; Maundi et al. 2006). International organizations, friendly states, and NGOs need to develop the sense among the parties that current policy is heading to costly deadlock and that problems and perceptions are better handled positively. This is a circular effort since external parties need to use entry to gain entry, as Secretary-General Perez de Cuellar and his SRSG Alvaro de Soto did in 1990–2 in the conflict between the FMLN and the Salvadoran government, using their official positions to gradually develop a role between the conflicting parties, and then to use that role to prevent escalated conflict. Early discussions need organization rather than insistence; as the dialog digs deeper into conflict it may require more insistent pressures for attendance and agreement. Third parties arranging dialog to head off violence cannot be limited to good counsel; they are likely to need to provide incentives against defection from the path of reconciliation. Too little pressure leaves the course of conflict costless, but too much pressure arouses a defensive reaction and closes the door to external attentions. As in any adolescent behavior, the best kind of pressure is peer pressure, so gathering parties to join in the call for a dialog can help in getting everyone to join.

Like separation, integration through dialog has its place in preventing conflict escalation once the immediate crisis is past. When formal institutions break down, dialog has a role as a supplementary house of parliament, bringing conflicting parties together until the formal institutions can take over. Dialog is appropriate when the government as a party to the conflict loses its position of conflict manager in normal politics and the interests of all the sides need to be incorporated in ending violence and restoring a functioning political system. It provides a forum for open discussion among parties in an effort to reach a consensus; unlike elected assemblies, it does not involve strict measures of representation or votes, but rather looks for an exchange of ideas without winner or loser. It can contain acceptable ways for parties to back down. One of the keys to successful transition in Arab Spring countries has been the use of dialog, even when elected assemblies exist to draft constitutions. In Tunisia, Yemen, and Libya dialogs (with differences among the three) moved the process forward, convened either by the government as in Libya, or by a UN mediator as in Yemen, or by civil society groups such as the national labor union in Tunisia. Dialog is such an attractive concept that governments in Egypt, Syria, and Algeria have tried to appropriate it for their own purposes, but the parties were not tricked. Preventing conflict through the establishment of a new political system is such an important process that it exceeds the legitimacy of even an elected assembly and calls for an integrative dialog of all strains of civil society to create a new social contract.

Dialog is not a brief one-shot activity; it needs sustained attention to overcome hardened perceptions and reverse sharpened policies, and that requires repeated, not too far spaced meetings, a suspension of actions that might be interpreted as hostile, and an effort to use external events positively, as an occasion to meet, explain, and work out common responses. Measures to be accomplished include integrative structural changes to give a hard look at grievances and images, both formally and in civil society, where Track 2 is best suited. Local, culturally and historically based practices are frequently available to provide the framework for dialog, first on the local and then on the national (and even international) level. Indigenous institutions and dispute resolution methods that have often been developed over centuries to defuse conflict can be revived, updated, and adopted to fit current situations. Such historic and cultural legitimization removes the onus of face-losing for the parties in calling for and submitting to dialog. Each party must find ways to explain to its public that it is sitting down with and then assuaging the very party that it claimed was posing an existential threat.

The longer-term need is for measures of communication to create an atmosphere of conference and a sense of security for the confronting parties. Confidence- and security-building measures (CSBMs), giving pre-announcement of troop exercises for example, reduce suspicion and prevent spiraled reactions and security dilemmas from swinging into operation. If responsible sovereignty is based on the politics of inclusion, not exclusion, then integration is a requirement for forestalling conflict, and corrective integration, or affirmative action, may be a necessary form to take. The purpose of integration is to lock communities into the governing system so that its functioning depends on suspending the conflict and learning to work together. It involves creating self-government by association; bringing the targeted population into collective, not separate, governance; and opening the roles from which they felt excluded. The premise is that the involvement in governance of the whole will win rebels and separatists away from efforts to take over or secede from the state, although alternative or complementary strategies may be useful to have on hand if the winning effect of inclusion is not foolproof.

Integration in various degrees is the ultimate goal of prevention, whether it be as conflict transformation or simply the ability to live as good neighbors next door or as co-lodgers (even with separate rooms) under the same roof. Like separation, it involves immediate pre-crisis measures and then long-term prevention:

Immediate measures:
- Open exchanges to convey goals, needs, and fears to head off the crisis, as when Strobe Talbott went to India and Pakistan to defuse the Kargil crisis in 1999, or when the US and China parlayed over the Hainan crisis in 2001, or when the US got Morocco and Spain talking in the Perejil/Leila island crisis in 2002 and Turkey and Greece talking in the Imia/Kardak island crisis in 1995.

Long-term measures
- Repeated crises and long-term rivalries can bear their own lessons of counterproductivity leading to a cooperative turnabout, as in the Chilean–Argentinian rivalry that was then tempered in the Andean Group, or in the capital example of the German–French conflict that ended in the European integration agreements.
- Track II dialog efforts can reform attitudes and lead to conflict settlements, as Herbert Kelman's Palestinian–Israeli dialog sessions that contributed to the Oslo negotiations and Harold Saunders' Tajik dialog that fed into the Tajik conflict settlement.

More than separation, measures of integration eventually require a strong change of attitude along with structural change, although in many cases, former warring enemies were able to govern together before they actually changed their attitudes. Examples include Mozambique, Kenya, Cambodia, Northern Ireland, and Burundi, as well as Colombia, Lebanon, South Africa, and Nepal. Admittedly, in some of these cases, structural change did not change attitudes very well or very fast. In politics, anything is possible, even if not guaranteed to go smoothly. In all cases, this integration followed rather than prevented violent conflict and some sort of formal agreement to end it, but it did prevent the crisis from going on for longer.

CHAPTER SIX

Measures of Late (and Earliest) Post-Crisis Prevention

Prevention must not stop once escalation and violence are prevented. It is still needed on the downslope of a conflict, to close the circle and keep it from happening all over again. It needs to ensure both that the settlement is adequate and respected and that new causes do not arise, in the same way as Boutros Ghali spoke of peace-building as both healing and preventing. There are indications that countries that have had a civil war have a nearly 50 percent chance of having another one within five years, so that the quality of the settlement is a crucial element in preventing a relapse (Collier et al. 2003). The preventive attention, once violence has been brought under control, can be divided into management and resolution, implementation and monitoring, prevision and reconstruction, and reconciliation and remediation.

When agreements are made to put an end to a conflict, a basic element in preventing recidivism is the substance of the settlement: whether the elements of *management and resolution* are adequate for the satisfaction of the conflicting parties. Management is merely the prelude to resolution, as it indicates that the parties have put down their weapons, the basic means of bringing their grievances to each other's attention, but it does not indicate that they are ready to resolve those grievances. Conflict management may take the form of a temporary truce, a ceasefire, a more formal long-term agreement to prevent further violence, or a set of accepted practices for handling or preventing a momentary outcome to the conflict.

While ceasefires can be attempted during the negotiations to end the conflict, they are not likely to become fully operative until the parties have an idea of what the final settlement will look like (Mahieu 2007).

Management is supposed to give the parties the time and space to work on resolution, but since it removes the pressure of violence, it may last a long time, growing as a source of much frustration. Notable conflict management measures such as the 1948 ceasefire in the Middle East, the 1952 ceasefire in the Korean War, the 1964–74 truce in Cyprus, the 1991 ceasefire in the Western Sahara, and the 1994 truce around Nagorno-Karabakh have not led to the promised resolution, for all their apparent stability, and they leave a dangerous situation of compounded conflict. It is tempting to confuse the suspension of violence and escalation with the resolution of the conflict, but prolonged ceasefire is a false prevention and may actually contribute to instability, and eventually renewed violence, if not turned to resolution. Real prevention requires taking up the respite of management to craft a durable solution.

This means addressing the initial grievances that gave rise of the conflict, but also the grievances that have arisen in the course of the conflict itself by the multifarious process of escalation already described. Addressing grievances does not mean going back to dig up all the root causes; the original and subsequent issues will provide enough material for an agenda. Grievance resolution seems to have been bypassed in much of the literature on durability (Gartner & Mellin 2009) but it is crucial, both logically and empirically (Arnson & Zartman 2005). Also neglected is the fact that addressing past grievances does mean paying attention to more recent damages to relations produced by and during the conflict itself. A Palestinian solution has to face the right of return, not only for the original refugees half a century ago but for their expanding descendency, and will also have to deal with Jewish colonies. A Bosnian solution dealt, imperfectly, with the scars of past relations among the three communities but also with fresh wounds from the war. Cypriot, Colombian, and Karabakhchi resolution will have to deal with the grievances of an unacceptable political situation, but also with the property rights of expelled populations and the damages of the expulsion. Unless management turns to resolution and such secondary grievances are addressed, prevention of a relapse has not been addressed.

Implementation and monitoring require equal attention for preventing new outbreaks if conflicts managed and resolved are to be really managed and resolved. Prevention is not like baking a cake, which is done when it is done; rather, the proof of prevention is in the leading of the parties into a new level of positive stability. The natural human tendency is to declare victory, with self-congratulations, and to go on to other conflicts, leaving the previous one to disappear or resume on its own. The stability of ceasefires depends on UN Charter Chapter VI.5 PKF observation measures, more frequently than on Chapter VII "PMF" intervention. There were 15 successive peace agreements in the Liberian civil war (1989–97) because the parties signed them and went home to fight some more, without any concern for their implementation (Mutwol 2009).

Implementation and monitoring constitute crucial and neglected links between successful post-crisis prevention and "normal politics" (Hampson 1996; Stedman et al. 2002). Parties emerging from conflict are unlikely to be able to monitor their own performance and assure compliance. For these reasons, preventive agreements need not only to contain implementation commitments and schedules from conflicting parties but also to record monitoring commitments from third parties – states, international organizations, and/or

NGOs. Monitoring requires sufficient numbers of observers with appropriate mandates and rules of engagement, operating on sufficient budgets, with continuing diplomatic and civilian attention to the problems of carrying out the initial agreement. It also requires coordination among the monitors – who also need coordination when adopting earlier preventive measures – so that duplication, competition, and undercutting do not appear as corollaries of monitoring. Studies seem to show that provision of military monitors is the largest factor in assuring the durability of peace agreements (Walter 2002).

The Angolan civil war, which had ideological and ethnic identity dimensions, outlived its Bicesse settlement in 1991 in part because UN monitoring was carried out on a shoestring, as UN SRSG Margaret Anstee (1996) complained; the 1994 peace agreement in Mozambique lasted for two decades in part because of the large sums provided to RENAMO to hold to its word and to its soldiers for demobilization, disarmament, reinsertion, and reintegration (DDRR). The monitoring of the 1999 Lusaka Agreement by the UN Mission to the Democratic Republic of Congo (MONUC) was deficient on every count – mandate, rules of engagement, money, troops – until MONUSCO was given a mandate in 2013 to take the offensive and clear out the rebel forces. After a series of inadequate ECOWAS and UN monitoring forces in Sierra Leone, the UN Armed Mission in Sierra Leone (UNAMSIL) got a shot in the arm from a British intervention and the international community stepped in with economic and technical assistance. Haiti provides both negative and positive examples: UN intervention (MICIVIH) after the 1991 coup against Jean-Bertrand Aristide and then US-led intervention upon his restoration in 1994 were followed by the diminution and withdrawal of external support by the end of the decade, whereas the restoration of a democratic regime in 2000 was followed by the reinstallation of civilian and economic commitments to continue support for the new regime for an extended period of time, until all was undone by the hurricane of 2008 and the earthquake of 2010. The complex structure for monitoring the 2014 Mindanao Comprehensive Peace Agreement is a major key to its success.

Prevision and reconstruction are needed to prevent backsliding and to build new bases for handling past issues and future conflicts. Conflict settlements need to provide mechanisms and procedures for handling left-over grievances that may reappear in the cracks of the agreement and also new conflicts uncovered by the agreement that might emerge. Any commercial contract includes dispute settlement provisions; conflict settlements require the same in order to prevent dislocation of the resolution measures as they take shape. Grievance procedures, truth and reconciliation measures, and transitional justice mechanisms are all continuing aspects of a peace agreement designed to handle loose ends left over from the conflict. Prevention of recurrence means looking beyond the agreement into potential unresolved issues.

Preventive attention necessitates an intense surge of effort and finance; each success piles up further responsibilities to continue a high level of attention, political and economic. A conflict has engendered serious setbacks in the economy and development of the affected society, leaving it simply incapable of providing reconstruction by itself: the destruction is not over just because the conflict is. Without continuing attention from the same third parties who helped bring about the settlement, these efforts to end conflict will predictably collapse if left to their own devices. They need sustained international attention over a substantial period of time, since the conflict-torn societies are too weak and chaotic to bear the burdens of reconstruction. Without reconstruction, programs to return combatants to civilian life (DDRR) will have no economy into which to reintegrate the demobilized fighters. Reconstruction requires a long commitment from external agencies, who are used to leaving the parties on their own economically as well as politically once an agreement is signed. IFIs and national governments alike need to keep the file open until the conflict area is back on its feet. Nonetheless, too hasty assurances of economic aid without corresponding responsibility of the new authorities runs the danger of installing habits of dependency and corruption. IFIs were alert to run to the aid of the new Congolese government after the fall of Mobutu in 1996 but not awake to the inherent corruption in the new regime and the possibility of using the assistance for purposes of shaping up the new incumbents to provide good governance along with sound development.

State-building after unprevented conflicts is the institutionalized form of Boutros Ghali's "peace-building." State capacities for handling past remnants and future revivals of conflict return to the business of normal politics and the institutions of good governance (Call & Wyeth 2008). International agencies have a role in assisting new states to build their capacity, but it is not without consequences. The debate is whether being thrown into the pond and forced to swim is preferable to being given floaters and in the process taught to over-rely on outside assistance. While the first builds capacity on the job and encourages national ownership of the process and results, it is also prone to serious mistakes for lack of experience; the second inhibits those very advantages while avoiding the disadvantage. The problem was posed clearly in the necessary and helpful role of the EU and UN assistance in the case of Kosovo, which enabled the new country to take part in some international cooperation efforts for lack of recognition, but which left the new state with a crutch habit (Tahiri 2010).

Reconciliation and remediation are the measures that seal successful efforts to prevent further conflicts. Both are long processes and so need special emphasis, lest it be thought that conflicts are isolated incidents with neither antecedents nor consequences, neither causes nor impacts, and that negative prevention completes the job (Ricoeur 2000; Rosoux 2009). Interdependent projects need relations to be renewed and work to be launched, and overarching identities and loyalties need to be nurtured, to contain the identities in conflict. European construction gradually overcame Franco-German enmity, economic enterprise overshadowed UN–Vietnam war memories, the spirit of Ubuntu prevailed over racism in South Africa. The examples stand out and they take time to take hold. Crucial to their success is an overarching and shared project. Atonement and forgiveness, too, are key elements in burying the conflict, and they require specific gestures, not simply passive page turning. Wounds untreated fester rather than becoming scars; as scars never disappear, they cannot be ignored and need gentle treatment. Targeted parties have real grievances, a discriminatory aspect to the deprivations they suffer, but targeting parties are scapegoating or reacting to some underlying problem. Frequently these are found in the societal inequalities and structural causes of conflict, returning the cycle of prevention back to the beginning.

Conflict fatigue and focus on the common project of national construction, carefully guided by national leadership, have provided the basis for programs of reconciliation, even if imperfect, in South Africa, Sri Lanka, Rwanda, and Liberia in the 2000s; it is still absent in Bosnia-Herzegovina, Yemen, Afghanistan, Turkey, Nigeria, and Iraq. Local self-government and increased national attention to development have provided the context for attempts at reconciliation and remediation in Alto Adige (South Tyrol) in Italy, Kosovo, Casamance in Senegal, Bougainville, Cabinda in Angola, and even Euskadi in Spain. In a number of important cases, identity-based violence has remained frozen – in some cases for a long time – without any progress in reconciliation, as in Cyprus, Northern Ireland, Ethiopia–Eritrea, Nagorno-Karabakh, Ivory Coast, Rwanda, and Burundi. Reconciliation is an active challenge to be worked on with deliberate programs in such cases if the parties are not to fall back into conflict again; frozen conflicts do not naturally sublimate into the air but can crack open with deep violence to call attention to their suspended state and unmet expectations.

There is an ongoing debate about the structures and attitudes behind differing views of reconciliation, vaguely associated with the two halves of the modern world. The West sees reconciliation centered on accountability, the East on healing. The debate continues between those who see the mind of reconciliation in the search for justice and those who find its heart in mercy, or, more deeply, between those for whom justice is the grounding of healing and those who see healing as the meaning of justice (Cobban 2007; Schirch 2013; Anstey & Rosoux 2015). The matter returns to considerations of separation vs integration, through measures that keep alive a sense of identity and awareness as victims vs those that foster an overarching common identity and community – in fact, between those that look back, however correctively, and those that look ahead, above all constructively. The first is primarily a Western or Northern approach, although the second is found in corrective or reformative notions of imprisonment. The second is the basis of the African, Middle Eastern, and Asian (but not Latin American) notion of restorative justice, in which the criminal is a social deviant who must be reintegrated into the social tissue of the community (Zartman 2003). The two approaches start from different premises and there is no basis for judging between them, but the methods and consequences of the two are profoundly different. One wants punishment to change cultures of impunity; the other looks to reintegration to restore the fabric of society. One requires an acknowledged criminal code, the other a cohesive community. Neither satisfies the other, nor are the two easily synthesized in their fundamental basis. Yet each has something to say to the other, as the Truth and Reconciliation Commission (TRC) in South Africa tried to express. Reconciliation requires the impossible integration of both justice and healing for prevention to be durable.

Efforts at reconciliation must come from within the society, as changes in attitudes, but they can be encouraged from the outside, notably by NGOs more than by external official actions, providing changes in structures. It takes a brave change of attitudes of a few leaders to change structures that mandate or facilitate changes of attitudes among the many. Truth and reconciliation commissions are an applicable institution in many cases; internal and external NGOs can also hold sessions conducive to reconciliation. Joint learning experiences for youth, either within integrated educational institutions or in special programs abroad, can also be helpful, but they must be accompanied by organized follow-up exercises and new integrative situations to return to. The key to effective reconciliation is a common project that engages the formerly conflicting parties in cooperative efforts, creates interdependence, and focuses their attention on a common goal of joint benefit. Governmental programs carefully designed to help former conflicting parties to learn to work together are also useful. If any of these projects is crudely or prematurely carried out, the result can revive and exacerbate conflict, so care and monitoring need to be exercised.

The ultimate step in the punitive notion of reconciliation as justice is to identify the most guilty and responsible individuals and bring them to justice. Coercive or judicial accountability, the removal of bloody-fingered incumbents, needs to be considered where ethnic repression and genocide can be unambiguously traced to the long rule of an egregious dictator or rebel. Judicial accountability can be conducted by legitimate national authorities after the conflict but must take pains not to be simply a victor's justice. It can also come as universal jurisdiction exercised for universal standards by individual states or ultimately by the International Criminal Court (ICC). It is a necessary option in order to prevent the implantation of a culture of impunity that underlies the pursuit of conflict. The national heroic status accorded to the political entrepreneur in identity conflicts, whether victorious or – curiously – defeated, tends to encourage emulation and, if necessary, another try. International judicial enforcement of the ban on genocide and similar crimes against humanity works best as a threat to counter this tendency, although like any threat, it works best when an only occasional use has enough impact to make the threat credible throughout.

Preventing more serious conflict sometimes depends on removing the ruler; hopes of reforming him are vain; mere power-sharing only prolongs the pain. Although incumbent rulers are sacred objects in international relations, respecting their claim to power in such cases only assures continued killing. Mass murderers have been removed from the outside on occasion, when their subjects were not up to the job, but then the onus and the action have lain on individual states, as in the cases of Bernard Coard in Grenada in 1983, Ferdinand Marcos in the Philippines in 1986, Manuel Noriega in Panama in 1989, Jean-Claude Duvalier and Raoul Cédras in Haiti in 1986 and 1945, respectively, and Saddam Hussein in Iraq in 2003, discretely applauded by the international community. Yet until Assad and Mugabe are removed – or in the past Qaddafi, Mobutu, Taylor, Savimbi – there is no end to the mass murder they pursue. There are three non-military ways of removing an egregious ruler – vote him out, talk him out, or buy him out (or a combination thereof). The military alternative is to take him out. Removal by election has the strong advantage of providing a successor and thereby limiting the dangers of a political vacuum, but it too often needs active intervention by external patrons to take effect. In any case, no action to enforce accountability on a sitting ruler should be undertaken in the absence of a mechanism to provide a legitimate successor, for the vacuum created will inevitably create even more deadly ethnic conflict. External intervention following an election was instrumental in the deposition of Laurent Gbagbo in Ivory Coast, Marcos, and Cédras – and arguably of Duvalier in Haiti. If elections are to be regarded as a valued means of stability and succession, there should be no hesitation over intervention to enforce them when necessary; a few crucial enforcements work to reduce the need for similar actions in subsequent instances. However, even with a legitimate election, the removal of the powerful authoritarian leader can leave a vacuum that only chaos can fill, as the events of post-Qaddafi Libya and post-Saleh Yemen show, and as those who look to a post-Assad Syria fear. The more egregious the ruler, the greater the risks in his removal.

It is difficult to assess the use of judicial and coercive accountability preventively, as it is hard to find instances where the threat of indictment kept an identity conflict from arising. As individual punishment and a deterrent to the culture of impunity, however, judicial accountability can also operate as a strong impediment to peaceful conclusion of conflict, as leaders who know they will be tried anyhow are unlikely to sign a peace agreement. As a result, indictments should be issued only once the subject is already captured. In an instance of popular (non-judicial) accountability, CNN reports of the violent overthrow of Nicolae Ceaușescu at the end of 1989 moved Beninois dictator Mathieu Kérékou to give way to the Sovereign National Conference (CNS) his country invented in 1990. Cases of failure are clear enough: the threat of indictment by the International Criminal Court in 2008 did not prevent Sudanese President Bashir from pursuing a policy that some states have termed genocide in Darfur or Kony of the Lord's Resistance Army from similar operations in northern Uganda (and then the Democratic Republic of Congo and Southern Sudan as well). The clear lesson is that prevention is far more effective in earlier stages of conflict than when it has reached its ultimate stages; the damage of violent conflict is deep and difficult to overcome.

Post-crisis and post-agreement prevention involve both immediate and long-term commitments if the conflict – handled either by pulling back from crisis or by pulling ahead after settlement – is to be effectively prevented from returning in the future.

Immediate Alerts for Prevention
- Conflict management contains the promise of conflict resolution and requires immediate efforts for the completion of the process to prevent relapse.
- Post-crisis and -conflict agreements require attention to faithful implementation and attentive monitoring.
- Settlements on conflicts past require provisions for dispute settlement mechanisms for future incidents to be effective.

Long-term Provisions for Prevention
- Resolution needs to handle both original causes and more recent grievances arising from the course of the conflict if it is to prevent recidivism.
- Post-conflict areas need committed help in both political and economic reconstruction to prevent backsliding into conflict.
- Reconciliation depends on conscious effort to provide both justice and healing.

- Reconciliation, reconstruction, and transformation require common projects to orient cooperation and to structure relations that prevent conflict.
- Post-conflict reconstruction is the time to think of structure that can channel and undergird changes in attitudes over conflict issues and situations.

Prevention after crisis or settlement is an ongoing process that returns attention to the beginning of the list – long-term norms, mid-term mechanisms, even pre-crisis methods of prevention. Prevention does not end when the current phase of conflict ends; it merely changes nature. If "crisis hangover" is not cured, the cycle resumes, as Collier's figures show. Prevention is a state of mind, an attitude that needs to be the focus of policy, from the beginning and not just in the later stages of conflict.

CHAPTER SEVEN

Conclusions: The Elusive Quest for Prevention

Prevention will remain an impelling frontier for evolving international and internal political relations activity for a long time. Galvanizing atrocities will create new pressures for "Never again" and for searches for new, more effective measures before the fact. This will lead to more effective red lines, new tools for keeping them in place, new actors to increase effectiveness, and new research and insights into the way humans and societies react when normal processes go awry. Knowledge about the subject has increased over the past two decades; it would be fascinating to count how many conflict escalations and violence have been preempted as a result, but there are some things beyond the reach of quantification. New (or revived) types of conflicts have burst into media and policymakers' attention, obviously not prevented in outbreak or in escalation. There is more work to be done – new imperatives to be faced in approaching the challenge, new tools to be used to improve the practice, new types of parties to be recruited as agents in the performance, and new knowledge to be developed about the nature and practice of prevention (and of the conflicts, escalation, and violence it seeks to prevent).

The Search for New Imperatives

In a world that is continually reorganizing its life and penetrating human society to a greater degree than ever before, there is no end to new aspects of conflict that will be seen as appropriate subjects for prevention. There is no expectation that conflict prevention will be legislated or violence effectively outlawed, or that prevention will ever be complete. But there is undeniably a growth in the areas of daily collective and even personal life that fall under attempts at normalization and standardization. As the world gets smaller (and warmer) and its population larger, the pressure to reduce anarchy and aggression mounts, against rising contrary challenges.

In the field of immediate concern over the prevention of conflict, it is the norms governing security conflicts that are the first target of new imperatives, as the first line of prevention. The international community has undertaken an extraordinary revision of the norms of sovereignty, through the doctrine of R2P. The established powers of the West, the coalition of the sometimes willing, are the leaders of this revision, as newly aroused to protect endangered world citizenry; the emerging powers of the BRICS (Brazil, Russia, India, China, South Africa) rise in constraint, if not opposition, as defenders of the old notion of sovereignty as the protection of the state; and the lesser countries stand by as the grass that gets trampled when elephants fight (Rosenberg 2013). It is imperative that the guidelines for legitimate operation of the norm of sovereignty be further sharpened, lest the procedures for conflict prevention themselves become a subject for conflict escalation. Norms of responsibility for the protection of people are not to be expected to be any more absolute than is the norm of sovereignty as protection of the state, whose debates have filled law books and commentaries. But the growing focus on human security beyond state security poses new opportunities for operationalization (Hamburg 2002, 2010; Wolff & Yakinthou 2012; Hamburg & Hamburg 2013).

In a related area, the persisting appearance of collapsed states continues to pose questions over the responsibility of the international community in conflicts apparently beyond the cover of R2P. By the third R2P pillar, the international community has the responsibility to protect populations when the state's efforts are insufficient in their responsibility for the need to protect. But what if there is no state? In 2015, conditions in Libya, Mali, Syria, Central African Republic, Northern Nigeria, South Sudan, Afghanistan, Honduras, Guatemala, and Somalia qualified, and still others had struggling governments in charge primarily of the national capital area; South America and Asia seem to have fewer qualifying cases. With the state in disarray, there are no pieces to work with. State collapse leaves not only large areas ungoverned, and thus open to all sorts of unregulated conflict behavior, but also rapacious gangs in charge of the nominal (and internationally recognized) state apparatus and also other nodes of power (Clunan & Trinkunas 2010). The nodes are busy and satisfied the way they are – in a pervasive S5 situation. When the hyenas ravage, even the elephants suffer. State failure, a way station to collapse in extreme cases, has become the subject of a wide range of scholarship, accompanied by academic conflict over its identification and causes, but at least in this situation there is a state that needs supporting (Rotberg 2003). In state collapse, the state needs to be reinvented, on the job, in a form that fits local conditions (Zartman 1995). To deal with this situation before it happens is a new challenge for conflict prevention.

Similarly, the conditions for the recognition of a new state need greater regularization rather than being left to an ad hoc political process. Political process it will always be, just as the definition of statehood and the role of recognition has been the subject of long debates and longer exegesis, but states and movements should be left with a clearer notion of what they have to aim for to qualify. The condition that new EU members must be free of disputes with other EU neighbors was removed by political blackmail by Greece in regard to Cyprus, eliminating the most effective inducement to settlement of the Cyprus conflict. On the other hand, the EU rule has been helpful in attenuating conflict elsewhere, notably in regard to the Serbia–Kosovo dispute. Intractable conflicts, as over Palestine, Kurdistan, Kashmir, and Balochistan, need clearer norms and strong adherence to the norms (as indeed to the norm of non-conquest) by the international community as an adjunct of prevention efforts.

The attachment of Crimea to Russia after its detachment from Ukraine in 2014, preceded by the detachment of Abkhazia and South Ossetia from Georgia under Russian auspices, brought to the fore the conditions for moving boundaries and transferring territories. Currently, when a powerful state wants neighboring territory, it can take it, a reversion to an age thought to be past. In the same year, the horror – in the West at least – at Hamas missiles rained down on Israeli territory and the condemnation of the occupying power as merely excessive in its response reversed the attitudes during World War II when occupation was condemned as inexcusable and resistance lauded. These incidents highlight the fact that there is no mechanism for legitimizing territorial transfers, as Russian claims to be protecting Russian *speakers* and to be legalized by a referendum after the occupation vitiated the expression of public support as a justification. There has to be a better way to legitimize transfers and avoid abuses.

The conflict with nature over climate change has already posed a challenge to the development of imperatives for prevention. Norms governing behavior in the climate conflict may well be produced some day, for protection if not prevention, and probably too late. But immediate awareness and decisive action are becoming urgent, not only on the global warming issue itself but for the international conflicts that inundation, water deprivation, and crop failures feed (Edenhofer et al. 2014). Although seemingly a direct conflict with nature, like earthquake prevention, climate change is really a conflict among the responsible human agencies over a reaction of nature to their activities. Here a change in attitudes is necessary to precede a change in normative and operative structures, and the means will have to be found to pressure and finally perhaps enforce compliance in such an area of global cause and concern. One way regimes are formed is by first enunciating principles and gradually tightening the levels of constraint and the means of enforcing compliance, as occurred in the Ozone Treaty sequence from Vienna in 1985 to Montreal in 1987 to London in 1990, but this process has become bogged down (Benedick 1991; Chasek 2003). As some states feel more and more compelled to take action and others equally compelled to resist, conflict stakes rise and hostilities spread to other, often unrelated matters. As a conflict between a public (climate change) and a private (development) good, the need for prevention is acute (CIGI 2015).

Other regimes involving the same type of conflict are in a shambles, laying open the conflicts within their particular areas of focus. The nuclear arms regime shows great cracks in its non-proliferation and test ban controls. The regime is a conflict prevention measure, but in the process it is a bitter subject of conflict, which in turn risks destroying its prevention capabilities and opens the door to a number of new Nuclear Weapons Capable States (NWCS), particularly in volatile regions such as the Middle East. Alongside, a regime for the prohibition of biological weapons is needed to complete the ABC (atomic, biological, chemical) weapons regime, and the chemical segment needs teeth.

Demographic and economic (under)developments in the near future carry some explosive combinations. A youth bulge, particularly for ages 20 to 30, combined with education just enough to raise expectations, and economies producing 20 percent unemployment (and 40 percent among the youth) have combined to create anomic uprisings from West Africa in the 1990s to the Mediterranean countries in the 2010s as harbingers of more to come. The political reactions to these revolts – the Sovereign National Conferences (CNS) in West Africa and the Arab Spring in North Africa and the Fertile Crescent – brought a few democratic results in Benin and Tunisia, but authoritarianism and anarchy were more prevalent. The tinder for pyromaniacs is available for violent conflict, and even where the conflict does not escalate all the way to violence, it can be debilitating for the development of sound governance (Koppell & Sharma 2003; Arnson & Zartman 2005). Prevention is a broad and complex challenge.

Another area of conflict prevention that presses for attention concerns conflicts over depleting natural resources. Population pressure (also exacerbated by climate change in tropical regions) raises issues over the land tenure system in much of the developing world, where traditional ownership norms clash with modern legal systems, with no established practices on how to combine the two. Traditional norms themselves are unable to handle clashes between tribal (collective) ownership and longstanding labor claims (Boone 2014). The many regimes governing the prevention of depletion of fish and wildlife need to be amalgamated onto a global or at least species and geographic continent or basin basis, in the image that CITES on endangered species has created. Similarly, prevention is called for in conflicts over the depletion of water resources, where there are few norms, regimes, or regulations to govern allocation and contain claims.

Information and communication technology (ICT) is a new double-faced area of concern, both as a subject of conflict and as an agent of prevention (DeNardis 2014; Stauffacher 2014). Cyber conflict has become a major arena of covert operations among states, as a means of locating intelligence, as a weapon of disruption, and as a means of security and defense. Its use as the latter justifies its use as the former, and so the cycle of conflict escalates. But as a means of prevention, it is both a direct agent in the development of warning, awareness, and timely action, and a subject of new norms and their enforcement. Transparency, confidence, and security-building mechanisms (TCSBMs) expand the original focus on confidence-building alone to encompass the whole range of regime activities into this new area, where the operative details of prevention remain to be worked out, with urgency. Governance through the urgent creation of a system of norms is required in order to prevent ragged conflict.

As for the operation of prevention itself, the imperviousness of bureaucracies, politicians, and citizen audiences to the warning signals of rising conflict is often shocking. The post-World War II world is many times reminded that people are human beings no matter where they live, and the enormous human cost of conflict in the Sahel from Mali to North and South Sudan, the Fertile Crescent from Israel and Lebanon to Syria to Iraq, and the Himalayan Triangle from Afghanistan and Pakistan through India and China is a matter of prime concern and policy motivation. Audiences have been turned on by scenes of violence on television, and then turned off as those scenes become too common and routine. Yugoslavia in the 1990s was said to be a matter of primordial habits, Rwanda was merely "what they do" in Africa, and Syria in the 2010s just the way "those Arabs" behave toward each other. The imperative is to live and act by global norms that dictate a preventive response to such behavior, not an ethno-targeting dismissal.

Hand in hand with that imperative is the need to work for solutions, not simply negative preventions. The absence of norms for handling ethnic disputes, state collapse, and land tenure conflicts has been noted. In such areas, prevention is still working on its negative face, of stopping and avoiding; the challenge of positive prevention, of providing pro-active guidelines and solutions, is awaiting its insights.

Search for New Mechanisms

The search for new mechanisms of prevention looks for structures for formulation, application, and enforcement. Norms and practices emerge from public discussion before they become enunciated in some documentary form and adopted and put into practice. A number of new mechanisms have appeared in recent decades – new regimes of various degrees of authority such as the new Law of the Sea (1982), the Framework Convention on Climate Change (1992), the Guidelines on IDPs (1998), truth and reconciliation commissions, IAEA, UN SRSGs and PKFs (not provided for in the Charter), the International Criminal Court (1998), and the remarkable efforts of the OSCE High Commissioner on National Minorities and the Conflict Prevention Center and the UN Assistant Secretaries-General on Displaced Persons and the Prevention of Genocide.

The existing mechanism that needs most improvement is arguably the UN Security Council. Repeated blocking of otherwise consensual action by single-party or two-party vetoes is as much a derogation of the spirit of UN operating principles as is single-party intervention; the use of coalitions of the willing to carry out needed preventive actions is a properly creative response. Reforms of UNSC composition are unlikely, but rules of procedure that would give the forum more flexibility could be helpful in enacting preventing measures (although not entirely likely because of the organization's composition). Other UN bodies work on a decision rule of consensus or unanimity minus one, an extension of the abstention rule that could facilitate positive action.

A standard mechanism for inserting at least a pause in escalatory spirals is an imposed suspension, as used in US labor strikes. There has been much progress in slowing down the sort of sudden response and crisis escalation that started World War I, although the June War in 1967 was launched by a similar escalation based on false intelligence on both capabilities and intentions (Parker 1993, 1996). IAEA and OPCW inspections – and Comprehensive Test Ban Treaty Organization inspections, when the treaty is ratified – are an important element in assuring atomic weapons regimes, although they need greater authority against tactics of sovereignty. Had they been able to overcome Saddam Hussein's ill-considered diplomatic games, they could have assured the absence of weapons of mass destruction and removed the excuse – and possibly the initiation – of the Iraq War (2003); the same goes for North Korea and Iran.

Another mechanism for interrupting the spiral of escalation is the awareness by the escalator itself that it has achieved some success and that it is time to pull back or at least to pause. Escalation can become a reverse entrapment, an end in itself rather than a means, with the escalating party unable to recognize when it has started to achieve its goals and can use its own reverse momentum to pull, rather than push, the other side to agreement. The dynamics of the US sanctions campaign against Iran is an eloquent case, as is the Russian covetousness campaign over Ukraine. Such a reversal of pressure should not become precipitous, of course, lest the other side see it as *its* end rather than as a means to full prevention and agreement. At the same time, sanctions must stay in place until some results occur and not be lifted just to create a nice atmosphere. Threats of escalated sanctions have their place as pressure to produce results, after which they should be relaxed, gradually. The debate over the partial lifting of sanctions against Serbia before 1998 and against Iran in 2013–15 is an example.

A difficult and daring mechanism would be the revival of the institution of UN trusteeship to help collapsed states (Helman & Ratner 1992). The odor of revived colonialism and the bureaucratic inefficiency of international organizations provide the narrow limits within which such a reform would have to operate. The third limit in the barrel would be the terrain in which the trustee would have to operate; it is simply dauntingly dangerous for any agency, whether the French or American army or a UN trustee, to try to restore law and order in Centrafrique, Syria, Iraq, Somalia, Afghanistan, or eastern Congo, yet attempts are being made.

Mechanisms of enforcement run up against sovereignty in the state system. Enforcement depends on the constraints that states agree to impose on themselves. Therefore the mechanism of enforcement lies in the solutions negotiated with attention to the interests of the parties involved, either in specific outcomes to a conflict situation or in general responses to a type of situation. Both depend on the reciprocity encased in the prevention arrangement; in specific conflict agreements, each party depends on the interest that the other has in holding the agreement for the first to receive satisfaction for its interests, whereas in longer term, more generic agreements, parties find their interest in compliance in the expectation that the other will find its interest in compliance too, reciprocally, now and on future occasions.

The profoundest limitation on new mechanisms is the *modus operandi* of the international system. Trapped within the extremes of interstate anarchy and world government, any system of conflict prevention must work on the intermediate level of institutionalized interstate cooperation and must expect to live by the rules they impose on others, *mutatis mutandis* (Ikenberry 2001). Those who look for appropriate mechanisms in an ultimate supranational authority ignore the twin dangers of top-level inefficiency and tyranny; those who want simply to leave it up to the wisdom of the states – or effectively, the governments of the moment – mistake the solution for the problem. Whatever is done must operate on the states – and just as strongly, on rebel movements – and provide them with channels and opportunities to manage and resolve conflict without endangering the system which depends on them for implementation. The state is both judge and jury, and also criminal and policeman, all at the same time, and will be for a while. It must learn to exchange self-interest for cooperative (but not self-abnegating) interest, if the self-organizing World System is to avoid the jungle of anarchy. So much has been done, after all, underscoring what remains to be done to tighten the system of World Self-Order.

As prevention looks for new material to work with if it is not to simply return to *Lord of the Flies* (Golding 1954), it can look most productively at traditional local customs for managing conflict. Traditional societies long developed their own practices and norms for conflict prevention and escalation; the community served to prevent conflict in the first place and provided systems of accountability and healing. They have found effectiveness in eastern Congo (Autessere 2010), West Africa (Adebayo et al. 2014), and Palestine (Abu Nimer 2003). When the problem is that there is no state to work with, in or about, the beginnings of the answer can be to think small, at the local level. What is needed, however, is an existing community of some sort within which conflict prevention can operate to rebuild social tissue ruptured by conflict (Zartman 2003). Community has been weakened by modernization, and if there is any effort at a replacement, it is on the national level as state-nations seek to become the forum for its functions. It doesn't work. The search for mechanisms needs a functional replacement on the subnational level that can update traditional structures and functions. Efforts such as Infrastructures for Peace, including both revived and refitted traditional practices and local peace committees (LPCs), are an initial step adopted by the OSCE and promoted by NGOs, to establish "infrastructures for peace" as local networks building on social practices to prevent the spread and escalation of conflict (OSCE 2012; UNDP 2013; Unger et al. 2013; van Tongeren 2013). The next, and necessary, step is to link these grassroots activities to national governance systems so that they do not remain autonomous unrecognized feet separate from the body politic.

Search for New Agents

Although it is the prime agent of prevention, the state can benefit from multiple assistants. A notable addition to the agents of conflict prevention in the post-World War II era is the rise of NGOs into an area that was long off-bounds. As noted, the unofficial terrain is where norms and regimes are initiated and debated, and when states then act on the basis of their leaders' perception of what is possible and permissible, the unofficial terrain becomes alive again to evaluate the action and its results (Stein 2000). In the various issue areas and mechanisms of prevention, NGOs have as active a role as do states. Other areas, such as awareness and mediation, have seen a growing civil society role to complement state action with activities the state cannot perform as well. For the most part, states are needed to render processes and results official, but NGOs can be singularly effective in smoothing ethnic relations, promoting human rights, encouraging democratization, facilitating good governance, softening population displacement, promoting attention and attentiveness, providing mediatory functions, and facilitating implementation – in sum, in working with people as opposed to with states.

The most important qualification to be observed on NGO work alongside states in conflict prevention (Track II diplomacy) is respect and coordination. NGOs can do things that states cannot, notably in working with populations and civil societies before, during, and after the prevention efforts, and states can do things that NGOs cannot, as noted, but the two can completely undermine each other's efforts if they do not work together. (The same is true regarding multiple mediation by states, where mediator competition leads to outbidding by the mediated party and a destruction of good works; Crocker et al. 1999; Vuković 2015b.) NGOs are helpful in preparing the terrain by working on parties' attitudes and on implementing agreements by monitoring and civil society assistance.

NGOs are particularly useful in creating conditions that reduce the terrain for conflict. Notable is the work of Transparency International and of human rights organizations such as Amnesty International, Human Rights Watch, and international human rights leagues, all of which lift the lid on states' (and movements') inner practices. Organizations such as Freedom House, Fund for Peace and the IFIs that evaluate governance practice have a more broad-brush and less well-established practice; similarly failing states' indices, already noted, are a work in progress that contributes broadly to the prevention of conflict. More of such work, particularly in the area of ethnic relations, would be helpful, but indices still remain to be worked out.

Agency can only be public or private, but cooperation can take new forms. Increased use of NGOs puts unusual strains on resources. Standby teams for diplomatic as well as military duty have been set up in conjunction with the UNDPA Mediation Support Unit, with increasing success. The Carter Center's International Negotiation Network (INN) depended on availability and proved useful on occasion. Blue Hats, along with Blue Helmets, have been proposed to help develop administrative skills in post-conflict situations on a short-term basis; police (Blue Caps) have also been seconded from national police duties to fill in in post-conflict situations and provide training. The Intergovernmental Panel on Climate Change (IPCC) and the UNDPA Academic Advisory Council on the Mediation Initiative bring private expertise to bear on conflict situations to inform professional practitioners. These agencies mix public and private personnel to capitalize on both; unfortunately they do not meet a dominating need in post-conflict situations for lasting assistance, but on the other hand their temporary nature prevents them from being a habit-forming crutch.

Search for New Knowledge

Conflict prevention remains an exciting and relevant field for the search for new knowledge. The uncertainty of the causal chain and the fallibility of foresight have been highlighted from the beginning. Better understanding of what causes conflict to emerge from its passive shell and climb the steps of escalation is necessary for more effective prevention. Such dynamics as the security dilemma and entrapment still escape effective interruption and remedy. While new work is being done on why rebellions arise (Collier et al. 2003; Arnson & Zartman 2009) and why people engage in them (Lichbach 1995; Sambanis 2002), the etiology is still not well enough understood to counter the causes and satisfy the demands at the same time; frequently, the people are the ones who are engaging in their side of normal politics (articulating and aggregating demands) and it is the government that is waging conflict against them.

New knowledge will give better predictions; nonetheless, human beings have the ineffable capacity both to do stupid things and to practice inspired creativity, in addition to following studied regularities of behavior. A study of political forecasting showed that experts were wrong 25 percent of the time when they claimed to be absolutely certain (Tetlock 2005). That means that they were right three-quarters of the time, an astoundingly high figure for an activity subject to popular derision. It all depends on expectations. New knowledge on data, regularities, and prediction will work on that 25 percent, although it will discover new irregularities at the same time, and hopefully will reduce stupidity and increase creativity.

In conflicts with or over nature, despite the scientific reluctance to be certain about anything, conclusive evidence of facts and effects has been developed, but the challenge to scientists is to make their knowledge acceptable to the public and convincing to interest groups. Both of these needs are beyond the control of scientists (understood as "natural") but not of social scientists, who need to work on local hustings, on media publicizing scientific data, and on affected businesses to develop an awareness of complementary interests. It is relevant to recall that businesses opposed a ban on substances shown to deplete ozone until they saw a chance to profit from manufacture and sales of non-depleting substitutes (Lang 1989; Benedick 1991).

Prevention is a pressing concern as the system of World Order undergoes sharp shocks in the early twenty-first century. The norm against conquest has been shaken by Russia in Ukraine and Israel in Palestine and the methods of interruption, separation, and integration have wobbled. The norm against mass murder of one's own population has been trashed by Bashir in Sudan and Assad in Syria, and the mechanisms of awareness, de-escalation, stalemate and ripening have been left in the bag, unused. Ethnic and religious (often mixed) wars in Central Africa, Syria, Iraq, Afghanistan, Pakistan, both Sudans, Burundi, Burma, Thailand, and Ukraine have moved toward genocide. The non-proliferation, world trade, and climate change regimes have frayed at the edges with large loopholes in the middle. The Cold War blockade of the UN security and preventive machinery by Russia and China has returned, bereft of ideology but just for reasons of power rivalry. Conflict and security as world-shaping interstate matters have re-emerged from the history files of the last century, alongside anomies of terrorizing gangs, sometimes with a message, sometimes without a cause, such as Boko Haram, the various al-Qaeda franchises in the Maghreb, the Arabian Peninsula, Egypt and elsewhere, ISIS (the "Islamic State"), among others, but also thugs in Honduras and Guatemala, for whom prevention is as elusive as solution.

In this World in search of Order, there is a crying need to focus on prevention. Crisis management is only a part that comes too late, conflict management is another part that is incomplete without resolution, but prevention is the frame for the whole picture. More than periodic toolkits, a change of attitudes toward the field and philosophy of prevention is needed if a sound system of World Order is to be reinvigorated. That is the purpose of this book.

Notes

INTRODUCTION: THE FATAL ATTRACTION OF
PREVENTION

1 Other treatments of conflict prevention have made their
attempts at visual presentations. Lund (1996: 38) has presented
a life-history of a conflict as a smooth Bell curve that others
have often reproduced. It does not see conflict as a cycle and
its categories or measures appear mutually exclusive. Hopp-
Nishanka (2013: 5) presents a more realistic, bumpier depiction
of conflict stages, with peace efforts. Miall et al. (1999) includes
lots of diagrams, with a conflict hump (p. 11) and a management
"hourglass" (p. 12), but the two have not been combined. Major
et al. (2012: 94) presented a Conflict Management Cycle that
includes a quadrant on Crisis Prevention separate from Conflict
Management, Mediation, and Intervention and Peacebuilding.
Figure 1 seeks to combine the Conflict Cycle in its variations with
the typology of prevention efforts at various phases of the conflict,
as is pursued in this book.

CHAPTER 1: THE INEVITABILITY AND VALUE OF
CONFLICT

1 The book *Preventing Genocide: A Blueprint for US Policymakers*
(Albright & Cohen 2008), by a task force led by Madeleine
Albright and William Cohen, is essentially a forceful call for
leadership and commitment, with institutional assistance.
2 Also termed the "Full Plate Problem" (Jentleson 2000).
3 Actually Yugoslavia presented a dangerous certainty to many
people at the time.

CHAPTER 2: THE UBIQUITY OF PREVENTION

1 Maritime boundaries are more complex because the criteria are open to a great range of interpretation.
2 "Ethnic" and "national" will be used here interchangeably or as appropriate.
3 My "tribe" of Pennsylvania Dutchmen (or Germans) who came to Eastern America from southwest Germany in the early eighteenth century still retains its archaic language and literature, its Protestant religion, its territorial attachment, and its identity, even though weakened on all these counts; it has never demanded any special self-determination and in fact prefers farming over politics.

CHAPTER 3: NORMS FOR LONG-TERM PREVENTION

1 Bercovitch (2011) similarly talks of antecedent, concurrent, and consequent phases.
2 The term is used here in its international sense, as referenced, and not in the domestic sense, of an administration or type of government, as in "regime change," discussed below. See Krasner (1983), Levy et al. (1995: 272), Hasenclever et al. (1997), Spector & Zartman (2003).
3 The situation is quite comparable to medical measures of prevention against epidemics. Gradually, the world comes to the consensus that a particular disease can be controlled, even eradicated, and its outbreak prevented. Here and there, frequently in traditional societies, the work of the preventing medical teams will be hindered and refused; this has been the case in prevention efforts on ebola, malaria, river blindness, and polio, among others. But the norm of prevention is maintained and the international community persists in enforcing it.
4 It bears noting that self-determination need not mean full sovereignty but only a determination by the referent group themselves of the manner by which they choose to be governed. The same ellipsis arises in connection with decolonization. UNGA resolutions 1541 (1960) and 2625 (1970).
5 None of the UN agencies has formally adopted even the Guiding Principles on Internal Displacement, of which the Commission

on Human Rights only "took note." How much further are
we from an actual UNGA adoption of a set of democratic
"guidelines"?

6 Actually it is not officially contested, since it has been officially
accepted and endorsed by 199 UN member states on a number of
occasions, although in some cases with "further questions" and
other restrictions and hesitations.

7 The General Assembly and Security Council adopted and
reaffirmed, respectively, the endorsement of the R2P principle in
the 2005 World Summit Conference Outcome, paragraphs 138
and 139, A/60/1 and S/1674 (2006).

CHAPTER 4: MECHANISMS OF MID-TERM
PREVENTION

1 Critics, notably Kleiboer (1997), would do well to read the
literature again, which does not promise success but only a
situation ripe to be activated for the beginning of negotiations.
Nor is it tautological, since there are plenty of indicators of a ripe
moment not seized and of ways of ripening; see Zartman & de
Soto (2010).

References

Abed, George T. & Sanjeev Gupta 2002. *Governance, Corruption, and Economic Performance*. Washington, DC: IMF.

Abu Nimer, Mohammed, 2003. "Traditional Conflict Management in the Middle East," in I. William Zartman (ed.) *Traditional Cures for Modern Conflicts*. Boulder, CO: Lynne Rienner.

Adebayo, Akanmu, Brandon Lundy, Jesse Benjamin, & Joseph Kingsley Adjei (eds) 2014. *Indigenous Conflict Management Strategies in West Africa: Beyond Right and Wrong*. Lanham, MD: Lexington.

Adelman, Howard 1998. "Difficulties in Early Warning," in Klaas van Walraven (ed.), *Early Warning and Conflict Prevention: Limitations and Possibilities*. The Hague: Kluwer.

Adler-Nissen, Rebecca 2014. "Stigma Management in International Relations: Transgressive Identities, Norms, and Order in International Society," *International Organization* LXVIII(1): 143–76.

African Leadership Forum 1991. *The Kampala Document*. Kampala: ALF.

Albin, Cecilia 1991. "Negotiating Indivisible Goods: The Case of Jerusalem," *Jerusalem Journal of International Relations* 13(1), 45–76.

Albright, Madeleine & William Cohen (eds) 2008. *Preventing Genocide: A Blueprint for US Policymakers*. United States Institute of Peace and United States Holocaust Memorial Museum.

Albright, Madeleine & Brontislaw Geremek 2003. *Threats to Democracy: Prevention and Response*. New York: Council on Foreign Relations.

Anderlini, Sanam & David Nyheim 1999. "Preventing Future Wars," *Conflict Trends*. 1: 20–3.

Annan, Kofi 1998. "Press Briefing," http://www.un.org/press/en/1998/19980224.SGSM6470.html

Annan, Kofi 2002. *UN Prevention of Armed Conflict: Report of the Secretary-General*. New York: United Nations.

Anstee, Margaret 1996. *Orphan of the Cold War: The Inside Story of the Collapse of the Angolan Peace Process 1992–1993.* New York: St. Martin's Press.

Anstey, Mark 1993. *Practical Peacemaking: A Mediator's Handbook.* Cape Town: Juta.

Anstey, Mark 1999. *Managing Change, Negotiating Conflict.* Cape Town: Juta.

Anstey, Mark & Valerie Rosoux (eds) 2015. *Reconciliation and Negotiation* (in press).

Anstutz, Mark 2005. *The Healing of Nations: The Promise and Limits of Political Forgiveness.* Lanham, MD: Rowman & Littlefield.

Arnson, Cynthia & I. William Zartman (eds) 2005. *Rethinking the Economics of War: The Intersection of Need, Creed, and Greed.* Washington, DC: Woodrow Wilson Center Press.

Autesserre, Severine 2008. "The Trouble with Congo," *Foreign Affairs* LXXXVII(3): 94–110.

Autesserre, Severine 2010. *The Trouble with the Congo.* Cambridge: Cambridge University Press.

Avenhaus, Rudolf & Thomas Krieger 2014. "Errors of the First and Second Kind," in Mordechai Melamud, Paul Meerts, & I. William Zartman (eds) *Banning the Bang or the Bomb? Negotiating the Nuclear Test Ban Regime.* Cambridge: Cambridge University Press, pp. 253–69.

Avenhaus, Rudolf & Gunnar Sjöstedt (eds) 2009. *Negotiated Risks: International Talks on Hazardous Issues.* Heidelberg: Springer-Verlag.

Avenhaus, Rudolf, Victor Kremenyuk, & Gunnar Sjöstedt (eds) 2002. *Containing the Atom: International Negotiations on Nuclear Security and Safety.* Lanham, MD: Lexington.

Ayissi, Anatole 2001. "Territorial Conflicts: Claiming the Land," in I. William Zartman (ed.) *Preventive Negotiation.* Lanham, MD: Rowman & Littlefield.

Azar, Edward 1990. *The Management of Protracted Social Conflict.* Aldershot: Dartmouth.

Bagla, Pallava 2010. "Along the Indus River, Saber Rattling over Water Security," *Science* 328: 1226–7.

Baldwin, Clive, Chris Chapman & Zoë Gray (eds) 2007. *Minority Rights: The Key to Conflict Prevention.* London: Minority Rights International.

Ballentine, Karen & Jake Sherman 2003. *The Political Economy of Armed Conflict: Beyond Greed and Grievance.* Boulder, CO: Lynne Rienner.

Ban, Ki-moon 2009. *Report of the Secretary-General: Implementing the Responsibility to Protect*, A 63/677, 12 January, ¶45.

Ban, Ki-moon 2010. *Report of the Secretary-General: Early Warning, Assessment and the Responsibility to Protect*. UN doc. A/64/864, July 14.

Barkan, Elazar 2000. *The Guilt of Nations: Restitutions and Negotiating Historical Injustices*. New York: Norton.

Barnett, Michael & Martha Finnemore 2004. *Rules for the World: International Organizations in Global Politics*. Ithaca, NY: Cornell University Press.

Barrett, Scott 2003. *Environment and Statecraft*. Oxford: Oxford University Press.

Bar-Siman-Tov, Yaacov (ed.) 2004. *From Conflict Resolution to Reconciliation*. Oxford: Oxford University Press.

Bartoli, Andrea 2009. "NGOs and Conflict Resolution," in Jacob Bercovitch, Victor Kremenyuk, & I. William Zartman (eds) *The Sage Handbook of Conflict Resolution*. Thousand Oaks, CA: Sage.

Bazerman, Max 1984. "Escalation of Commitment in Individual and Group Decision Making," *Organizational Behavior and Human Performance* 33(2): 141–52.

Bazerman, Max 1994. *Judgment in Managerial Decision Making*. New York: Wiley.

Bazerman, Max H. & Margaret A. Neale 1992. *Negotiating Rationally*. New York: Free Press.

Bellamy, Alex 2011. "Mass Atrocities and Armed Conflict: Links, Distinctions, and Implications for the Responsibility to Prevent," Muscatine, IA: The Stanley Foundation, February.

Benedick, Richard Elliot 1991. *Ozone Diplomacy: New Directions in Safeguarding the Planet*. Cambridge, MA: Harvard University Press.

Bercovitch, Jacob (ed.) 1996. *Resolving International Conflicts*. Boulder, CO: Lynne Rienner.

Bercovitch, Jacob (ed.) 2002. *Studies in International Mediation*. New York: Palgrave.

Bercovitch, Jacob 2007. "Mediation in International Conflicts," in I. William Zartman (ed.) *Peacemaking in International Conflicts*. Washington, DC: United States Institute of Peace.

Bercovitch, Jacob 2009. "Mediation and Conflict Resolution," in Jacob Bercovitch, Victor Kremenyuk, & I. William Zartman (eds) *The Sage Handbook of Conflict Resolution*. Thousand Oaks, CA: Sage.

Bercovitch, Jacob 2011. *Theory and Practice of International Mediation: Selected Essays*. New York: Routledge.

Bercovitch, Jacob & Jeffrey Z. Rubin (eds) 1992. *Mediation in International Relations: Multiple Approaches to Conflict Management*. Basingstoke: Palgrave Macmillan.

Bercovitch, Jacob, Victor Kremenyuk, & I. William Zartman (eds) 2009. *The SAGE Handbook of Conflict Resolution*. Thousand Oaks, CA: Sage.

Berdal, Mats & David Malone (eds) 2000. *Greed and Grievance: Economic Agendas in Civil War*. Boulder, CO: Lynne Rienner.

Bhattacharjee, Yudhijit 2011. "Army Missed Warning Signs," *Science* 332(6025): 27.

Bilder, Richard 2007. "Adjudication," in I. William Zartman (ed.) *Peacemaking in International Conflicts*. Washington, DC: United States Institute of Peace.

Blechman, Barry & Brian Finlay 2012. "What Climate Control Can Learn from Past Efforts to Limit Nuclear Dangers," in Ruth Bell & Micah Ziegler (eds) *Building International Climate Cooperation*. Washington, DC: World Resources Institute.

Bodansky, Daniel 1995. "Customary (and not so Customary) International Environmental Law," *Indiana Journal of Global Legal Studies* III(1): 105–19.

Bombande, Emmanuel 2007. "Conflicts, Civil Society Organizations and Community Peacebuilding Practices in Northern Ghana," in Steve Tonah (ed.) *Ethnicity, Conflicts and Consensus in Ghana*. Accra: Woeli Publishing Services.

Boone, Catherine 2014. *Property and Political Order in Africa*. Cambridge: Cambridge University Press.

Boutros Ghali, Boutros 1992a. *An Agenda for Peace*. S/23500, January 31. New York: United Nations.

Boutros Ghali, Boutros 1992b. *An Agenda for Peace*. A47/277-S24111, June 17. New York: United Nations.

Boutros Ghali, Boutros 1995. *An Agenda for Peace*. A/50/60-S/1995/1, January 3. New York: United Nations.

Bowen, M. 1987. "The Escalation Phenomenon Reconsidered," *Academy of Management Review* 12: 52–66.

Brecher, Michael 1992. *Crises in World Politics: Theory and Reality*. Oxford: Pergamon.

Brecher, Michael 1996. "Crisis Escalation: Model and Findings," *International Political Science Review* XVII(2): 215–30.

Brecher, Michael & Jonathan Wilkenfeld 1997. *A Study of Crisis*. Ann Arbor, MI: University of Michigan Press.

Brockner, Joel & Jeffrey Z. Rubin 1985. *Entrapment in Escalating Conflicts*. New York: Springer Verlag.

Brooks, Sean P. 2008. "Enforcing a Turning Point and Imposing a Deal," *International Negotiation* XIII(3): 415–42.

Brown, Michael & Richard Rosecrance (eds) 1999. *The Costs of Conflict*. Lanham, MD: Rowman & Littlefield.

Burton, John 1990. *Conflict: Resolution and Prevention*. New York: St Martin's Press.

Call, Charles, with Vanessa Wyeth 2008. *Building States to Build Peace*. Boulder, CO: Lynne Rienner.

Carment, David & Albrecht Schnabel 2003. *Conflict Prevention: Path to Peace or Grand Illusion?* Tokyo: United Nations University Press.

Cede, Franz 2009. "The Settlement of International Disputes by Legal Means," in Jacob Bercovitch, Victor Kremenyuk, & I. William Zartman (eds) *The Sage Handbook of Conflict Resolution*. Thousand Oaks, CA: Sage.

Chandra, Kanchan & Steven Wilkinson 2008. "Measuring the Effect of 'Ethnicity,'" *Comparative Political Studies* XL(4/5): 515–63.

Chasek, Pamela S. 2003. "The Ozone Depletion Regime," in Bertram Spector and I. William Zartman (eds) *Getting it Done: Post-Agreement Negotiations and International Regimes*. Washington, DC: United States Institute of Peace.

CIGI 2015. *Political Obstacles to More Effective Agreement*. Waterloo, Canada: Centre for International Governance and Innovation.

Cincotta, Richard 2008/2009. "Half a Chance: Youth Bulges and Transition to Liberal Democracy," Environmental Change and Security Project Report, 13: 10–18. Washington, DC: Woodrow Wilson Center for International Scholars.

Clunan Anne & Harold Trinkunas 2010. *Ungoverned Spaces: Alternatives to State Authority in an Era of Softened Sovereignty*. Stanford, CA: Stanford University Press.

Cobban, Alfred 1944. *National Self-Determination*. Chicago, IL: University of Chicago Press.

Cobban, Helena 2007. *Amnesty after Atrocity? Healing Nations after Genocide and War Crimes*. Boulder, CO: Paradigm.

Cohen, J. 1999. *Conflict Prevention in the OSCE: An Assessment of Capacities*. The Hague: Clingendael.

Cohen, Roberta 2011. "Lessons Learned from the Development of the Guiding Principles on Internal Displacement," The Crisis Migration Project, Institute for the Study of International Migration, Georgetown University.

Collier, Paul & Anke Hoeffler 2000. "Greed and Grievance in Civil War," World Bank Policy Research Paper 2355. Washington, DC: World Bank.

Collier, Paul, V. L. Elliott, Havard Hegre, Anke Hoeffler, Marta Reynal-Querol, & Nicholas Sambanis 2003. *Breaking the Conflict Trap: Civil War and Development Policy*. Washington, DC: World Bank and Oxford: Oxford University Press.

Conca, K. 2005. *Governing Water: Contentious Transnational Politics and Global Institution Building*. Cambridge, MA: MIT Press.

Cortright, David (ed.) 1997. *The Price of Peace: Incentives and International Conflict Prevention*. Lanham, MD: Rowman & Littlefield.

Coser, Lewis 1956. *The Functions of Social Conflict*. New York: Free Press.

Cranna, Michael (ed.) 1994. *The True Cost of Conflict: Seven Recent Wars and Their Effects on Society*. New York: New Press.

Crawford, Beverly & Ronnie Lipschutz (eds) 1999. *The Myth of Ethnic Conflict*. Los Angeles, CA: University of California Press.

Crocker, Chester A. 1993. "Strengthening African Peacemaking and Peacekeeping," in David Smock (ed.) *Making War and Waging Peace: Foreign Intervention in Africa*. Washington, DC: United States Institute of Peace.

Crocker, Chester A., Fen Osler Hampson, & Pamela Aall (eds) 1999. *Herding Cats: Multiparty Mediation in a Complex World*. Washington, DC: United States Institute of Peace.

Cross, John 1969. *The Economics of Bargaining*. New York: Basic Books.

Cunliffe, Philip (ed.) 2011. *Critical Perspectives on the Responsibility to Protect*. New York: Routledge.

Darby, John 2001. *The Effects of Violence on Peace Processes*. Washington, DC: United States Institute of Peace.

Darby, John (ed.) 2006. *Violence and Reconstruction*. Notre Dame, IN: Notre Dame Press.

Davies, James C. 1962. "Toward a Theory of Revolution," *American Sociological Review* 27(1): 5–18.

de Callières, François 2002 [1716]. *De la manière de négocier avec les souverains*. Geneva: Droz.

DeNardis, Laura 2014. *The Global War for Internet Governance*. New Haven, CT: Yale University Press.

De Soto, Alvaro 1999. "Ending Violent Conflict in El Salvador," in Chester A. Crocker, Fen Osler Hampson, & Pamela Aall (eds) *Herding Cats: Multiparty Mediation in a Complex World*. Washington, DC: United States Institute of Peace.

Deng, Francis & Roberta Cohen 1998. *Guiding Principles on Internal Displacement*. New York: United Nations.

Deng, Francis & I. William Zartman 2002. *A Strategic Vision for Africa: The Kampala Movement*. Washington, DC: Brookings Institution Press.

Deng, Francis, Sadikiel Kimaro, Terrence Lyons, Donald Rothchild, & I. William Zartman 1996. *Sovereignty as Responsibility: Conflict Management in Africa*. Washington, DC: Brookings Institution Press.

Diehl, Paul (ed.) 1998. *A Road Map to War: Territorial Dimension of International Conflict*. Nashville, TN: Vanderbilt University Press.

Djalal, Hasjim & Ian Townsend-Gault 1999. "Managing Potential Conflict in the South China Sea," in Chester A. Crocker, Fen Osler Hampson, & Pamela Aall (eds) *Herding Cats: Multiparty Mediation in a Complex World*. Washington, DC: United States Institute of Peace, pp. 107–34.

Downie, Christian 2014. *The Politics of Climate Change Negotiations*. Cheltenham: Edward Elgar.

Dutton, Peter 2007. "Carving Up the East China Sea," *Naval War College Review* 60(2): 49–72.

Dutton, Peter 2009. "Charting a Course: US-China Cooperation at Sea," *China Security* 5(1): 11–26.

Dutton, Peter 2010. *Military Activities in the EEZ: A US-China Dialogue*. Newport, RI: US Naval War College.

Ebbesen, Ebbe B. & Vladimir J. Konečni, 1980. "On the External Validity of Decision-Making Research: What Do We Know About Decisions in the Real World?" in T. S. Wallsten (ed.) *Cognitive Processes in Choice and Decision Behavior*. Hillsdale, NJ: Lawrence Erlbaum Associates, pp. 21–45.

Edenhofer, Ottmar et al. (eds) 2014. *Climate Change 2014: Mitigation of Climate Change, Working Group III Contribution to the Fifth Assessment Report of the Intergovernmental Panel on Climate Change*. Cambridge: Cambridge University Press.

Edkins, Jenny 2003. *Trauma and the Memory of Politics*. Cambridge: Cambridge University Press.

Elbadawi, Ibrahim & Nicholas Sambanis 2000. "Why Are There So Many Civil Wars in Africa?" *Journal of African Economies* 9(3): 244–69.

Elgie, Robert 2007. "Varieties of Semi-Presidentialism and their Impact on Nascent Democracies," *Taiwan Journal of Democracy* 3(2): 53–71.

Elhance, Arun P. 1996a. *Conflict and Cooperation over Water in the Aral Sea Basin*. New York: Social Science Research Council.

Elhance, Arun P. 1996b. "Hydropolitcs: Conflict and Cooperation in International River Basins," in Daniel Deudney and Richard Matthews (eds) *Contested Grounds: Conflict and Security in the New Environmental Politics*. Albany, NY: State University of New York Press.

Enserink, Martin 2001. "Rapid Response Could Have Curbed Foot-and-Mouth Epidemic," *Science* 294: 26–7.

Evans, Gareth 1994. "Cooperative Security and Intrastate Conflict," *Foreign Policy* 96: 3–20.

Evans, Gareth 2008. *The Responsibility to Protect: Ending Mass Atrocity Crimes Once and For All*. Washington, DC: Brookings Institution Press.

Evans, Gareth & Mohamed Sahnoun (eds) 2001. *The Responsibility to Protect*. Ottawa: International Commission on Intervention and State Sovereignty.

FAO 1987. Agreement on the Action Plan for the Environmentally Sound Management of the Common Zambezi River System signed at Harare, 28 May 1987. Available at: http://www.fao.org/docrep/w7414b/w7414b0j.htm

Faure, Guy Olivier 2014. "South-China Sea: Options for Negotiations," *PINPoints* 40: 18–26.

Faure, Guy Olivier & I. William Zartman (eds) 2010. *Negotiating with Terrorists: Strategy, Tactics and Politics*. Abingdon: Routledge.

Festinger, Leon 1957. *A Theory of Cognitive Dissonance*. New York: Row, Peterson & Company.

Finlay, Brian 2014. *Southern Flows: Weapons of Mass Destruction and the Developing South*. Muscatine, IA: Stanley Foundation and Stimson.

Finnemore, Martha & Kathryn Sikkink 1998. "International Norm Dynamics and Political Change," *International Organization* 52(4): 887–917.

Fisher, Roger, Bruce Patton, & William Ury 1982. *Getting to Yes: Negotiating an Agreement Without Giving In*. Boston, MA: Houghton Mifflin.

Fixdal, Mona (ed.) 2015. *Mediation in the Middle East*. Special issue of *International Negotiation* 20(3).

Fortna, Virginia Page 2004a. "Does Peacekeeping Keep Peace? International Intervention and the Duration of Peace After Civil War," *International Studies Quarterly* 48: 269–92.

Fortna, Virginia Page 2004b. *Peacetime: Ceasefire Agreements and the Durability of Peace*. Princeton, NJ: Princeton University Press.

Frederick, Bryan 2012. "The Sources of Territorial Stability," doctoral dissertation. Washington, DC: Johns Hopkins University School of Advanced International Studies.

Friedheim, Robert 1993. *Negotiating the New Ocean Regime*. Columbia, SC: University of South Carolina.

Fuller, Thomas 2014. "Thailand's Political Tensions," *New York Times*, April 15.

G-8 2000. "G-8 Myazaki Initiatives for Conflict Prevention," Kyushu-Okinawa Summit meeting, July 13.

Gao, Zhiguo & Bing Bing Jia 2013. "The Nine-Dash Line in South China Sea," *American Journal of International Law* 107(1): 98–124.

Garcia, Denise 2011. *Disarmament Diplomacy and Human Security: Norms, Regimes and Moral Progress in International Relations*. New York: Routledge.

Garcia, Denise & Monica Herz 2014. "Anticipating the Future: Preventive Multilateral Norms and the Impact on International Security." Catholic University of Rio de Janeiro.

Gartner, Scott Sigmund & Molly Mellin 2009. "Assessing Outcomes," in Jacob Bercovitch, Victor Kremenyuk, & I. William Zartman (eds) *The Sage Handbook of Conflict Resolution*. Thousand Oaks, CA: Sage.

George, Alexander 1983. *Managing US-Soviet Rivalry: Problems of Crisis Prevention*. Boulder, CO: Westview.

George, Alexander, David Hall, & William Simons 1971. *The Limits of Coercive Diplomacy*. New York: Little Brown.

Gilbert, Daniel 2006. *Stumbling on Happiness*. New York: Knopf.

Ginifer, Jeremy, Espen Barth Eide and Carsten Rønnfeldt (eds) 1999. *Preventive Action in Theory and Practice: The Skopje Papers*. Oslo: Norwegian Institute of International Affairs.

Goertz, Gary & Paul Diehl 1992. *Territorial Changes and International Conflict*. New York: Routledge.

Golding, William 1954. *Lord of the Flies*. London: Faber & Faber.

Goldstein, Joshua 2011. *Winning the War on War*. New York: Dutton.

Gordon, David 1971. *Self-Determination and History in the Third World*. Princeton, NJ: Princeton University Press.

Grindle, Merilee S. 2005. *Good Enough Governance Revisited: A Report for DFID with reference to the Governance Target Strategy Paper, 2001.*

Gurr, Ted Robert 1970. *Why Men Rebel.* Princeton, NJ: Princeton University Press.

Gurr, Ted Robert 1993. "Why Minorities Rebel: A Global Analysis of Communal Mobilization and Conflict since 1945," *International Political Science Review* 14(2): 161–201.

Haas, Ernest 1968. *Collective Security and the Future International System.* Denver, CO: University of Denver.

Hamburg, David 2002. *No More Killing Fields: Preventing Deadly Conflict.* Lanham, MD: Rowman & Littlefield.

Hamburg, David 2010. *Preventing Genocide.* Boulder, CO: Paradigm.

Hamburg, David & Beatrix Hamburg 2004. *Learning to Live Together: Preventing Hatred and Violence in Child and Adolescent Development.* Oxford: Oxford University Press.

Hamburg, David with Eric Hamburg 2013. *Give Peace a Chance.* Boulder, CO: Paradigm.

Hampson, Fen Osler 1996. *Nurturing Peace.* Washington, DC: United States Institute of Peace.

Hampson, Fen Osler & David M. Malone 2002. *From Reaction to Conflict Prevention: Opportunities for the UN System.* Boulder, CO: Lynne Rienner.

Hancock, Landon E. & Christopher Mitchell 2007. *Zones of Peace.* Bloomfield, CT: Kymarian.

Harris, Gardiner 2012. "As Tensions in India Turn Deadly, Some Say Officials Ignored Warning Signs," *New York Times,* July 29.

Harris, Peter & Ben Reilly (eds) 1998. *Democracy and Deep-Rooted Conflict: Options for Negotiators.* Stockholm: IDEA.

Hasenclever, Andreas, Peter Mayer, & Volker Rittberger 1997. *Theories of International Regimes.* New York: Cambridge University Press.

Hayes, Richard, Stacey Kaminski, & Steven Beres 2003. "Negotiating the Non-Negotiable: Dealing with Absolute Terrorists," in I. William Zartman (ed.) *Negotiating with Terrorists,* special issue of *International Negotiation,* 8(3): 9–25.

Hayner, Priscilla 2001. *Unspeakable Truths: Confronting State Terror and Atrocity.* New York: Routledge.

Helman, Gerald R. & Steven R. Ratner 1992. "Saving Failed States," *Foreign Policy,* 89: 3–20.

Henehan, Marie & John Vasquez 2006. "The Changing Probability of

Interstate War 1816–1992," in Raimo Väyrynen (ed.) *The Waning of Major War: Theories and Debates*. London: Routledge.

High-Level Panel on Threats, Challenges and Change 2004. *A More Secure World: Our Shared Responsibility*. Report to the Secretary-General. New York: United Nations.

Hobbes, Thomas (1964 [1651]) *The Leviathan*. New York: Washington Square Press.

Holl, Jane (ed.) 1997. *Preventing Deadly Conflict*. New York: Carnegie Commission on Preventing Deadly Conflict.

Holsti, Kalevi Jaakko 1991. *Peace and War: Armed Conflicts and International Order, 1648–1989*. Cambridge: Cambridge University Press.

Homans, Charles 1961. *Social Behavior*. New York: Harcourt, Brace, Jovanovich.

Hopmann, P. Terrence 1996. *The Negotiation Process and the Resolution of International Conflicts*. Columbia, SC: University of South Carolina.

Hopmann, P. Terrence 2001. "Disintegrating States: Separating without Violence," in I. William Zartman (ed.) *Preventive Negotiation*. Lanham, MD: Rowman & Littlefield.

Hopmann, P. Terrence 2014. "Conflict Management in Mindanao," Johns Hopkins University, SAIS, Washington, DC.

Hopp-Nishanka, Ulrike 2013. "Giving Peace and Address," in Barbara Unger, Stina Lundström, Katrin Planta, & Beatrix Austin (eds). *Peace Infrastructures: Assessing Concept and Practice*. Berghof Dialog Series 10. Berlin: Berghof Foundation.

Horowitz, Donald, 1985. *Ethnic Groups in Conflict*. Los Angeles, CA: University of California Press.

Howard, Lise Morjé 2007. *UN Peacekeeping in Civil Wars*. Cambridge: Cambridge University Press.

Huth, Paul 1996. *Standing Your Ground: Territorial Disputes and International Conflict*. Ann Arbor, MI: University of Michigan Press.

Ikenberry, G. John 2001. *After Victory*. Princeton, NJ: Princeton University Press.

Ikle, Fred Charles 1964. *How Nations Negotiate*. New York: Harper & Row.

Ikle, Fred Charles 1971. *Every War Must End*. New York: Columbia University Press.

Janis, Irving 1972. *Victims of Groupthink*. Boston, MA: Houghton-Mifflin.

Jentleson, Bruce 1994. *With Friends Like These: Reagan, Bush, and Saddam, 1982–1990*. New York: Norton.

Jentleson, Bruce 2000. *Opportunities Missed, Opportunities Seized*. Lanham, MD: Rowman & Littlefield.

Jones, Bruce, Thomas Wright, Jeremy Shapiro, & Robert Keane 2014. *The State of the International Order*. Policy Paper 33. Washington, DC: Brookings Institution.

Kacowicz, Arie 1994. *Peaceful Territorial Change*. Columbia, SC: University of South Carolina Press.

Kahler, Miles & Barbara Walter (eds) 2006. *Territoriality and Conflict in an Era of Globalization*. Cambridge: Cambridge University Press.

Kahneman, Daniel 2011. *Thinking, Fast and Slow*. New York: Farrar, Straus & Giroux.

Kahneman, Daniel & Amos Tversky 1995. "Conflict Resolution: A Cognitive Perspective," in K. Arrow, R. H. Mnookin, L. Ross, A. Tversky, & R. Wilson (eds) *Barriers to Conflict Resolution*. New York: Norton, pp. 44–61.

Kanet, Roger & Edward Kolodziej (eds) 1991. *The Cold War as Cooperation*. Basingstoke: Macmillan.

Kaufman, Chaim 1996. "Intervention in Ethnic and Ideological Civil Wars: What Can Be Done and What Can't," *Security Studies* 6(1): 62–100.

Kaufmann, Daniel 2003. *Rethinking Governance: Empirical Lessons Challenge Orthodoxy*. Washington, DC: World Bank.

Kautilya 1960 [−320]. *Arthasastra* (R. Shamasastry trans). Mysore: Mysore Printing & Publishing House.

Kawachi, Ichiro & S.V. Subramanian (eds) 2008. *Social Capital and Health*. New York: Springer.

Kawachi, Ichiro, Bruce Kennedy, Kobertley Lochner, & Deborah Prothro-Stuth 1997. "Social Capital, Income Inequality, and Mortality," *American Journal of Public Health* 87(9): 1491–8.

Kennedy, John F. 1960. Third Kennedy–Nixon Presidential Debate, 13 October.

Kissinger, Henry 1964. *A World Restored*. New York: Crosset & Dunlop.

Kleiboer, Marieke 1997. *International Mediation*. Boulder, CO: Lynne Rienner.

Koenigsberg, Richard 2009. *Nations Have the Right to Kill: Hitler, the Holocaust and War*. New York: Library of Social Sciences.

Koppell, Carla, with Anita Sharma 2003. *Preventing the Next Wave of*

Conflict. Washington, DC: Woodrow Wilson International Center for Scholars.

Korula, Anna 2003. "The Regime against Torture," in Bertram I. Spector & I. William Zartman (eds) *Getting It Done: Post-Agreement Negotiations and International Regimes*. Washington, DC: United States Institute of Peace.

Krasner, Stephen (ed.) 1983. *International Regimes*. Ithaca, NY: Cornell University Press.

Kremenyuk, Victor (ed.) 2002. *International Negotiation*. San Francisco, CA: Jossey-Bass.

Kress, Moshe & R. Szechtman 2009. "Why Defeating Insurgencies Is Hard," *Operations Research* 57(3): 578–85.

Kriesberg, Louis & Bruce W. Dayton 2012. *Constructive Conflicts: From Escalation to Resolution*, 4th edn. Lanham, MD: Rowman and Littlefield.

Kuhn, Thomas 1962. *The Structure of Scientific Revolutions*. Chicago, IL: University of Chicago Press.

Kuperman, Alan (ed.) 2015. *Shocks in Africa*. Philadelphia, PA: University of Pennsylvania Press.

Laibson, David 1997. "Golden Eggs and Hyperbolic Discounting," *Quarterly Journal of Economics* 112(2): 443–78.

Lake, David & Donald Rothchild 1998. *The International Spread of Ethnic Conflict*. Princeton, NJ: Princeton University Press.

Lang, Winfried, 1989. *Internationaler Umweltschutz: Völkerrecht und Aussenpolitik zwischen Ökonomie und Ökologie*. Vienna: Orac.

Larémont, Ricardo 2014. *Revolution, Revolt and Reform in North Africa*. New York: Routledge.

Lateef, Sarwar 1990. "Issues of Governance in Borrowing Members," Memorandum, World Bank, December 21.

Lateef, Sarwar (ed.) 1991. Managing Development: The Governance Dimension. World Bank, August 29.

Lax, David & James Sebenius 1986. *The Manager as Negotiator*. New York: Free Press.

Leatherman, Janie, William DeMars, Patrick D. Gaffney, & Raimo Väyrynen (eds) 1999. *Breaking Cycles of Violence: Conflict Prevention in Intrastate Crises*. West Hartford, CT: Kumarian.

Lederach, John Paul 1997. *Building Peace: Sustainable Reconciliation in Divided Societies*. Washington, DC: United States Institute for Peace.

Lemarchand, René 1982. *The World Bank in Rwanda*. Bloomington, IN: University of Indiana, African Studies Program.

Lemkin, Raphael 1944. *Axis Rule in Occupied Europe: Laws of Occupation, Analysis of Government, Proposals for Redress.* Washington, DC: Carnegie Endowment for International Peace.

Levy, Marc, Oran Young, & Michael Zürn 1995. "The Study of International Regimes," *European Journal of International Relations* 1(3): 267–330.

Lichbach, Mark 1995. *The Rebel's Dilemma.* Ann Arbor, MI: University of Michigan Press.

Lijphart, Arild 1977. *Democracy in Plural Societies.* New Haven, CT: Yale University Press.

Loewenstein, George 1989. "Anomalies in Intertemporal Choice: Evidence and an Interpretation." Working paper, Division of Research, Harvard Business School.

Loewenstein, George 1992. "Anomalies in Intertemporal Choice: Evidence and an Interpretation," *Quarterly Journal of Economics* 107(2): 573–97.

Lorenz, Edward 1972. "Predictability: Does the Flap of a Butterfly's Wings in Brazil Set Off a Tornado in Texas?" Speech to the American Academy for the Advancement of Science, December 29.

Lorenz, Edward 1993. *The Essence of Chaos.* Seattle, WA: University of Washington Press.

Lund, Michael 1996. *Preventing Violent Conflicts: A Strategy for Preventive Diplomacy.* Washington, DC: United States Institute for Peace.

Lund, Michael 2000. *UN Preventive Measure: A Prototype Manual for Practitioners in Potential Conflict Situations.* UN Framework Team.

Lund, Michael 2009. "Conflict Prevention: Theory in Pursuit of Policy and Practice," in Jacob Bercovitch, Victor Kremenyuk, & I. William Zartman (eds) *The Sage Handbook of Conflict Resolution.* Thousand Oaks, CA: Sage.

Lund, Michael & Guenola Rasamoelina (eds) 2000. *The Impact of Conflict Prevention Policy: Cases, Measures, Assessments.* Conflict Prevention Network Yearbook. Baden-Baden: Nomos.

Luttwak, Edward 1999. "Give War a Chance," *Foreign Affairs* 78(4): 36–44.

Mahieu, Sylvie 2007. "When Should Mediators Interrupt a Civil War? The Best Timing for a Ceasefire," *International Negotiation* 12(2): 207–28.

Major, Claudia, Tobias Pietz, Elisabeth Schöndorf, & Wanda Hummel 2012. "The Crisis Management Toolbox," in Eva Gross, Daniel

Hamilton, Claudia Major, & Henning Riecke (eds) *Preventing Conflict, Managing Crisis: European and American Perspectives.* Washington, DC: Center for Transatlantic Relations.

Matthews, Richard 1995. *If Men Were Angels: James Madison and the Heartless Empire.* Lawrence, KS: University Press of Kansas.

Maundi, Mohammed O., I. William Zartman, Gilbert Khadiagala, & Kwaku Nuamah 2006. *Getting In: Mediators' Entry into the Settlement of African Conflicts.* Washington, DC: United States Institute for Peace.

McDermott, Rose 2009. "Prospect Theory and Negotiation," in Rudolf Avenhaus & Gunnar Sjöstedt (eds) *Negotiated Risks: International Talks on Hazardous Issues.* Heidelberg: Springer-Verlag.

Meerts, Paul 2005. "Entrapment in International Negotiations," in I. William Zartman & Guy Olivier Faure (eds), *Escalation and Negotiation in International Conflicts.* Cambridge: Cambridge University Press.

Melamud, Mordechai, Paul Meerts, & I. William Zartman (eds) 2014. *Ban the Bang or the Bomb? Negotiating the Comprehensive Test Ban Treaty.* Cambridge: Cambridge University Press.

Merrills, John G. 2011. *International Dispute Settlement.* Cambridge: Cambridge University Press.

Mezran, Karin & Alice Alunni 2015. "Libya," in I. William Zartman (ed.) *Arab Spring: Negotiating in the Shadow of the Intifadat.* Athens, GA: University of Georgia Press.

Miall, Hugh, Oliver Ramsbotham, & Tom Woodhouse 1999. *Contemporary Conflict Resolution.* New York: Wiley.

Micaud, Charles A., Leon Carl Brown, & Clement Henry Moore 1964. *Tunisia: The Politics of Modernization.* New York: Praeger.

Midlarsky, Manus 1992. *The Internationalization of Communal Strife.* New York: Routledge.

Mitchell, C.R. 2000. *Gestures of Conciliation.* New York: St Martin's/ Macmillan.

Mitchell, C.R. & Keith Webb (eds) 1988. *New Approaches to International Mediation.* Santa Barbara, CA: Greenwood.

Mnookin, Robert 2010. *Bargaining with the Devil.* New York: Simon & Schuster.

Montville, Joseph (ed.) 1990. *Conflict and Peacemaking in Multiethnic Societies.* Lanham, MD: Lexington.

Mooradian, Moorad & Daniel Druckman 1999. "Hurting Stalemate or Mediation? The Conflict over Nagorno-Karabakh, 1990–95," *Journal of Peace Research* 36(6): 709–27.

Morel, Michel, M. Stavropoulou, & J.-F. Durieux 2012. "The History and Status of the Right Not To Be Displaced," *Forced Migration Review*, 41: 5–7.

Moss, R.H. et al. 2013. "Hell and High Water: Practice-Relevant Adaptation Science," *Science* 342: 696–8.

Mutwol, Julius 2009. *Peace Agreements and Civil Wars in Africa.* Amherst, NY: Cambria.

Nash, John N. 1950. "Equilibrium Points in n-Person Games," *Proceedings of the National Academy of Sciences of the United States of America* 36(1): 48–9.

NBI 2015. *Nile Basin Agreement.* Entebbe, Uganda: Nile Basin Initiative.

Nicolson, Harold 1964. *Diplomacy.* Oxford: Oxford University Press.

Nordquist, Kjell-Åke 2001. Boundary Conflicts: Drawing the Line. In I. William Zartman (ed.) *Preventive Negotiation: Avoiding Conflict Escalation.* Lanham, MD: Rowman & Littlefield.

Norlén, Tova 2015. *Sacred Stones and Religious Nuts: Managing Territorial Absolutes.* Athens, GA: University of Georgia Press.

Normile, D. 2011. "Japan Disaster: Scientific Consensus on Great Quake Came Too Late," *Science* 332: 22–3.

North, Douglass 1990. *Institutions, Institutional Change and Economic Performance.* Cambridge: Cambridge University Press.

Nuamah, Kwaku 2008. *Sources of Leverage in Third-Party Mediation: The Cases of Ghana, Peru-Ecuador and the Ethiopia-Eritrea Conflicts.* Baltimore, MD: Johns Hopkins University.

O'Donnell, Guillermo & Philippe Schmitter 1986. *Transitions from Authoritarian Rule: Tentative Conclusions about Uncertain Democracies.* Baltimore, MD: Johns Hopkins University Press.

Olson, Mancur 1968. *The Logic of Collective Action.* New York: Schocken.

OSCE 2012. *OSCE Guide on Non-Military Confidence-Building Measures (CBMs).* Vienna: Organization for Security and Cooperation in Europe.

Parker, Richard 1993. *The Politics of Miscalculation in the Middle East.* Bloomington, IN: Indiana University Press.

Parker, Richard (ed.) 1996. *The Six-Day War.* Gainesville, FL: University Press of Florida.

Peck, Connie 1998. *Sustainable Peace: The Role of the UN and Regional Organizations in Preventing Conflict.* Lanham, MD: Rowman & Littlefield.

Peck, Connie 2009. "United Nations Mediation Experience," in Jacob

Bercovitch, Victor Kremenyuk, & I. William Zartman (eds) *The SAGE Handbook of Conflict Resolution*. Thousand Oaks, CA: Sage.

Pillar, Paul 1983. *Negotiating Peace*. Princeton, NJ: Princeton University Press.

Posen, Barry 1993. "The Security Dilemma, and Ethnic Conflict," in Michael Brown (ed.) *Ethnic Conflict and International Security*. Princeton, NJ: Princeton University Press.

Postel, Sandra 2015. "Nile *River* Nations Agree to Cooperate," *National Geographic*.

Pruitt, Dean G. 1981. *Negotiation Behavior*. New York: Academic Press.

Pruitt, Dean G. & Peter J. Carnevale 1993. *Negotiation in Social Conflict*. Buckingham: Open University Press.

Pruitt, Dean G. & Sung Hee Kim 2004. *Social Conflict: Escalation, Stalemate, and Settlement*, 3rd edn. New York: McGraw-Hill.

Prunier, Gerard 1994. *The Rwanda Crisis*. New York: Columbia University Press.

Raskin, A.H. 1987. "The Newspaper Strike," in I. William Zartman (ed.) *The 50% Solution*. New Haven, CT: Yale University Press.

Raven, Bertrand & Arie Kuglanski 1970. "Conflict and Power," in Paul Swingle (ed.) *The Structure of Conflict*. Waltham, MA: Academic Press.

Reynolds, James F. et al. 2007. "Global Desertification: Building a Science for Dryland Development," *Science* 316: 847–51.

Richelieu, Cardinal du Plessis 1947 [1638]. *Testament politique*. Paris: Laffont.

Ricoeur, Paul 2000. *La mémoire, l'histoire, l'oubli*. Paris: Seuil.

Risse, Thomas, Stephen Ropp, & Kathryn Sikkink (eds) 2013. *The Persistent Power of Human Rights: From Commitment to Compliance*. Cambridge: Cambridge University Press.

Rosenau, James 1964. *International Aspects of Civil Strife*. Princeton, NJ: Princeton University Press.

Rosenberg, Sheri P. 2013. *A Common Standard for Applying the Responsibility to Protect*. Cardozo Law School, Holocaust, Genocide and Human Rights Program.

Rosoux, Valerie 2001. *Les usages de la mémoire dans les relations internationales*. Brussels: Bruylant.

Rosoux, Valerie 2009. "Reconciliation as a Peace-Building Process," in Jacob Bercovitch, Victor Kremenyuk, & I. William Zartman (eds) *The Sage Handbook of Conflict Resolution*. Thousand Oaks, CA: Sage.

Ross, Denis 2004. *The Missing Peace*. New York: Farrar, Straus, Giroux.

Rothchild, Donald 1997. *Managing Ethnic Conflicts in Africa*. Washington, DC: Brookings Institution Press.

Rubin, Jeffrey Z. (ed.) 1981. *The Dynamics of Third Party Intervention*. New York: Praeger.

Rubin, Jeffrey Z. & Joel Brockner 1975. "Factors Affecting Entrapment in Waiting Situations: The Rosencrantz and Guildenstern Effect," *Journal of Personality and Social Psychology*, 31: 1054–63.

Rubin, Jeffrey Z. & Bert Brown 1975. *The Social Psychology of Negotiating and Bargaining*. New York: Academic Press.

Salton, Herman 2014. *The United Nations, Leadership and Genocide*. New York: Routledge.

Sambanis, Nicholas 2002. "A Review of Recent Advances and Future Directions in the Literature on Civil War," *Defense and Peace Economics* 14(3): 215–43.

Schaller, Dominik J. & Jürgen Zimmerer (eds) 2009. *The Origins of Genocide: Raphael Lemkin as a Historian of Mass Violence*. London: Routledge.

Schirch, Lisa 2013. "Separate Tracks, Common Goals," *Building Peace* 2: 17–20.

Schnabel, Albrecht & David Carment (eds) 2004. *Conflict Prevention from Rhetoric to Reality* (2 vols). Lanham, MD: Lexington Books.

Schwenk, Charles R. 1986. "Information, Cognitive Biases, and Commitment to a Course of Action," *Academy of Management Review* 11: 298–310.

Sebenius, James 1984. *Negotiating the Law of the Sea*. Cambridge, MA: Harvard University Press.

Shehadi, Kamal 1993. Ethnic Self-Determination and the Break-Up of States. *The Adelphi Papers* 33(283): 3–10.

Shubik, Martin 1971. "The Dollar Auction Game: A Paradox in Noncooperative Behavior and Escalation," *Journal of Conflict Resolution* 15(1): 109–11.

Silver, Nate 2012. *The Signal and the Noise: Why So Many Predictions Fail – and Some Don't*. New York: Penguin.

Simmons, Beth 1999. *Territorial Disputes and their Resolution*. Peaceworks 27. Washington, DC: United States Institute of Peace.

Simmons, Beth 2005. "Forward-Looking Dispute Resolution," in I. William Zartman & Victor Kremenyuk (eds) *Peace vs Justice*. Lanham, MD: Rowman & Littlefield.

Sjösted, Gunnar 1993. *International Environmental Negotiations*. Thousand Oaks, CA: Sage.

Sjösted, Gunnar & Ariel Penetrante 2013. *Climate Change Negotiations.* New York: Routledge.

Skaperdas, Stergios, Rodrigo Soares, Alys Willman, & Stephen C. Miller 2009. *The Costs of Violence.* Washington, DC: World Bank.

Smoker, Paul 1964. "Fear in the Arms Race," *Journal of Peace Research* 1(1): 55–63.

Spector, Bertram I. 2005. *Fighting Corruption in Developing Countries: Strategies and Analysis.* Bloomfield, CT: Kumarian Press.

Spector, Bertram I. 2008 *Negotiating Peace with Integrity: Anticorruption Strategies in Post-Conflict Societies.* Potomac, MD: Center for Negotiation Analysis.

Spector, Bertram I. 2009. *Fighting Corruption in Countries Rebuilding After Conflict: A Democracy and Governance Program Brief.* Washington, DC: Management Systems International (for USAID).

Spector, Bertram I. & I. William Zartman (eds) 2003. *Getting It Done: Post-Agreement Negotiations and International Regimes.* Washington, DC: United States Institute of Peace.

Spector, Bertram I., Gunnar Sjöstedt, & I. William Zartman (eds) 1994. *Negotiating International Regimes: Lessons Learned from the United Nations Conference on Environment and Development (UNCED).* Dordrecht: Graham & Trotman.

Sriram, Lekha & Karin Wermester (eds) 2003. *From Promise to Practice: Strengthening UN Capacities for the Prevention of Violent Conflict.* Boulder, CO: Lynne Rienner.

Staub, Ervin 1989. *The Roots of Evil.* Cambridge: Cambridge University Press.

Staub, Ervin 2000. "Preventing Genocide," *Other Voices* 2(1): 1–11.

Staub, Ervin 2003. *The Psychology of Good and Evil: Why Children, Adults and Groupings Help and Harm Each Other.* Cambridge: Cambridge University Press.

Staub, Ervin 2011. *Overcoming Evil: Genocide, Violence and Terrorism.* Oxford: Oxford University Press.

Stauffacher, Daniel 2014. *Presentation on "Preventing Cyber Conflict" at the United Nations,* ICT4Peace Foundation. Available at: www.ict 4peace.org

Stavropoulou, Maria 2010. "The Kampala Convention and Protection from Arbitrary Displacement," *Forced Migration Review* 36: 62–3.

Staw, Barry M. & Jerry Ross 1987. "Behavior in Escalation Situations: Antecedents, Prototypes, and Solutions," *Research in Organizational Behavior* 9: 39–78.

Stedman, Stephen John 2000. "Spoiler Problems in Peace Processes," in Paul Stern and Daniel Druckman (eds) *International Conflict Resolution After the Cold War*. Washington, DC: National Academy Press.

Stedman, Stephen John, Donald Rothchild, & Elizabeth Cousens (eds) 2002. *Ending Civil Wars: The Implementation of Peace Agreements*. Boulder, CO: Lynn Rienner.

Stein, Janice 2000. "New Challenges to Conflict Resolution," in Paul Stern & Daniel Druckman (eds) *International Conflict Resolution after the Cold War*. Washington, DC: National Academy Press.

Steiner, Barry 2004. *Collective Preventive Diplomacy*. Albany, NY: SUNY Press.

Stenelo, Lars 1972. *Mediation in International Negotiations*. Stockholm: Studentlitteratur.

Sultany, Nimer (ed.) 2003. *Citizens without Citizenship: Israel and the Palestinian Minority 2000–2002*. Haifa: The Arab Center for Applied Social Research.

Susskind, Lawrence 1994. *Environmental Diplomacy: Negotiating More Effective Global Agreements*. Oxford: Oxford University Press.

Svensson, Isak & Peter Wallensteen 2010. *The Go-Between: Jan Eliasson and the Style of Mediation*. Washington, DC: United States Institute of Peace.

Sweden 1997. *Strategi för konfliktförebyggande och konflikthantering*. Stockholm: Foreign Ministry Ds 1997:18.

Sweden 1999. *Preventing Violent Conflict – A Swedish Action Plan*, Stockholm: Foreign Ministry Ds 1999:24.

Tahiri, Edita 2010. "International Statebuilding and Uncertain Sovereignty," doctoral dissertation, University of Pristina.

Tetlock, Phillip 2005. *Expert Political Judgment: How Good Is It? How Can We Know?* Princeton, NJ: Princeton University Press.

Thaler, Farah 2010. *Atrocity Prevention and US National Security*. Policy Dialogue Brief, 51st Strategy for Peace Conference, Muscatine, IA: Stanley Foundation.

Theiss, Johan 2015. "The NATO Negotiations," in I. William Zartman (ed.) *Arab Spring: Negotiating in the Shadow of the Intifadat*. Athens, GA: University of Georgia Press.

Themnér, Otto & Peter Wallensteen 2014. "Armed Conflict 1946–2013," *Journal of Peace Research* 51(4): 541–54.

Tilly, Charles 2003. *The Politics of Collective Violence*. Cambridge: Cambridge University Press.

Toch, Hans 1965. *The Social Psychology of Social Movements*. Indianapolis, IN: Bobbs-Merrill.

Toft, Monica 2003. *The Geography of Ethnic Violence*. Princeton, NJ: Princeton University Press.

Touval, Saadia 1994. "Why the UN Fails," *Foreign Affairs* 73(5): 44–57.

Touval, Saadia & I. William Zartman (eds) 1985. *International Mediation in Theory and Practice*. Boulder, CO: Westview.

Trolldalen, Jon Martin 1992. *International Environmental Conflict Resolution: The Role of the United Nations*. New York: UNITAR.

Tuchman, Barbara 1994. *The Guns of August*. New York: Random House.

Tutu, Desmond 1999. *No Future Without Forgiveness*. New York: Doubleday.

Tversky, Amos & Daniel Kahneman 1981. "The Framing of Decisions and the Psychology of Choice," *Science* 211(4481), 453–8.

UNDP 2013. "Issue Brief: Infrastructure for Peace," February 27, available at: www.undp.org/content/dam/undp/library/crisis%20prevention/Issue_brief_infrastructure_for_peace_27022013.pdf

Unger, Barbara, Stina Lundström, Katrin Planta, & Beatrix Austin (eds) 2013. *Peace Infrastructures: Assessing Concept and Practice*. Berghof Handbook Dialogue Series 10. Berlin: Berghof Foundation.

Ury, William 1991. *Getting Past No: Negotiating in Difficult Situations*. New York: Bantam Books.

Uvin, Peter 1998. *Aiding Violence: The Development Enterprise in Rwanda*. West Hartford, CT: Kumarian.

Valencia, Mark, Jon Van Dyke, & Noel Ludwig 1997. *Sharing the Resources of the South China Sea*. The Hague: Kluwer Law International.

van de Stoel, Max 1994. Keynote speech, Seminar on Early Warning and Preventive Diplomacy, Warsaw, January 12; *ODIHR Bulletin* 2: 7–13.

van Tongeren, Paul 2013. "Background Paper on Infrastructures for Peace." International Civil Society Network on Infrastructures for Peace.

van Tongeren, Paul, Malin Brenk, Marte Hellema, & Juliette Verhoeven 2005. *People Building Peace II: Successful Stories of Civil Society*. Boulder, CO: Lynne Rienner.

van Walraven, Klaas (ed.) 1998. *Early Warning and Conflict Prevention: Limitations and Possibilities*. The Hague: Kluwer Law International.

van Walraven, Klaas & Jurjen van der Vlagt 1996. *Conflict Prevention and Early Warning in the Political Process of International Organizations*. The Hague: Clingendael.

Varshney, Ashutosh 2003. *Ethnic Conflict and Civil Life: Hindus and Muslims in India*. New Haven, CT: Yale University.

Vasquez, John A. 2010. *Territory, War and Peace*. New York: Routledge.

Vasquez, John A. & Brandon Valeriano 2009. "Territory as a Source of Conflict and a Road to Peace," in Jacob Bercovitch, Victor Kremenyuk, & I. William Zartman (eds) *Sage Handbook on Conflict Resolution*. Thousand Oaks, CA: Sage, pp. 193–209.

Verstegen, Suzanne 1999. *Conflict Prognostication: Toward a Tentative Framework for Conflict Assessment*. The Hague: Clingendael.

Vuković, Sinisa 2015a. "Serbia: Moderation as a Double-Edged Sword," in I. William Zartman (ed.) *Arab Spring: Negotiating in the Shadow of the Intifadat*. Athens, GA: University of Georgia Press.

Vuković, Sinisa 2015b. *International Multiparty Mediation and Conflict Management*. New York: Routledge.

Wallensteen, Peter (ed.) 1998. *Preventing Violent Conflicts: Past Record and Future Challenges*. Department of Peace and Conflict Research, Uppsala University.

Wallensteen, Peter 2007. *Understanding Conflict Resolution*. Thousand Oaks, CA: Sage.

Wallensteen, Peter, Birger Heldt, Mary B. Anderson, Stephen John Stedman, & Leonard Wantchekon 2000. *Conflict Prevention through Development Cooperation*. Department of Peace and Conflict Research, Uppsala University.

Walter, Barbara 2002. *Committing to Peace: The Successful Settlement of Civil War*. Princeton, NJ: Princeton University Press.

Walton, Richard & Robert McKersie 1965. *A Behavioral Theory of Labor Negotiations*. New York: McGraw-Hill.

Waterbury, J. 1979. *Hydropolitics of the Nile Valley*. Syracuse, NY: Syracuse University Press.

White, Ralph K. 1984. *Fearful Warrior: A Psychological Profile of US–Soviet Relations*. New York: Free Press.

Whyte, Glen 1986. "Escalating Commitment as a Course of Action," *Academy of Management Review* 11: 33–50.

Wiegand, Krista (ed.) 2014. *Mediation in Interstate Disputes*. Special issue of *International Negotiation* 19(2).

Wolff, Stefan & Christalla Yakinthou 2012. *Conflict Management in Divided Societies*. New York: Routledge.

Woodward, Susan L. 1995. *Balkan Tragedy: Chaos and Dissolution After the Cold War*. Washington, DC: Brookings Institution Press.

Wright, Nicholas & James Schoff 2014. "China and Japan's Real Problem: Enter the Fairness Dilemma," *The National Interest*, November 2.

Young, Oran 1967. *The Intermediaries: Third Parties in International Crises*. Princeton, NJ: Princeton University Press.

Young, Oran (ed.) 1975. *Bargaining: Formal Theories of Negotiation*. Champaign, IL: University of Illinois Press.

Zacher, Mark 2001. "The Territorial Integrity Norm: International Boundaries and the Use of Force," *International Organization* 55(2), 215–50.

Zartman, I. William 1965. "The Politics of Boundaries in North and West Africa," *Journal of Modern African Studies* 3(2): 155–74.

Zartman, I. William (ed.) 1974. *The 50% Solution*. New York: Doubleday Anchor.

Zartman, I. William 1989. *Ripe for Resolution: Conflict and Intervention in Africa*. Oxford: Oxford University Press.

Zartman, I. William 1991. "Negotiations and Pre-Negotiations in Ethnic Conflict: The Beginning, the Middle and the End," in Joseph Montville (ed.) *Conflict and Peacemaking in Multiethnic Societies*. Lanham, MD: Lexington.

Zartman, I. William (ed.) 1995. *Elusive Peace: Negotiating an End to Civil Wars*. Washington, DC: Brookings Institution Press.

Zartman, I. William (ed.) 1996. *Governance as Conflict Management*. Washington, DC: Brookings Institution Press.

Zartman, I. William 1998. "An Apology Needs a Pledge," *New York Times*, April 2.

Zartman, I. William 2000. "Ripeness: The Hurting Stalemate and Beyond," in Paul Stern and Daniel Druckman (eds), *International Conflict Resolution after the Cold War*. Washington, DC: National Academy Press.

Zartman, I. William (ed.) 2001. *Preventive Negotiations*. Lanham, MD: Rowman & Littlefield.

Zartman, I. William (ed.) 2003. *Traditional Cures for Modern Conflicts*. Boulder, CO: Lynne Rienner.

Zartman, I. William 2005a. *Cowardly Lions: Missed Opportunities to Prevent Deadly Conflict and State Collapse*. Boulder, CO: Lynne Rienner.

Zartman, I. William 2005b. "Analyzing Intractability," in Chester A. Crocker, Fen Osler Hampson, & Pamela Aall (eds) *Grasping the Nettle*. Washington, DC: United States Institute of Peace.

Zartman, I. William (ed.) 2009. *Imbalance of Power*. Boulder, CO: Lynne Rienner.

Zartman, I. William 2010. "Conflict Management as Cooperation," in I. William Zartman & Saadia Touval (eds) *International Cooperation*. Cambridge: Cambridge University Press.

Zartman, I. William (ed.) 2015. *Arab Spring: Negotiating in the Shadow of the Intifadat*. Athens, GA: University of Georgia Press.

Zartman, I. William and Maureen Berman 1982. *The Practical Negotiator*. New Haven, CT: Yale University Press.

Zartman, I. William and Alvero de Soto 2010. *Timing Mediation Initiatives*. Washington, DC: United States Institute of Peace.

Zartman, I. William and Guy Olivier Faure (eds) 2005. *Escalation and Negotiation in International Conflicts*. Cambridge: Cambridge University Press.

Zartman, I. William & Guy Olivier Faure (eds) 2010. *Engaging Extremists: Negotiating Ends and Means*. Washington, DC: United States Institute of Peace.

Zartman, I. William & Saadia Touval 2007. "Mediation in International Politics," in Chester A. Crocker, Fen Osler Hampson, & Pamela Aall (eds) *Leashing the Dogs of War*. Washington, DC: United States Institute of Peace.

Zartman, I. William, Mark Anstey, and Paul Meerts (eds) 2012. *The Slippery Slope to Genocide: Reducing Identity Conflicts and Preventing Mass Murder*. Oxford: Oxford University Press.

Zawahri, Neda and Andrea Gerlak (eds) 2009. *Negotiating International River Disputes to Avert Conflict and Facilitate Cooperation*. Special issue of *International Negotiation* 14(2).

Zoufal, Donald R. 2013. "Bosnia-Herzegovina and the Development of Democratic Policing," in Joseph R. Rudolph, Jr. & William J. Lahneman (eds) *From Mediation to Nation Building: Third Parties and the Management of Communal Conflict*. Lanham, MD: Lexington Books.

Suggestions for Further Reading

Prevention of Deadly Conflict rose to public – and hence published – attention in the 1990s, largely because of the prominence given it by the UN Secretary-General Boutros Boutros Ghali and also because of the new era of victory and good feeling occasioned by the end of the Cold War. Both of these influences were passing events, and scholarly and practitioners' focus leveled off, if not dwindled: The subject narrowly conceived remained broad-brush and then tended off into other topics for greater precision, and its practice was found to be sharply challenged by some discouraging exceptions to established efforts. At the same time, prompted by Rwanda, attention turned to the even broader but more shocking subject of genocide, where a number of arguable cases suddenly appeared on the screen at the end of the millennium. The work on genocide prevention has often tended to focus on final phases and pathologies with less analysis of antecedents. The work of violence prevention has tended to begin with violence, after its causes were past. As these various strands were pulled together throughout this book, pertinent references have been given. This final discussion takes stock of some, mainly the best, of them by topic, with attention above all to the post-Cold War period. Most of the contributions are by individual authors working on their own initiative but a good proportion are sponsored by various institutions and programs, usually devoted to a broader sweep of international relations into which deadly conflict prevention is folded.

Boutros Boutros Ghali's (1992) report to the UN General Assembly, Michael Lund's (1996) book with the US Institute of Peace and the work of the Carnegie Commission on Preventing Deadly Conflict (Holl 1997) began the contemporary approach to the subject. The first was a concise policy appeal, the second a comprehensive treatment of analysis and policy, and the third a detailed synthesis of the project's work. None is outdated a quarter of a century and many conflicts later, but much knowledge and experience has been developed in the interim.

Boutros Ghali's defining concern for prevention was expanded by his successor, Kofi Annan (2002), who spoke of the multi-tooled, multi-level, multi-actors effort needed as a culture of prevention. Annan launched the High-Level Panel on Threats, Challenges and Change (2004) which made strong recommendations, not only for the promotion of the Responsibility to Protect (R2P) but in an encompassing strategy for prevention of threats to both human and state security. His successor, Ban Ki-moon (2009, 2010), in turn, emphasized R2P from the Report and developed it further, underscoring the importance of the first two pillars (self-responsibility, assisting state responsibility) rather than the hotly debated third (intervention responsibility). R2P arose from the Brookings Africa Project (Deng et al. 1996), was launched in Canada by the International Commission on Intervention and State Sovereignty (Evans & Sahnoun 2001), promoted in the *Report to the UN Secretary-General* (High-Level Panel on Threats, Challenges and Change 2004), adopted by the Millennium Summit in 2005, and cogently discussed by Evans (2008).

Analysts from the outside have investigated further ways in which the UN agencies could refine their capabilities for conflict prevention. Peck (1998) presented a positive analysis and evaluation of the UN role in prevention, as part of the Carnegie Commission's series, and also as part of the PIN Program (Peck 2009). Sriram and Wermester (2003), in a study sponsored by the International Peace Academy (now Institute), analyze the course of conflict through gestation, triggers and escalation. Van Walraven & van der Vlagt (1996), of Clingendael, Netherlands, focused particularly on the role of early warning and the UN; volume 2 of Schnabel & Carment (2004) examines the possibilities for the UN and also regional organizations. Hampson and Malone (2002) emphasized a pro-active role for conflict prevention that could be open to the UN agencies. Lund (2000) has prepared a guide for UN practitioners in the preventing business.

Boutros Ghali's (1995) second series of reports to the UNGA broadened the concern for prevention to include aspects of development. The subject has been pursued at the World Bank by Paul Collier et al.'s (2003) team and other Bank projects. Although an economist, Collier has done great service in bringing political science to the attention of the Bank. Wallensteen et al. (2000) of the Peace and Conflict program at Uppsala University also analyzed the role of development in conflict prevention. Other works, by Ballentine and Sherman (2003), Berdal and Malone (2000), and Arnson and Zartman (2005) at the Wilson Center have further examined the economics of conflict in an effort to discover how to break the link between profiteering and warring. The costliness of conflict as opposed to prevention has been underscored in authoritative detail by Cranna (1994), Brown and Rosecrance (1999) and, in comparison with incentives for prevention, Cortright (1997), the last two books sponsored by the Carnegie Commission.

Others followed in the tradition of Lund, who continues to write on the subject (2009; with Rasmoelina 2000), by pursuing prevention through the escalation process. Leatherman et al. (1999), and also Sriram and Wermester (2003), move vigorously from early warning to early action. A creative juxtaposition of escalation and negotiation is presented by Zartman & Faure (2005), a study from the Processes of International Negotiation (PIN) Program at Clingendael, Netherlands. A major two-volume collection on many aspects of conflict prevention has been organized by Schnabel and Carment (2004), including some good discussions of early warning. Good evaluations of early warning were conducted at Clingendael by van Walraven (1998) and Verstegen (1999). Leatherman et al. (1999) also have a good discussion of early warning, among other subjects. Zartman (2005) analyzes instances of early warning that were neglected and the opportunities open for prevention at many stages. Steiner (2004) presents historical instances of historical preventive diplomacy.

In a different direction, the dedication to the "social medicine" of conflict of medical doctor David Hamburg (2002, 2010, with Hamburg 2004), former president of Carnegie Corporation, has carried him into inspiring works on preventing genocide. Social psychologist Erwin Staub (1989, 2000, 2003, 2011) has produced comprehensive and penetrating work on prevention not just of genocide but of the behavioral causes of the pathology, as has Edkins (2003). A study from the PIN Project edited by Zartman et al. (2012) investigates the socio-political dynamics of rising ethnic conflict as it heads toward the slippery slope to genocide. Reconciliation has received much discussion after the South Africa experience (Tutu 1999; Hayner 2001), reviving earlier important critical attention coming out of the Holocaust and then the Franco-German reconciliation (Rosoux 2009; Anstey & Rosoux 2015). Lederach (1997), Barkan (2000), Bar-Simon-Tov (2004), and Anstutz (2005) follow suit from different angles. Mitchell (2000) develops the theme of preventive conciliation in a most productive work; van

Tongeren et al. (2005) of the European Centre for Conflict Prevention present a number of cases studies of civil society in action to prevent conflict through conciliation and reconciliation at various stages.

The Carnegie Commission sponsored further collections on preventive diplomacy and negotiation edited by Jentleson (2000) and Zartman for the PIN Program (2001). USIP also sponsored a thick and rare collection of diplomats' accounts of preventive diplomacy, as well as conflict resolution and settlement, edited by Crocker et al. (1999). There is unusually little work on the preventive diplomacy practiced by the Special Representatives and Special Envoys of the UN Secretary-General (SRSG, SESG).

Ethnic conflict and its dangers of escalation have attracted much current scholarship. Besides the chapters in Zartman (2001) and Bercovitch et al. (2009), there have been significant works on the nature of ethnic conflict as a basis for analyzing its prevention. Two now classics have reopened broad attention to the need and ways to prevent ethnic conflict, following at a distance an earlier unique collection by Rosenau (1964), which, in its era, did not mention prevention: Montville (1990) brought many facts of analysis, with focused evaluation of Northern Ireland, Sri Lanka, and Sudan, and Horowitz (1985), rebutting Lijphart (1977), is the basic argument for overcoming ethnic divisions as the foundation for conflict prevention. Midlarsky (1992) and Lake and Rothchild (1998) analyze the tendency of ethnic conflict to spill over internationally, providing opportunities and obstacles to prevention efforts. Rothchild (1997) at Brookings examined both external and internal efforts to bring ethnic conflict under control. A seminal article that develops the concept of security dilemma to ethnic conflicts is Posen (1993).

Territorial conflict has a long history in classical treatments but the means to its prevention is a more recent subject of analysis. Kacowicz (1994), Huth (1996), Diehl (1998), Toft (2003), and Kahler and Walter (2006) all contain useful approaches to territorial conflict with relevant material for prevention of ownership conflicts.

The initial defining work on regimes is Krasner (1983), followed by a thorough and thoughtful evaluation of the ensuing debate by Hasenclever et al. (1997). After two decades of experience with regimes, a revision by Spector and Zartman (2003), a PIN and USIP book, presents them as recursive negotiations. Barnett and Finnemore (2004) examine the role of international bureaucracy in promoting norms. Risse et al. (2013) support the power of the human rights regime in affecting conflict behavior. Studies of environmental regimes began with practitioners' accounts such as Lang (1989) and Benedick (1991) and then after the UN Conference on Environment and Development (UNCED) (1992) saw fuller analyses such as Sjöstedt (1993), Spector et al. (1994), and Sjöstedt and Penetrante (2013) for the PIN Program. Among many ensuing works, particularly insightful ones are Susskind (1994), Barrett (2003), and Downie (2014).

Negotiation is, after all, the first and the last mechanism for preventing conflict by resolution, and also for temporarily diminishing it by management. The book that brought negotiation to the public attention was Fisher et al. (1982). More conceptual development of the subject was found in: Ikle (1964), a basic work drawn from current diplomacy; Walton and McKersie (1965), another defining work developing typologies; Cross (1969), a tight economic analysis; Pruitt (1981), an insightful use of social psychology; Zartman and Berman (1982), a conceptual development from diplomatic practice; Pillar (1983), a creative application of theory to history; Lax and Sebenius (1986), a study of negotiation for business; and Hopmann (1996), reviewing different approaches. Three collections of seminal articles from economics, social psychology and politics were Zartman (1974), Rubin and Brown (1975), and Young (1975). An encompassing collection on the subject is found in the PIN volume edited by Kremenyuk (2002). Subsequent developments of theory and practice have been developed by Zartman (1989) on the search for ripeness, and Anstey (1999) on preventing recidivism by managing change.

Mediation, negotiation with a third-party catalyst, needs to take over when direct negotiation between the parties fails. Early works did not draw much attention, despite their insights, largely because the Cold War standoff was not hospitable to mediation. Young (1967) developed principle, applied mostly to the UN. An early work, largely ignored, was Stenelo (1972). Rubin (1981), analyzing Kissinger's work in the Middle East, and Touval and Zartman (1985), drawing lessons from a number of cases, began a revived attention, and Bercovitch (1996, 2002, 2011) pursued a major data-gathering project. Anstey (1993) developed a helpful conceptual and applied analysis from a labor mediator's experience. Crocker et al. (1999) pursued the study with a wealth of direct practitioners' testimony, Svensson and Wallensteen (2010) plumbed insights from Jan Eliasson, and Zartman (1995) drew lessons from cases both managed and unmanaged.

What is surprising is that the wave of works on Conflict Management and Resolution pays little or no attention to Conflict Prevention, although for that matter the current wave of works on International Politics pays equally little attention to conflict management, resolution, and negotiation. Wallensteen (2007) is an insightful exception. It is important to head off conflicts before they call for attention in the ultimate stage of their course.

Index